T0291194

Lectures in Applied Environmental Economics and Policy

World Scientific Lecture Notes in Economics and Policy

ISSN: 2630-4872

Series Editors: Felix Munoz-Garcia *(Washington State University, USA)*
Ariel Dinar *(University of California, Riverside, USA)*
Dirk Bergemann *(Yale University, USA)*
George Mailath *(University of Pennsylvania, USA)*
Devashish Mitra *(Syracuse University, USA)*
Kar-yiu Wong *(University of Washington, USA)*
Richard Carpiano *(University of California, Riverside, USA)*
Chetan Dave *(University of Alberta, Canada)*
Malik Shukayev *(University of Alberta, Canada)*
George C Davis *(Virginia Tech University, USA)*
Marco M Sorge *(University of Salerno, Italy)*
Alessia Paccagnini *(University College Dublin, Ireland)*
Luca Lambertini *(Bologna University, Italy)*
Konstantinos Georgalos *(Lancaster University, UK)*

The World Scientific Lecture Notes in Economics and Policy series is aimed to produce lecture note texts for a wide range of economics disciplines, both theoretical and applied at the undergraduate and graduate levels. Contributors to the series are highly ranked and experienced professors of economics who see in publication of their lectures a mission to disseminate the teaching of economics in an affordable manner to students and other readers interested in enriching their knowledge of economic topics. The series was formerly titled World Scientific Lecture Notes in Economics.

Published:

For the complete list of volumes in this series, please visit
www.worldscientific.com/series/wslnep

World Scientific Lecture Notes in Economics and Policy – Vol. 19

Lectures in Applied Environmental Economics and Policy

Anastasios Xepapadeas
University of Bologna, Italy
Athens University of Economics and Business, Greece

World Scientific

NEW JERSEY · LONDON · SINGAPORE · BEIJING · SHANGHAI · HONG KONG · TAIPEI · CHENNAI · TOKYO

Published by

World Scientific Publishing Co. Pte. Ltd.

5 Toh Tuck Link, Singapore 596224

USA office: 27 Warren Street, Suite 401-402, Hackensack, NJ 07601

UK office: 57 Shelton Street, Covent Garden, London WC2H 9HE

Library of Congress Control Numbrt: 2024008425

British Library Cataloguing-in-Publication Data
A catalogue record for this book is available from the British Library.

World Scientific Lecture Notes in Economics and Policy — Vol. 19
LECTURES IN APPLIED ENVIRONMENTAL ECONOMICS AND POLICY

Copyright © 2024 by World Scientific Publishing Co. Pte. Ltd.

All rights reserved. This book, or parts thereof, may not be reproduced in any form or by any means, electronic or mechanical, including photocopying, recording or any information storage and retrieval system now known or to be invented, without written permission from the publisher.

For photocopying of material in this volume, please pay a copying fee through the Copyright Clearance Center, Inc., 222 Rosewood Drive, Danvers, MA 01923, USA. In this case permission to photocopy is not required from the publisher.

ISBN 978-981-12-9207-1 (hardcover)
ISBN 978-981-12-9253-8 (paperback)
ISBN 978-981-12-9208-8 (ebook for institutions)
ISBN 978-981-12-9212-5 (ebook for individuals)

For any available supplementary material, please visit
https://www.worldscientific.com/worldscibooks/10.1142/13810#t=suppl

Desk Editors: Aanand Jayaraman/Yulin Jiang/Sylvia Koh

Typeset by Stallion Press
Email: enquiries@stallionpress.com

About the Author

Anastasios Xepapadeas is currently Professor of Economics at the Department of Economics of the University of Bologna and Professor Emeritus at the Department of International and European Economic Studies of Athens University of Economics and Business. He is an elected international member of the US National Academy of Sciences, past president of the European Association of Environmental and Resource Economics and past Chair of the Board of Directors of the Beijer Institute of the Royal Swedish Academy of Sciences. He is co-editor of *Environmental and Resource Economics*, associate editor of *Proceedings of the National Academy of Sciences*, and member of the editorial committee of *Annual Review of Resource Economics*. He is past editor of *Environment and Development Economics*. He has published more than 150 papers in leading journals and collective volumes. His current research interests include Environmental Policy; Environmental Cost-Benefit Analysis; Sustainability; Economics of Climate Change; and Uncertainty and Robust Control.

Contents

Introduction

These lectures comprise the primary teaching material for the courses in applied environmental economics and policy which I have taught in master's and PhD programs and seminars in a number of universities. The lectures are divided into four parts: environmental cost–benefit analysis; ecosystem services; ecosystems, biodiversity, and the economy; and sustainability.

The first part introduces basic concepts in environmental cost–benefit analysis (CBA), which include the steps in conducting a CBA, and the welfare foundations of CBA. It goes on to explain discounting, which is a central concept of CBA, and the choice of the appropriate discount rate. The important but complex issue of the distribution of costs and benefits across different social groups is then addressed. Finally, the assessment of risk involved in CBA decision-making criteria, and the tools such as sensitivity analysis and Monte Carlo simulations which are used to assess this risk, are presented.

The second part of the lectures, which deals with ecosystem services, begins with a thorough discussion of the concept of total economic value in the context of the environment. It then addresses the concept of quasi-option value and the associated central issue in the management of ecosystem services: whether to preserve or convert. There follows a brief presentation of two landmark global initiatives focused on understanding and valuing the world's ecosystem services: the Millennium Ecosystem Assessment and The Economics of Ecosystems and Biodiversity. A number of examples of the broad range of information available in some widely used ecosystem service valuation databases are provided. Then, the various methods and approaches for valuing ecosystem services, along with their advantages and disadvantages, are explored. Revealed and stated preference valuation methods are presented and some of the important issues and challenges in the valuation of ecosystem services are discussed.

In the third part, the links between ecological and economic systems are explored. More specifically, the coevolution of these systems is presented and issues such as regime shifts, tipping points, policy issues, and the emergence of infectious diseases are discussed. This part concludes with a presentation of the economics of biodiversity where biodiversity-related issues such as metrics, valuation, conservation, and policy design are explored.

The fourth and final part of the lectures deals with sustainability. It covers issues such as how to define and measure sustainable development at the macro level. It then discusses the relatively new area of corporate sustainability and takes a brief look at environmental, social, and governance (ESG) reporting. This part concludes with a discussion of the concept of green economic growth and the UN sustainable development goals.

Part 1

Some Basics in Cost–Benefit Analysis

Chapter 1

Cost–Benefit Analysis: The Basic Concepts

1.1. Cost–Benefit Analysis

Cost–Benefit Analysis (CBA) is a technique for analyzing projects to determine whether carrying them out is in the public interest, or for choosing between two or more mutually exclusive projects.

For example:

o Should we go ahead with a new power plant?
o How do we choose between a new motorway and a hydroelectric scheme?
o Are we going to introduce policies to improve air or water quality?
o How do we address climate change?
o How do we protect societies from expected climate change damages?

CBA assigns a monetary value to each input used by a project and to each output resulting from a project. The values of the inputs and outputs are then compared.

1.1.1. *What is CBA?*

CBA is a systematic approach used to evaluate the pros and cons of a project or decision. It helps decision-makers determine whether the benefits of a particular course of action outweigh its costs. Its fundamental characteristics are briefly described as follows.

Cost–benefit analysis:

- involves identifying and quantifying all the relevant costs and benefits associated with a project. These can be both tangible (e.g., monetary costs and financial gains) and intangible (e.g., social and environmental impacts). By quantifying these factors, a more objective comparison can be made.
- takes into account the concept of the time value of money, recognizing that a euro received today is worth more than a euro received in the future. It involves discounting future costs and benefits to present value to enable comparisons.
- provides a common metric (usually monetary) to compare costs and benefits. By converting all factors into a single currency, it becomes easier to assess whether the benefits justify the costs.
- focuses on comparing the changes in costs and benefits between different alternatives, including the *status quo* or "do nothing" alternative, and looks at the differences brought about by each option.
- attempts to include all relevant costs and benefits, even if they might be challenging to quantify. This ensures that important aspects are not overlooked. For example, clean air and good health are clearly valuable, but it is a challenge to precisely determine the benefits of a program that would yield cleaner air and better health at some cost.
- uses risk assessment analysis to test the robustness of the results, since some inputs in a cost–benefit analysis may be uncertain or subject to change. The risk assessment analysis helps understand how variations in key variables can affect the outcome.
- aims to be transparent and objective, relying on data, clear assumptions, research, and sound economic principles. This helps in avoiding biases and subjective judgments that could influence the results.

- tries to incorporate and monetize externalities — the unintended positive or negative consequences that affect parties not directly involved in a project into the analysis — even though they might be difficult to quantify.

1.1.2. *A formal definition*

CBA seeks to maximize the present value of all benefits less that of all costs, subject to specified constraints. The main issues to be addressed are:

(1) Which costs and which benefits are to be included?
(2) How are the costs and benefits to be evaluated?
(3) At what discount rate are future benefits and costs to be discounted to obtain the present value (the equivalent value that one is receiving or giving up today when the decision is being made)?
(4) What are the relevant constraints?

1.1.3. *Investment decision by a private firm*

In project appraisal, there is generally a distinction between investments undertaken by private firms and investments undertaken by the public sector. The main difference is the type of benefits and costs included in each case.

In investments undertaken by private firms:

(1) Only the private benefits and costs that can be measured in financial terms are to be included.
(2) Benefits and costs are the financial receipts and outlays as measured by market prices. The difference between them is reflected in the firm's profits.
(3) The market rate of interest is to be used for discounting the annual profit stream.
(4) The main constraint is the funds constraint or capital availability associated with the financial status of the firm.

1.1.4. *Social cost–benefit analysis*

In contrast, in projects undertaken by the public sector:

(1) All benefits and costs are to be included, consisting of private and social, direct and indirect, tangible and intangible.

(2) Benefits and costs are given by the standard principles of welfare economics. Benefits are based on the consumer's willingness to pay for the project. Costs are what the potential losers from a project are willing to receive as compensation for giving up the resources.

(3) The social discount rate (which includes the preferences for the welfare of future generations) is to be used for discounting the annual net benefit stream.

(4) Constraints are included in the objective function. For example, income distribution considerations are to be included by weighting the consumer's willingness to pay according to an individual's ability to pay or income. A capital availability constraint is handled by using a premium on the cost of capital, that is, the social price of capital is calculated which would be different from its market price.

(5) Social CBA means that included in the evaluation are the effects of the project on **all the individuals in society** not just the parties directly involved (the consumers and the producers of the project). For example, everyone would be affected if the project caused any environmental impacts.

(6) Social CBA recognizes that distributional effects are being included along with the efficiency effects. Without the distributional effects, one is making an economic rather than a social evaluation.

(7) Social CBA emphasizes that market prices are not always good indices of individual willingness to pay. A social price would therefore mean that the market price was being adjusted to include effects that the market does not record or records imperfectly.

1.1.5. *The economic effects of a project*

The economic effects of a project undertaken by a private company or the public sector include benefits and costs to the following:

- the owner/operator — private company,
- the economy (e.g., local, regional, national, or European).

These benefits and costs correspond to:

- profits or losses recorded by a private or public company,
- direct effects on local, regional, or national economies (e.g., incomes, employment, and trade balance),
- indirect and induced effects (e.g., skills and knowledge spillovers),
- environmental benefits and costs and the value of resource use.

Countries should undertake investments which are efficient at the level of the national economy. Thus, it is necessary to evaluate how different investment projects affect the national economy, irrespective of whether ownership of the investment project is private or public.

1.1.6. *CBA, environmental economics, and resource valuation*

Using CBA in the context of policies and projects with significant environmental impacts can raise some concerns and involves certain limitations. While CBA is a valuable decision-making tool, it may not fully capture the complexities and externalities associated with environmental issues. Some of the key concerns are summarized below.

Difficulty in valuing intangible environmental benefits: Environmental impacts often involve intangible benefits like improved air quality, biodiversity preservation, or preservation of ecosystem services. Quantifying these intangible benefits in monetary terms can be challenging and may not fully reflect their true value to society.

Use of unadjusted market prices for environmental goods: CBA often relies on market prices to evaluate environmental goods and services. However, market prices may not reflect their true ecological importance or scarcity and may need to be adjusted to approximate their true social valuation.

Discounting future environmental impacts: CBA typically involves discounting future costs and benefits to present value. However, if the discount rate is fixed and relatively high, this approach may undervalue long-term environmental benefits that materialize years or decades into the future, especially in intergenerational contexts. Declining discount rates could, to some extent, alleviate this problem.

Neglecting distributional effects: CBA focuses on overall net benefits, but it may overlook distributional effects, meaning that while the project might be beneficial overall, certain communities or vulnerable groups could bear a disproportionate burden of negative environmental impacts.

Uncertainty and complexity: Environmental impacts are often characterized by uncertainty and complexity. Predicting the extent and consequences of environmental changes can be challenging, and this uncertainty may not be adequately addressed in a standard CBA.

Externalities and spillover effects: Environmental projects and policies can lead to positive or negative externalities, impacting parties not directly involved in the decision. These external effects may not be fully considered or accounted for in a traditional CBA.

Inadequate scope: CBA may not capture all relevant environmental factors or might only focus on immediate impacts rather than considering broader and longer-term ecological and systemic consequences.

Valuing pluralism: Different stakeholders may have diverse perspectives on environmental values. CBA relies on aggregating these values into a single metric, which can lead to conflicts between various groups and value systems.

It is important to be aware of these issues and to complement the CBA with alternative methods, when they can help, to provide a more comprehensive understanding of the environmental impacts of policies and projects. Additionally, adopting a precautionary approach when dealing with significant environmental impacts can help ensure that potential risks are carefully considered and minimized.

1.1.7. *Steps in a CBA*

Conducting a CBA entails a number of distinct steps (see, for example, Zerbe and Bellas (2006) and European Commission (2015) for more detailed coverage), which can be summarized as follows:

(1) **Description of the context**: This step describes the social, economic, political, and institutional context in which the project will be undertaken. The main features are associated with country or regional socioeconomic conditions, institutional aspects, and existing infrastructures.

(2) **Definition of objectives**: The objectives of the project should be defined. Regional and sectoral needs should be identified and should be aligned with more general development strategies.

(3) **Identifying the alternatives**: This step examines alternative projects that might attain the objectives, using as a benchmark for comparison the "do nothing" (*status quo*) option. Altering the scale or the duration of the project might be a relevant alternative. For example, a vaccination program that fails a CBA nationally might pass a CBA if analyzed only in a region with a high incidence of the associated disease.

(4) **Setting out assumptions**: It is necessary to set out clear assumptions about expected demand and costs, market conditions, inflation or interest rates. The assumptions should be transparent and it should be possible to use them in order to replicate the results.

(5) **Identification of the project**: The physical elements and activities associated with the project should be clearly identified, along with the body responsible for implementation, the impact area, and the final beneficiaries and stakeholders.

(6) **Assessment of technical feasibility and environmental sustainability**: Technical feasibility and environmental sustainability should be clearly stated and should include environment and climate change impacts, technical design and cost estimates, options analysis, and demand analysis.

(7) **Calculating financial and economic/social profitability**: This step is the core of CBA. It includes the estimation of the flow of costs and benefits associated with the project, along with calculations of criteria which will indicate whether the project is to be accepted or rejected. The detailed steps of how the financial profitability as well as the economic/social profitability are calculated are described below step 9.

(8) **Identifying and accounting for risk and uncertainty**: The failure to deal with risk or uncertainty is perhaps the most common shortcoming in CBA. Many aspects of a project may be subject to uncertainty and these sources of uncertainty should be identified as completely as possible and risk adjustments should be incorporated into the financial and economic/social analysis.

Suggested steps to deal with risk and uncertainty

(a) **Sensitivity analysis**: Identification of critical variables, elimination of deterministically dependent variables, elasticity analysis, choice of critical variables, and scenario analysis.

(b) **Monte Carlo simulations**: Use assumptions about probability distribution for each critical variable:

- calculation of the distribution of the performance indicator, typically financial net present value and economic net present value,
- discussion of results and acceptable levels of risk,
- discussion of ways to mitigate risks.

(c) **Qualitative analysis**: Qualitative assessment of risks, their severity, and proposals for mitigating specific types of risk.

(9) **Conduct a post-project analysis**: After completing a project, a follow-up analysis during the operational stage should be carried out. This could provide information about the quality

of the pre-project analysis and help guide future evaluations. If the post-project analysis indicates large deviations from the predictions of the pre-project analysis, the project might be abandoned.

We now look more analytically at the calculation of the financial and economic/social profitability mentioned in step 7 above, which is conducted in two parts.

Financial analysis

The *financial analysis* should be based on the discounted cash flow approach using market prices. The European Union suggests a benchmark real financial discount rate of 4%. A system of tables should show cash inflows and outflows related to total investment costs, total operating costs, and revenues.

Indicators for the evaluation of the project, such as net present value (NPV), internal rate of return (IRR), and benefit–cost ratio (B/C) should be calculated. Sources of finance and financial sustainability should be determined. Financial return on national capital should be calculated with a possible distinction between returns on public and private national capital.

Future cash flows are the key factor for calculating the evaluation indicators or criteria. A schematic picture of cash flows is presented in Figure 1. The arrows (on top) indicate benefits or inflows at given points in time, while the arrows (on the bottom) indicate costs or outflows.

The *evaluation criteria or indicators* used for the financial analysis include (1) net present value, (2) NPV calculation, (3) internal rate of return, (4) IRR calculation, and (5) benefit–cost ratio.

(1) Net present value

- $C_0, \ldots, C_{k-1}$: Investment or construction cost during construction period.
- $B_t - C_t$: Benefits or revenues less operating costs = net cash flow.

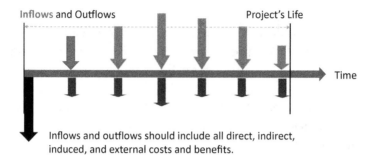

Figure 1: Cash flows.

- r: Discount rate — cost of capital or required rate of return:

$$\text{NPV}(r) = -C_0 - \frac{C_1}{(1+r)} - \cdots - \frac{C_{k-1}}{(1+r)^{k-1}} + \sum_{t=k}^{T-1} \frac{B_t - C_t}{(1+r)^t}.$$

Decision rule: $\begin{cases} \text{NPV} > 0 \text{ Accept} \\ \text{NPV} < 0 \text{ Reject.} \end{cases}$

(2) NPV calculation

Assume that the construction period is just 1 year. Then, if the cash flow is assumed to occur at the beginning of each period, the NPV is calculated as

$$\text{NPV}(r) = -C_0 + \frac{B_1 - C_1}{(1+r)} + \frac{B_2 - C_2}{(1+r)^2} + \cdots + \frac{B_{T-1} - C_{T-1}}{(1+r)^{T-1}}.$$

If the cash flow is assumed to occur at the end of each period, the NPV is calculated as:

$$\text{NPV}(r) = -\frac{C_1}{(1+r)} + \frac{B_2 - C_2}{(1+r)^2} + \frac{B_3 - C_3}{(1+r)^3} + \cdots + \frac{B_T - C_T}{(1+r)^T}$$

Calculation of NPV using Excel

NPV(rate, value1, [value2],...). The NPV function syntax has the following arguments:

- **Rate** (required). The rate of discount over the length of one period.
- **Value1, value2,** ... Value1 is required, subsequent values are optional. Value represents the cash flow.

(3) Internal rate of return

The IRR(i) is the maximum interest which can be paid on borrowed funds to finance the project when the project's receipts are used to repay principal and interest:

$$i : -C_0 - \frac{C_1}{(1+i)} - \cdots - \frac{C_{k-1}}{(1+i)^{k-1}} + \sum_{t=k}^{T-1} \frac{B_t - C_t}{(1+i)^t} = 0.$$

Decision rule: $\begin{cases} i > r \ \text{Accept} \\ i < r \ \text{Reject}. \end{cases}$

(4) IRR calculation

Cash flow for a project with 1 year construction period with flows occurring at the beginning of the period is

$$i : -C_0 + \frac{B_1 - C_1}{(1+i)} + \frac{B_2 - C_2}{(1+i)^2} + \cdots + \frac{B_{T-1} - C_{T-1}}{(1+i)^{T-1}} = 0,$$

or cash flow occurring at the end of the period is

$$i : \frac{-C_1}{(1+i)} + \frac{B_2 - C_2}{(1+i)^2} + \frac{B_3 - C_3}{(1+i)^3} + \cdots + \frac{B_T - C_T}{(1+i)^T} = 0.$$

Calculation of IRR using Excel (end of period)

IRR(values, [guess]). The IRR function syntax has the following arguments.
Values (required). An array or a reference to cells that contain the cash flow:

○ Values must contain at least one positive value and one negative value to calculate the IRR.
○ The IRR uses the order of values to interpret the order of cash flows. Be sure to enter your cost and benefit values in the sequence you want.
○ If an array or reference argument contains text, logical values, or empty cells, those values are ignored.

Guess (optional). A number that you guess is close to the result of the IRR.

(5) Benefit–cost ratio (B/C)

- Benefits per monetary unit of costs in present value terms:

$$B = \sum_{t=0}^{T-1} \frac{B_t}{(1+r)^t}, \quad C = \sum_{t=0}^{T-1} \frac{C_t}{(1+r)^t}.$$

Decision rule: $B/C = \frac{B}{C} = \begin{cases} B/C > 1 & \textit{Accept} \\ B/C < 1 & \textit{Reject.} \end{cases}$

- Profitability index (PI)

$$B' = \sum_{t=0}^{T-1} \frac{B_t - C_t}{(1+r)^t}$$

Decision rule: $PI = \frac{B'}{C_0} \begin{cases} PI > 1 & \textit{Accept} \\ PI < 1 & \textit{Reject.} \end{cases}$

- The time horizon must be consistent with the economic life of the main assets. The appropriate residual value must be included in the accounts in the end year.
- General inflation and relative price changes must be treated in a consistent way.

Economic/social analysis

CBA requires an investigation of a project's net impact **on economic welfare**. This is done through the following steps:

- Fiscal corrections are used to remove effects from taxes, tariffs, and subsidies.
- Observed market prices are converted into accounting (or shadow) prices, which better reflect the social opportunity cost of the good, by removing distortions from domestic markets, international trade, and subsidies.
- Externalities such as **environmental benefits and costs** and non-market impacts are taken into account and given a monetary value.
- Indirect effects are included if relevant (i.e., if not already captured by shadow prices).

- Costs and benefits are discounted with a real social discount rate and economic performance indicators are calculated (economic NPV, economic IRR, and B/C).

1.2. The Welfare Foundations of Cost–Benefit Analysis

1.2.1. *Basic concepts*

- CBA is about comparing the gains and losses (benefits and costs) of undertaking a new project or policy.
- These gains and losses need to be measured.
- One fundamental requirement is that all gains and losses thought to be relevant are measured in the same units, otherwise they cannot be added together (aggregated), either across people or over time. The unit of measurement in CBA is money, but the conceptual basis is utility:

$$
\text{NPV}(r) = -C_0 - \frac{C_1}{(1+r)} - \cdots - \frac{C_{k-1}}{(1+r)^{k-1}} + \sum_{t=k}^{T-1} \frac{B_t - C_t}{(1+r)^t}.
$$

1.2.2. *Willingness to pay*

Willingness to pay (WTP) is the most that a person is **willing to pay** to acquire more of something desirable or less of something undesirable. WTP is a measure of what an increase in the quantity of something good is worth to an individual. Following the approach in Pearce *et al.* (2006, p. 45):

- Consider an individual in an initial state of well-being U_0 that they achieve with a money income Y_0 and an environmental quality level of $E_0 : U_0(Y_0, E_0)$.
- Suppose there is a proposal to improve environmental quality from E_0 to E_1. This improvement would increase the individual's well-being to $U_1 : U_1(Y_0, E_1)$.
- We need to know by how much the well-being of this individual is increased by this improvement in environmental quality, i.e., $U_1 - U_0$.

- WTP: $U_0(Y_0 - WTP, E_1) = U_0(Y_0, E_0)$. This is the amount that a person is willing to pay to attain environmental quality E_1 and after the payment be at the same utility level as with income Y_0 and environmental quality E_0.
- WTP is called **compensating variation**, which is the amount of Y that can be taken from an individual after a change such that they are as well off as they were before the change.

1.2.3. *Willingness to accept*

Willingness to accept (WTA) is the least that a person is willing to accept in compensation for giving up something desirable or tolerating something undesirable. WTA is the minimum compensation for a decrease in the utility of an individual. Following again the approach in Pearce *et al.* (2006):

- Suppose we ask how much an individual would be willing to accept in terms of additional income to forego the improvement in environmental quality and still have the same level of well-being as if environmental quality had been increased.
- WTA: $U_1(Y_0 + WTA, E_0) = U_1(Y_0, E_1)$. This is the amount that a person is willing to accept to forego the improvement in environmental quality E_1 and after the payment be at the same utility level as with income Y_0 and environmental quality E_1.
- WTA is termed **equivalent variation**, meaning that, if a change does not occur, the amount of Y that would have to be given to the individual to make them as well off as if the change did take place. For a more detailed analysis of the concepts of compensating and equivalent variation, see Pearce *et al.* (2006).
- The monetary measure of the value of the change in well-being could be infinite if no amount of money could compensate the individual for not experiencing the environmental improvement.
- Differences between social and private marginal costs and benefits, willingness to pay, and consumer and producer surplus — which are fundamental in the welfare foundations of CBA — are shown in Figures 2–5. For more details regarding private and social marginal costs and benefits, see Hanley and Barbier (2009).

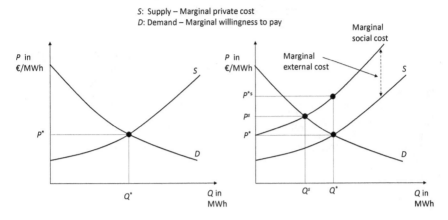

Figure 2: Private, social, and external costs in a market for energy.

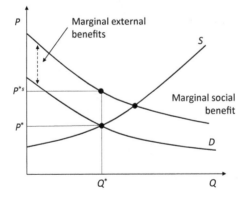

Figure 3: Private, social, and external benefits in a market for a good which embodies external benefits.

1.2.4. *The Kaldor–Hicks compensation principle*

A Pareto improvement occurs if, after a change (e.g., acceptance of a project), at least one individual is better off and nobody is worse off relative to the state before the change. In CBA, there will always be individuals who are better off, those who benefit from the project

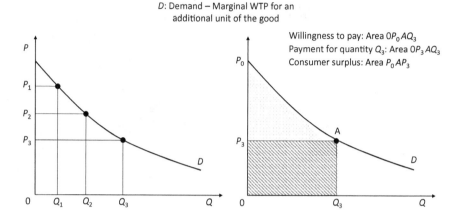

Figure 4:   Willingness to pay and consumer surplus.

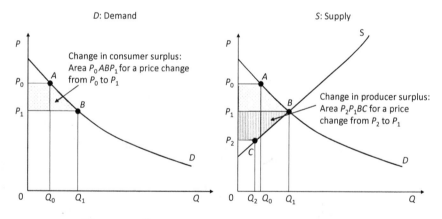

Figure 5:   Change in consumer and producer surplus.

(e.g., farmers for an irrigation project), and individuals who will be worse off (e.g., taxpayers who pay for the irrigation project). This means that the Pareto improvement criterion cannot be applied in a CBA.

The Kaldor–Hicks test examines whether a project brings about a potential Pareto improvement. This means that those who would be better off as a result of the increase in well-being due to the project are willing to pay more, in aggregate, to have the project go ahead than those who would be worse off from the project would demand in compensation for allowing it to occur (see also Hanley and Barbier, 2009):

- If the maximum aggregate WTP of the gainers (the social benefit) is greater than the aggregate minimum WTA of the losers (the social cost), the project will increase the net gains in human well-being.

  o That is, the **gains** in human well-being (benefits) due to the project will exceed the **losses** (costs) in human well-being.

- No compensation is actually paid to losers; we simply ask whether the gainers could compensate the losers, and still be better off.
- Implementing the Kaldor–Hicks test consists of adding up the benefits of a project across all those who will gain and then comparing this aggregate sum of benefits with the aggregate sum of costs.
- Costs include WTA or WTP to tolerate or to avoid losses, losses in consumers' or producers' surplus, and any changes in external costs and benefits resulting from the project, such as an increase in air pollution or a reduction in ecosystem services.
- Taxes, subsidies, or any other transfer payments are not real resource costs and are not taken into account in CBA.

1.2.5. *The decision rule and the Kaldor–Hicks test*

The NPV rule is consistent with the Kaldor–Hicks test, as shown in the following. Consider the standard NPV rule:

$$\text{NPV}(r) = -C_0 - \frac{C_1}{(1+r)} - \cdots - \frac{C_{k-1}}{(1+r)^{k-1}} + \sum_{t=k}^{T-1} \frac{B_t - C_t}{(1+r)^t}$$

$$= \sum_{t=0}^{T-1} \frac{B_t}{(1+r)^t} - \sum_{t=0}^{T-1} \frac{C_t}{(1+r)^t}.$$

Accept if $\text{NPV}(r) > 0$.

In the context of the Kaldor–Hicks test, the NPV rule for $i = 1, \ldots, N$ individuals can be written as

$$\text{NPV}_i(r) = \sum_i \sum_{t=0}^{T-1} \frac{WTP_{i,t}^G}{(1+r)^t} - \sum_i \sum_{t=0}^{T-1} \frac{WTP_{i,t}^L}{(1+r)^t} > 0,$$

$$PV(WTP^G) - PV(WTP^L) > 0,$$

where i is the ith individual, benefits are measured by WTP to secure the benefit (G refers to gainers), and costs are measured by WTP to avoid the cost (L refers to losers). Since the present value of the gainers' WTP exceeds that of the losers, the project is accepted.

If the "losers" from the project or policy have legitimate property rights to what they lose, then WTP (losers) should be replaced by WTA (losers):

$$\text{NPV}_i(r) = \sum_i \sum_{t=0}^{T-1} \frac{WTP_{i,t}^G}{(1+r)^t} - \sum_i \sum_{t=0}^{T-1} \frac{WTA_{i,t}^L}{(1+r)^t} > 0,$$

$$PV(WTP^G) - PV(WTA^L) > 0.$$

1.2.6. *Aggregation rules*

To obtain the aggregate WTP and WTA, the individuals WTP_i and WTA_i are summed across individuals in accordance with the aggregation rule which defines "society" as the sum of all individuals. Typically, "society" is equated with the sum of all individuals in a nation, state, or region:

- The aggregation process may need to take into account income or wealth differences across individuals. If region B is poor and region A is rich, allowance might be made for the likelihood that 1 euro of gain/loss to B will have a higher utility than 1 euro of gain/loss to A.
- Introduce distributional or equity weights, ω_i, associated with costs and benefits accruing to different income groups,

$$\omega_i = \left(\frac{Y}{Y_i}\right)^{-\sigma},$$

where Y is the overall mean income, Y_i is the mean income of group i, and σ is the elasticity of marginal social utility of income. (See also Chapter 3, Section 3.1.)

1.2.7. *Risk and uncertainty*

Risk and uncertainty can be incorporated by using expected values if the probability distribution of stochastic variables is known (the case of risk) or by using max-min expected value criteria and robust control methods if probability distributions are not known (the case of uncertainty). More specifically:

- Assume known probabilities (risk) and risk neutrality: Use the expected value of net benefits

$$\sum_j p_j B_j,$$

  where p_j is the probability that net benefits will take the value B_j.
- Assume known probabilities (risk) and risk aversion: Use the expected utility of benefits

$$\sum_j p_j U(B_j).$$

- Unknown probabilities (uncertainty, Knightian uncertainty): Use robust control or smooth ambiguity methods.
- Practical rule for parameter uncertainty: Use sensitivity analysis or Monte Carlo simulations.

1.2.8. *A generalized decision rule*

A generalized decision rule for NPV which takes into account distribution and uncertainty in costs and benefits can be written as

$$\text{NPV}(r(t)) = \sum_{i=1}^{N} \sum_{t=0}^{T-1} \frac{\omega_i \bar{B}_{i,t}(1 - eg_i)^t - \omega_i \bar{C}_{i,t}}{(1 + r(t))^t}$$

where ω_i is the distributional weight for income group i, $\bar{B}$, $\bar{C}$ are the expected benefits and costs, respectively, e is the elasticity of

WTP, g_i is the rate of growth of income for group i, and $r(t)$ is the time-dependent discount rate.

1.2.9. *Inflation*

In CBA, it is customary to use constant prices, i.e., prices fixed at a base year. Thus, WTP and WTA or benefits and costs should be expressed in real monetary terms with respect to a given base year. This means that any effects of inflation are netted out.

- When the analysis is carried out in constant prices, the financial or the social discount rate is to be expressed in real terms, while a nominal financial or social discount rate must be used with current prices.
- The formula for the calculation of the nominal discount rate, i, is
  - $(1 + i) = (1 + r)(1 + \pi)$, where i is the nominal rate, r is the real rate, π is the inflation rate, or
  - for the real discount rate, $r \approx i - \pi$.

In summary, CBA is a methodology that provides criteria that a decision-maker can use for accepting or rejecting investment projects. The methodology is general and can be used to evaluate both private and public projects, as well as projects with strong environmental components. CBA provides an important decision-making tool which is well founded in economic theory and its use by the public and the public sectors and international institutions is widespread.

References

European Commission. (2015). *Guide to Cost–Benefit Analysis of Investment Projects*. European Union.

Hanley, N., Barbier, E. (2009). *Pricing Nature: Cost–Benefit Analysis and Environmental Policy*. Cheltenham, UK: Edward Elgar Publishing.

Pearce, D., Atkinson, G., Mourato, S. (2006). *Cost–Benefit Analysis and the Environment: Recent Developments*. Paris: OECD Publishing.

Zerbe, R. O. Jr., Bellas, A. S. (2006). *A Primer for Benefit–Cost Analysis*. Cheltenham, UK: Edward Edgar Publishing.

Chapter 2

Discounting

2.1. Fundamental Concepts

Discounting refers to the process of assigning a lower weight, i.e., importance, to a unit of benefit or cost in the future than to that unit in the present time. The further into the future the benefit or cost occurs, the lower the weight attached to it (Pearce *et al.*, 2006). When long-term projects are evaluated (note that the vast majority of environmental, and especially climate-change-related, projects are long-term), the weights refer to the benefits and costs associated with future generations:

- The social discount rate (SDR) is the rate of decrease in the social value of public sector income or consumption over time. Two approaches for determining social discount rates are usually considered:

  (a) the social time preference (STP) approach and
  (b) the social opportunity cost (SOC) approach.

- The STP is the rate of decrease in the social value of consumption. It is also known as the consumption rate of interest (CRI).
- The SOC is usually identified with the real rate of return earned on a marginal project in the private sector.
- In CBA, and especially in environmental CBA, we concentrate on the STP (CRI).

Following Brent (2006), consider a simple two-period case where benefits today are negative (that is, they are costs C_0) and there are positive benefits in the next period B_1. Total benefits B could then be expressed as

$$B = -C_0 + B_1.$$

If C_0 is the basis for all the calculations (that is, the numeraire), the benefits can be weighted relative to C_0 using the time-dependent weights a_t (a_t is the value of a unit of benefits in any year t):

$$B = -a_0 C_0 + a_1 B_1.$$

Assuming a constant decline rate of the weights over time, the benefit stream can be expressed in today-value terms by dividing every term above by a_0. Then benefit stream B can be renamed the NPV and it can be represented by

$$\text{NPV} = -C_0 + \frac{a_1}{a_0} B_1, \quad \frac{a_1}{a_0} = \frac{1}{1+r}, \quad \text{NPV} = -C_0 + \frac{B_1}{1+r},$$

where r is the discount rate.

Therefore, in discounting, weights associated with benefits or costs accruing in the future are lower relative to weights associated with earlier periods. This leads to what could be considered a moral dilemma, which is explained below:

- Let the weight that is associated with a benefit or a cost occurring in any future year, t, be w_t. Discounting implies that $w_t < 1$. Moreover, discounting implies that the weight attached to, for example, 60 years in the future should be lower than the weight attached to 30 years in the future. The discounting formula is

$$w_t = \frac{1}{(1+r)^t}, \text{ or in continuous time, } w(t) = e^{-\rho t}.$$

Note that w_t, $w(t)$ is called the **discount factor** while r or ρ is the **discount rate**.

- If $r = 0.03$, then $w_{60} = 0.169$. This means that a gain or loss 60 years in the future would be valued at only 16.9% of its value now. Still using the 3% discount rate, this means that environmental

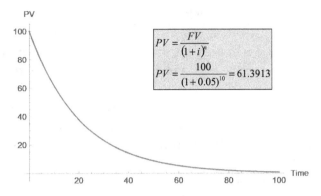

Figure 1: Present value.

damage 100 years from now would be valued at just 5% of the value that would be assigned to it if it occurred today. Moreover, if the discount rate is 10% (rather than 3%), environmental damage 100 years from now would be zero in present value terms.

The arithmetic illustrates the alleged "tyranny" of discounting.

- If the discount rate is relatively high, benefits accruing in the distant future, for example, benefits from preventing serious climate change, will have a very small present value now. This will make it difficult to accept projects that aim to prevent the impacts of climate change in the distant future, using CBA rules.

As shown in Figure 1, where FV stands for future value:

- €100 worth of benefits which will be received after 10 years have a present value now of €61.3913 at a 5% discount rate.
- After 50 years, they have a present value of €8.72.
- After 100 years, they have a present value of €0.76.

2.2. Zero Discounting

Zero discounting means that $r = 0$ and $w_t = 1$ for all t. This implies that the present and the future have the same weight and that all generations are regarded as equal over time (now and in the future):

- A low discount rate implies that higher future consumption is valuable, and therefore more investment should be undertaken by the present generation. A low discount rate also implies that more investment projects will be accepted relative to a higher discount rate.
- Zero discounting implies less consumption for the current generation. This applies to every generation so that each successive generation will have low consumption in order to invest more in the future.
- The maximin Rawlsian welfare criterion — which implies that the welfare of the worst-off individual will be maximized — would reject the zero discount policy (see Pearce *et al.* (2006) for more details regarding zero discounting).
- Not discounting creates a technical problem in optimizing infinite horizon models since in this case, welfare integrals or sums do not converge and the overtaking optimality criterion should be used.

2.3. The Social Discount Rate: The Ramsey Formula

The SDR can be defined by an equilibrium condition in two equivalent ways:

(1) Following Arrow *et al.* (2012, 2014) and considering a social planner who would be indifferent between €1 received at time t and €ε received today when the marginal utility of €ε today equals the marginal utility of €1 at time t, or

$$\varepsilon \cdot U'(c(0)) = e^{-\rho t} U'(c(t)) \cdot 1 \Rightarrow \varepsilon = \frac{e^{-\rho t} U'(c(t)) \cdot 1}{U'(c(0))} = 1 \cdot e^{-r_t t},$$

$$(1)$$

where r_t denotes the annual consumption discount rate between periods 0 and t and ρ is the utility discount rate.

Using the isoelastic utility function

$$U(c) = \frac{c^{1-\eta}}{1-\eta}, \quad U'(c) = c^{-\eta}, \quad \eta \geq 1$$

and taking logs, we obtain

$$-\rho t + \ln\left(\frac{U'(c(t))}{U'(c(0))}\right) + \ln 1 = -r_t t + \ln 1 \Rightarrow$$

$$r_t = \rho - \frac{1}{t}\ln\left(\frac{U'(c(t))}{U'(c(0))}\right) \Rightarrow$$

$$r_t = \rho - \frac{1}{t}\ln\left(\frac{c(t)^{-\eta}}{c(0)^{-\eta}}\right) \Rightarrow$$

$$r_t = \rho - \frac{1}{t}(-\eta\ln c(t) + \eta\ln c(0)).$$

$$\text{For } t \to 0, \quad r_t = \rho - (-\eta)\frac{d\ln c(t)}{dt} \Rightarrow$$

$$r_t = \rho + \eta g(t).$$

This is the Ramsey formula for discounting and $g(t)$ is the consumption rate of growth.

(2) Following Gollier (2007), and considering a marginal investment in a zero coupon bond of €1 which leaves the marginal utility of the representative agent unchanged, or

$$1 \cdot U'(c(0)) = e^{-\rho t}U'(c(t))e^{r_t t}, \tag{2}$$

where r_t is interpreted as per period rate of return at date 0 for a zero coupon bond maturing at date t.

- Taking logs in (2), we obtain

$$r_t = \rho - \frac{1}{t}\ln\left(\frac{U'(c(t))}{U'(c(0))}\right) \quad \text{or} \quad r_t = \rho - \frac{d}{dt}\ln U'(c(t)).$$

- Assuming a constant relative risk aversion utility function,

$$U(c(t)) = \frac{c^{1-\eta}}{1-\eta},$$

where η is both the coefficient of relative risk aversion and (minus) the elasticity of marginal utility with respect to consumption, we again obtain the Ramsey formula:

$$r_t = \rho + \eta g(t),$$

where $g(t) = \frac{dc(t)/dt}{c(t)}$ is the consumption rate of growth.

2.3.1. *Parameter interpretation*

- Utility discount rate, ρ: If one values future utilities less for reasons of impatience or hazard: $\rho > 0$.
- The wealth effect, ηg: The weight one places on the future depends on what state one will find oneself (or future generations) in the future. If society is richer in the future, $(g > 0)$, then less value will be placed on increments to consumption in the future, hence future benefits and costs are discounted. Society values projects that have payoffs in the future less if the future is richer and there is diminishing marginal utility. The higher the ηg, the higher the SDR. This promotes consumption now, relative to investment now and vice versa.
- The elasticity of marginal utility η can be interpreted as a parameter characterizing consumption smoothing, inequality aversion, and relative risk aversion. For more details, see Dasgupta (2008) and OECD (2018).

In the climate change literature, Cline (1992) uses $\rho = 0\%$ and $\eta = 1.5$, Nordhaus (1994) uses $\rho = 3\%$ and $\eta = 1$, and Stern (2006) uses $\rho = 0.1\%$ and $\eta = 1$ (see Table 1). Table 2, in which η is denoted

Table 1:   Implicit values of r in leading climate policy evaluations.

	$\rho(\%)$	η	$g(\%)$	$r(\%)$
Cline (1992)	0.0	1.5	1.3	2.05
Nordhaus (1994)	3.0	1.0	1.3	4.30
Stern (2006)	0.1	1.0	1.3	1.40

Table 2: Indicative SDR rates based on the STP approach.

Non-CF* countries	g	e	p	SDR
Austria	1.9	1.63	1.0	4.1
Denmark	1.9	1.28	1.1	3.5
France	2.0	1.26	0.9	3.4
Italy	1.3	1.79	1.0	3.3
Germany	1.3	1.61	1.0	3.1
Netherlands	1.3	1.44	0.9	2.8
Sweden	2.5	1.20	1.1	4.1
CF* countries	g	e	p	SDR
Czech Rep.	3.5	1.31	1.1	5.7
Hungary	4.0	1.68	1.4	8.1
Poland	3.8	1.12	1.0	5.3
Slovakia	4.5	1.48	1.0	7.7

Note: *CF: Cohesion Fund.

Source: European Commission (2008).

as e and ρ is denoted as p, shows SDR rates calculated using the SDR in certain EU countries.

2.4. The Social Opportunity Cost of Capital

In the Ramsey formula, r reflects the production possibilities in the economy, rather than the consumption possibilities reflected by the $\rho + \eta g$ part. Then $\rho + \eta g$ is the social time preference (STP) rate while r is the equilibrium social marginal productivity of capital in the economy, which reflects the SOC.

The SOC is the alternative rate of return that a government could obtain by investing public funds elsewhere in the economy or the cost of financing a public project from the capital markets (OECD, 2018).

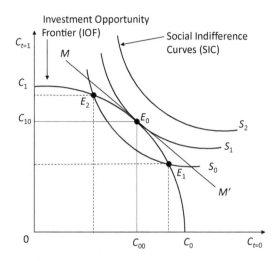

Figure 2:   Optimal consumption-investment choice in a two-period model.
Notes: Point E_0 is the social optimum where the IOF is tangential to the highest SIC. The slope of an SIC is the social time preference (STP) rate, while the slope of the IOF is the social opportunity cost of capital (SOC). At the social optimum, STP = SOC = the market rate of interest. At E_0, optimal first-period investment is C_0C_{00}, and consumption is $0C_{00}$. Optimal second-period consumption is $0C_{10}$. Point E_1 is not optimal. At this point, SOC > STP indicating that investment should be increased until the two rates are equalized. At E_2, STP > SOC and investment should be reduced.

In a deterministic competitive framework and in equilibrium (see Figure 2),

$$\text{SOC} = \text{STP} = \text{the market rate of interest.}$$

2.5.   The SOC as the SDR

The social discount rate can also be approximated by observed rates of return on relatively risk-free assets:

- The return on government bonds is a typical approach in determining the SDR. These bonds are considered to be relatively low-risk assets since they embody sovereign risk, have sufficient maturity, and represent the cost of government borrowing.

An example is the use of returns on bonds by the Norwegian and Dutch governments to approximate the SDR, with an added risk premium (OECD, 2018).

- The SOC is sometimes estimated using some weighted average of pre-tax rate of return to private capital, post-tax rate of return to consumer savings, and foreign financing, with the weights depending on the expected source of funds (Spackman, 2017).

2.6. The SDR under Risk

When future consumption is uncertain, the SDR formula becomes

$$r_t = \rho - \frac{1}{t} \ln \frac{EU'(c(t))}{U'(c(0))},$$

where E denotes the expectation operator.

If we expect to consume more in the future, that is, $Ec_t > c_0$, the marginal utility of one more euro in the future is smaller than the marginal utility of one more euro immediately: $U'(Ec(t)) < U'(c(0))$. This implies that

$$-\frac{1}{t} \ln \frac{EU'(c(t))}{U'(c(0))}$$

is positive. This positive wealth effect is increasing in the expected growth rate of consumption over the entire period $[0, t]$ and increasing in the rate at which marginal utility is decreasing with consumption, which is measured by the index of relative risk aversion, η.

The intuition is that higher expectation about future incomes reduces the willingness to save, thereby raising the SDR.

- If the logarithm of consumption follows a stationary Brownian motion

$$d \ln c_t = \mu dt + \sigma dz_t, \text{ which implies } \frac{dc}{c} = (\mu + 0.5\sigma^2)dt + \sigma dz,$$

where μ and σ are two scalars measuring, respectively, the mean and standard deviation of the change in log consumption, then the

Ramsey formula becomes (Gollier, 2007)

$$r_t = \rho + \eta\mu - 0.5\eta^2\sigma^2. \tag{3}$$

- The last term in equation (3) is a precautionary effect: uncertainty about the rate of growth in consumption reduces the discount rate, causing more savings in the present. The magnitude of the precautionary effect is, however, likely to be small, at least for the United States.
- Using annual data from 1889–1978 for the US, Kocherlakota (1996) estimated μ to be 1.8% and σ to equal 3.6%. This implies that the precautionary effect is 0.26%.
- The higher the uncertainty $(0.5\eta^2\sigma^2)$, the lower the SDR. This promotes investment now relative to consumption now as a precaution against future uncertain consumption and vice versa.

2.7. Project Risks and Discounting

In a number of countries (for example, France, Norway, and the Netherlands), the discount rate is adjusted to accommodate project risks. Project risks can be categorized into two main types, with one being relevant to the SDR and the other not:

(1) The first type, **unsystematic risk**, pertains to the uncertainty associated with inaccurately estimating the costs and benefits of a project. Within a specific project, certain elements may end up being more or less costly than anticipated due to unforeseen technical or other factors.

   These risks can be diversified across a portfolio of public projects. Asset pricing theory indicates that this type of risk should not impact the value of an asset or the appropriate discount rate.

(2) The second type of risk is **systematic risk**, which occurs when the uncertain costs and benefits of a project are correlated with the returns available in the overall macroeconomy.

   Systematic risk cannot be eliminated through diversification across different projects due to its macro-level nature.

When a project's net benefits are influenced by uncertainty in the broader macroeconomy, asset pricing theory suggests that the discount rate should be adjusted by adding a risk premium. This risk premium reflects the project's specific risk profile related to systematic risk, rather than the diversifiable risk. See OECD (2018) for more details.

2.8. The Ramsey Formula under Project Risk

The Ramsey formula can be extended to take into account project risk as described in OECD (2018, p. 209). Under the assumption that the project net benefits and consumption growth follow a bivariate normal distribution, incorporating project risk leads to a simple extension to the right-hand side of the Ramsey formula for a risky project j: SDR $= \rho + \eta\mu - 0.5\eta^2\sigma^2 + \eta^2\beta_j\sigma^2$.

The parameter β_j is the consumption beta, which measures the correlation (covariance) between the net benefits of project j and systematic risk associated with consumption growth:

- If $\beta_j = 1$, then a 1% increase in consumption growth will be expected to lead to a 1% growth in the project net benefits.
- If $\beta_j > 1$, then the project benefits are expected to increase by more than 1% when consumption grows by 1%, hence introducing proportionally more systematic risk than existing in the economy.
- If $\beta_j < 0$, the project reduces risk and has insurance properties.
- If $\beta_j = 0$, we are back to the Ramsey formula under risk.

2.9. The Capital Asset Pricing Model and the SDR

The capital asset pricing model (CAPM) can also be used in the approximation of the SDR. The CAPM pricing formula determines a required rate of return according to the risk associated with a specific asset. It includes a risk premium and can be used as a discount rate for a specific project. The CAPM asset return formula is

$$r_j = r_f + \beta_j(r_m - r_f),$$

where r_j is the required rate of return for asset j, r_f is the risk-free rate of return, r_m is the rate of return on the market/wealth portfolio, and β_j is the project beta, which reflects the correlation between asset j and the market portfolio. The risk premium for this project is given by the market premium $(r_m - r_f)$ multiplied by the project beta, β_j.

The risk premium will be positive when β_j is positive. The logic of this pricing formula is similar to the Ramsey formula under project risk except that the covariance is with a market portfolio of assets rather than consumption.

This formula for the SDR is project-specific but can be calculated by looking at suitable market returns and calculating the associated project betas (see Table 3).

Table 3:   Example of sector-level betas in the Indian market, 2006–2018.

Sector	Beta
Auto	0.818
Banking	1.165
Capital goods	1.983
Consumer durable	0.786
FMCG	0.594
Health	0.549
IT	0.785
Metal	1.212
Oil	1.012
Power	1.004
Realty	1.349

Notes: FMCG; Fast-moving consumer goods; IT: Information technology.
Data source: Gupta (2020).

The security market line is defined as

$$r_j = r_f + \beta_j(r_m - r_f), \quad \beta_j = \frac{\mathrm{Cov}_{j,m}}{(\sigma_m)^2} = \frac{\sigma_j \times \sigma_m \times \rho_{j,m}}{(\sigma_m)^2} = \frac{\sigma_j \times \rho_{j,m}}{\sigma_m},$$

where σ_j is the standard deviation of asset (or security) j's returns, σ_m is the standard deviation of returns of the market, $\rho_{j,m}$ is the correlation coefficient between the asset's returns and the market returns, and $\mathrm{Cov}_{j,m}$ is the covariance of returns of asset j and the market.

The accept/reject decision can be clarified with the help of Figures 3 and 4. The security market line (SML) in Figure 3 represents the relationship between the required rate of return — or the opportunity cost — of equity capital and the firm's beta. An all-equity firm should accept a project whose IRR is greater than the cost of equity capital and should reject a project whose IRR is less than the cost of equity capital. The acceptance region is the area above the SML, while the rejection region is the area below the SML.

Table 4 and Figure 4 provide an example of the use of the SML in project appraisal. Projects with positive NPV have an IRR which is above the SML for the specific β of the project.

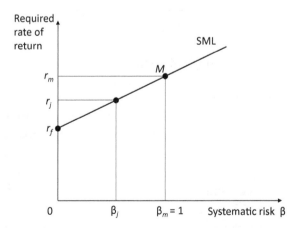

Figure 3: The security market line (SML).

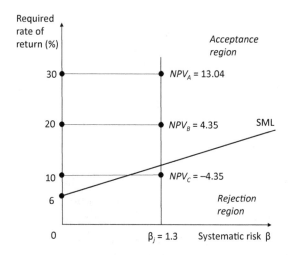

Figure 4: Accept/reject regions for the values in Table 4.

Table 4: Accept/reject decision and the SML.

Project	Project's β	Next year cash flow	IRR	NPV at 15%	Decision
A	1.3	130	30%	13.04	Accept
B	1.3	120	20%	4.35	Accept
C	1.3	110	10%	−4.35	Reject

2.10. Declining Discount Rates

According to Weitzman (2001), even if every individual believes in a constant discount rate, the widespread opinion on what it should be makes the effective social discount rate decline significantly over time:

- This means that using an uncertain but constant discount rate to calculate the expected net present value (ENPV) of a project is equivalent to calculating the NPV using a declining over time "certainty-equivalent" discount rate.

- Weitzman (2001) assumed that the uncertain discount rate is distributed according to a gamma density,

$$f(r) = \frac{\beta^\alpha}{\Gamma(\alpha)} r^{\alpha-1} e^{-\beta r},$$

where α, β are positive parameters which can be estimated from data. This approach leads to an effective discount rate, which is declining in time, of the form

$$r(t) = \frac{\mu}{1 + t\sigma^2/\mu}, \quad \mu = \frac{\alpha}{\beta}, \quad \sigma = \frac{\alpha}{\beta^2}.$$

- The declining certainty-equivalent discount rate result can be presented using a simpler approach following Cropper *et al.* (2014):

  o Assume that a flow of net benefits at time t, $Z(t)$ is discounted to the present at a constant exponential discount rate r. The present value of net benefits received at time t equals

  $$\text{NPV}(t \,|\, r) = Z(t) e^{-rt}.$$

  o Let the discount rate r be distributed as a random variable with a given density, then the expected NPV at time t can be calculated using an expected discount factor $p(t)$ as

  $$p(t) Z(t) = \text{E}(e^{-rt}) Z(t).$$

  o Then the certainty-equivalent discount rate $R(t)$ used to discount $Z(t)$ to the present time is defined by

  $$p(t) = e^{-R(t)t} = \text{E}(e^{-rt}).$$

  Taking logs and solving for $R(t)$, we obtain

  $$R(t) = -\frac{1}{t} \ln p(t) = -\frac{1}{t} \ln \text{E}[e^{-rt}].$$

  o To illustrate, assume that r is distributed according to a triangular distribution with $r = 1\%$, 4%, and 7%, with probabilities, 0.25, 0.5, and 0.25, respectively. Then the certainty-equivalent discount rate takes the values

$$t = 1: 0.039775 = -1 \cdot \ln[0.25e^{-0.01} + 0.5e^{-0.04} + 0.25e^{-0.07}],$$

$$t = 50: 0.0296694 = \left(-\frac{1}{50}\right) \cdot \ln[0.25e^{-0.01 \cdot 50} + 0.5e^{-0.04 \cdot 50}$$
$$+ 0.25e^{-0.07 \cdot 50}],$$

$$t = 100: 0.0228912 = \left(-\frac{1}{100}\right) \cdot \ln[0.25e^{-0.01 \cdot 100} + 0.5e^{-0.04 \cdot 100}$$
$$+ 0.25e^{-0.07 \cdot 100}].$$

- The time path of the certainty-equivalent discount rate is referred to as the **effective term structure**.
- The **instantaneous** certainty-equivalent discount rate, or **forward rate**, is defined by the rate of change in the expected discount factor:

$$-\frac{(dp(t)/dt)}{p(t)} = F(t).$$

This is the rate at which benefits in period $t + 1$ would be discounted back to period t. Figure 5 shows the **forward rate F_t** (solid line) and **the effective term structure R_t** (dashed line) resulting from the numerical example above.

The structure of the SDR for the UK economy, which has adopted a declining discount rate, is shown in Figure 6.

An example of the comparison between exponential and declining SDRs is shown in Figure 7, in which

$$D(t)^{\exp} = \frac{1}{(1 + 0.035)^t},$$

$$D(t)^{decl} = \frac{1}{(1 + 0.035t)^{0.035}},$$

$$D(100)^{\exp} = 0.032, \quad D(100)^{decl} = 0.949.$$

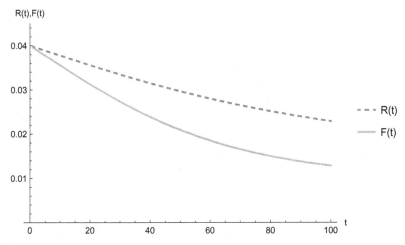

Figure 5: The term structure of the declining discount rate and the forward rate.

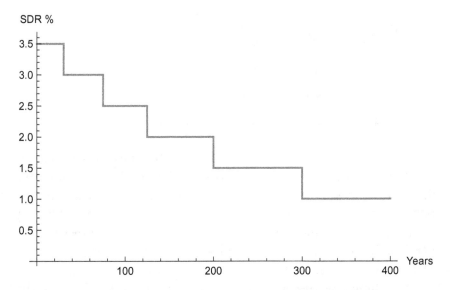

Figure 6: The UK effective term structure of the SDR.
Data source: Calculated from data from HM Treasury.

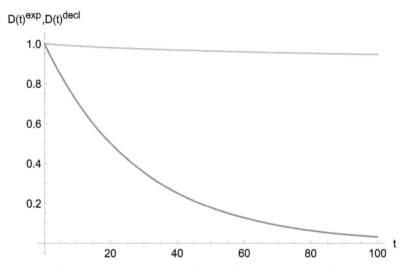

Figure 7:   Comparison: Exponential (bottom line) vs declining SDR (top line).

Consider a project with

$$C(0) = -0.5, \quad B(100) = 1, \text{ then}$$
$$\text{NPV}^{\text{exp}} = -0.5 + 0.032 * 1 < 0,$$
$$\text{NPV}^{decl} = -0.5 + 0.949 * 1 > 0.$$

Table 5 shows a comparison of the SDR and the concept on which it is based, for selected countries in the world. SDRs may vary depending on the type of investment being evaluated and the specific policy context. Additionally, different governments may use different methods to determine SDRs, so the rates may not be directly comparable. However, this table provides a general comparison of the SDRs used by these countries for public investments.

To summarize, discounting is at the core of CBA. Choosing the correct discount rate — especially for environmental projects for which benefits are expected in the long run, such as climate change-related projects — is of utmost importance and is directly related to sustainability. This chapter reviewed the main approaches in determining the appropriate discount rate, especially when benefits

Table 5: Social discount rate in selected countries.

Country	SDR (%)	SOC or STP	Source
Canada	10	SOC	Castillo and Zhangallimbay (2021)
Denmark	3.5	Both	Groom *et al.* (2022)
European Union	3	STP	Groom *et al.* (2022)
United Kingdom	3.5*	STP	Castillo and Zhangallimbay (2021)
France	4.5	SOC	Groom *et al.* (2022)
Germany	1	STP	Groom *et al.* (2022)
China	8	Both	Castillo and Zhangallimbay (2021)
India	12	SOC	Castillo and Zhangallimbay (2021)
Brazil	8.5	SOC	Groom *et al.* (2022)
Chile	6	SOC	Groom *et al.* (2022)

Notes: *Lower differentiated rates for projects of over 30 years.
Data sources: Castillo and Zhangallimbay (2021) and Groom *et al.* (2022).

are expected in the distant future and the project is affected by non-systematic risks.

References

Arrow, K. J., Cropper, M. L., Gollier, C., Groom, B., Heal, G. M., Newell, R. G., Nordhaus, W. D., Pindyck, R. S., Pizer, W. A., Portney, P. R., Sterner, T., Tol, R. S. J., Weitzman, M. L. (2012). How should benefits and costs be discounted in an intergenerational context? The views of an expert panel, Resources for the Future, RFF, DP-12-53.

Arrow, K. J., Cropper, M. L., Gollier, C., Groom, B., Heal, G. M., Newell, R. G., Nordhaus, W. D., Pindyck, R. S., Pizer, W. A., Portney, P. R., Sterner, T., Tol, R. S. J., Weitzman, M. L. (2014). Should governments use a declining discount rate in project analysis? *Review of Environmental Economics and Policy*, 8, 145–163.

Brent, R. (2006). *Applied Cost-Benefit Analysis* (2nd edn.). Cheltenham, UK: Edward Elgar Publishing.

Castillo, J. G., Zhangallimbay, D. (2021). The social discount rate in the evaluation of investment projects: An application for Ecuador. *CEPAL Review*, 134, 75–95.

Cline, W. R. (1992). *The Economics of Global Warming*. Washington, DC: Institute for International Economics.

Cropper, M. L., Freeman, M. C., Groom, B., Pizer, W. A. (2014). Declining discount rates. *American Economic Review: Papers and Proceedings*, 104, 538–543.

Dasgupta, P. (2008). Discounting climate change. *Journal of Risk and Uncertainty*, 37, 141–169.

European Commission (2008). *Guide to Cost Benefit Analysis of Investment Projects*. European Union.

Gollier, C. (2007). The consumption-based determinants of the term structure of discount rates. *Mathematical Financial Economics*, 1, 81–101.

Groom, B., Drupp, M. A., Freeman, M. C., Nesje, F. (2022). The future, now: A review of social discounting. *Annual Review of Resource Economics*, 14, 467–491.

Gupta, H. (2020). Stability of beta in various sectors in different phases of stock market. *Journal of Commerce & Accounting Research*, 9, 25–32.

Kocherlakota, N. (1996). The equity premium: It's still a puzzle. *Journal of Economic Literature*, 34, 42–71.

Nordhaus, W. D. (1994). *Managing the Global Commons: The Economics of Climate Change*. Cambridge, MA: MIT Press.

OECD (2018). *Cost–Benefit Analysis and the Environment: Further Developments and Policy Use*. Paris: OECD Publishing.

Pearce, D., Atkinson, G., Mourato, S. (2006). *Cost–Benefit Analysis and the Environment: Recent Developments*. Paris: OECD Publishing.

Spackman, M. (2017). Social discounting: The SOC/STP divide. Grantham Research Institute on Climate Change and the Environment, working paper 182. https://www.cccep.ac.uk/wp-content/uploads/2017/02/Working-paper-182-Spackman-Feb2017.pdf.

Stern, N. (2006). *The Economics of Climate Change: The Stern Review*. Cambridge, UK: Cambridge University Press.

Weitzman, M. L. (2001). Gamma discounting, *American Economic Review*, 91, 260–271.

Chapter 3

Distributional Issues and Benefits Transfer

3.1. Distributional Considerations

In project selection, cost–benefit analysis (CBA) aims to secure the most efficient allocation of scarce economic resources. This implies that individual projects are selected if discounted benefits exceed discounted costs.

If a set of potential projects is being considered, CBA seeks to select the subset that maximizes aggregate value subject to existing resource constraints. Investment projects, however, impact different income groups which could be either gainers or losers in the context of the Kaldor–Hicks test, and this introduces **distributional** consequences:

- Project evaluation related to environmental goods and services has important distributional implications because gainers and losers might belong to distinct income groups.
- It is well known from economic theory that efficiency and distribution are not always compatible. In this chapter, distributional considerations are included in standard CBA, and the trade-offs between efficiency and distribution are explored.
- To provide a clear example of these trade-offs, assume for simplicity that a project will affect only two distinct groups of individuals, 1 and 2. Let NB_1, NB_2 be the net benefits to each group.

Distributional considerations can be incorporated into the CBA by assigning a weight (a_i), $i = 1, 2$, to the net benefits received by each group. That is,

$$NB = a_1 NB_1 + a_2 NB_2.$$

- Conventional CBA assumes that $a_1 = a_2 = 1$. That is, weights of unity are assigned to the net benefits of each group regardless of which group is the gainers or the losers from the project.

3.1.1. *Distributional weights*

If more than one income group is affected by the project, then the criterion that incorporates distributional considerations is that a project should be undertaken if

$$\sum_i a_i NB_i > 0,$$

where a_i varies across income or social groups.

For example, assume two groups, 1 and 2. Group 1 receives the benefits and group 2 pays the costs of a project $B_1 = 200$, $C_2 = -100$. Conventional CBA implies that

$$NB_{project} = -100 + 200 > 0.$$

Break-even distributional weights are determined by asking the following question: What weight should be assigned to 1 and 2 so that the project's NPV is zero?

$$0 = NB_{project} = 200 - a_2 100 \Rightarrow a_2 = 2.$$

Thus, for a zero NPV, the loss of group 1 should be weighted twice as much as the gain of group 2:

$$0 = NB_1 + a_2 NB_2 \rightarrow a_2^* = \frac{NB_1}{NB_2}, \quad \text{with } NB_2 < 0.$$

For $a_2 = 3$, $a_1 = 1$,

$$NB_{project} = 200 - 3 \cdot 100 < 0.$$

Thus, the project is rejected.

3.1.2. *Explicit distributional weights*

One way to provide numerical estimates for distributional weights is to consider the relationship between the average income per capita in the economy and the average income per capita of a specific income or social group:

- In this way, explicit distributional weights can be defined as

$$a_i = \left(\frac{\bar{Y}}{Y_i} \right)^e,$$

where $\bar{Y}$ is the average or mean income per capita, Y_i is the income per capita of the ith group, and e is the elasticity of the marginal utility of income which reflects society's aversion to income inequality.
- In principle, e could range from $0 \leq e < \infty$, although conventional or "unweighted" CBA is equivalent to assuming $e = 0$, as this would result in $a_i = 1$.
- Figure 1 shows distributional weights when the average income per capita is 2, and the group income per capita varies from 0.5 to 3.

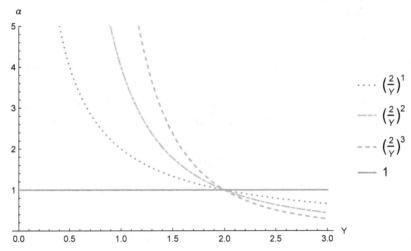

Figure 1: The relationship between distributional weights and income for $\bar{Y} = 2$ and $e = \{1, 2, 3\}$.

Table 1:   An example (distributional weights and CBA) $a_R = 0.75^e$, $a_P = 1.5^e$.

Degree of inequality aversion: e	Net benefits individual R	Net benefits individual P	Total net benefits
0	-200	100	-100
0.5	-173.2	122.47	-50.73
1	-150	150	0
2	-112.5	225	112.5

Notes: Negative net benefits correspond to costs. Total net benefits are calculated as $a_R \times (-200) + a_P \times 100$.

It is clear that for groups with average per capita income below 2, the distributional weight is greater than 1, while the opposite applies for groups with average per capita income greater than 2.

An example of the way in which distributional weights operate is provided in Table 1. For more details, see Pearce *et al.* (2006).

3.1.3.   *Distributional CBA and climate change damages*

The methodology described in the previous sections could be used to incorporate distributional considerations into damages from climate change across the globe.

If we assume that countries are divided into rich and poor countries, world damages from climate change can be defined as

$$D_{\text{WORLD}} = a_P D_P + a_R D_R.$$

The weights a_P and a_R are calculated as $a_i = \left(\frac{\bar{Y}}{Y_i}\right)^e$, where $\bar{Y}$ is (the global) average per capita income, Y_i is a (rich or poor) country's average per capita income (adjusted for differences in purchasing power across countries), and e is the elasticity of the marginal utility of income (see Table 2).

Table 2: Estimates of distributional weighted climate change damages (USD billions).

	Value of e			
	$e = 0$	$e = 0.5$	$e = 1.0$	$e = 2.0$
Poor countries	106	313.6	927.5	8,115.6
Rich countries	216	125.8	73.2	24.8
Total	322	439.3	1,000.7	8,140.15

Notes: The weights are calculated using World Bank data on GDP per capita (PPP current international \$) in 2021, which is \$54,758 for high-income countries, \$2,124 for low-income countries, and \$18,604 for the world. The weights are $a_H = 0.339^e$, $a_L = 8.75^e$. See also Pearce (2003) for estimates of damages between poor and rich countries when $e = 0$.

Then global damages (Pearce *et al.*, 2006) are as follows:

$$D_{\text{WORLD}} = D_P \times \left(\frac{\bar{Y}}{Y_P}\right)^e + D_R \times \left(\frac{\bar{Y}}{Y_R}\right)^e,$$

$$D_{\text{WORLD}} = \$106\text{bn} \times \left(\frac{\$3,333}{\$1,110}\right)^e + \$216\text{bn} \times \left(\frac{\$3,333}{\$10,000}\right)^e.$$

More generally, for n countries, the global damage from climate change will be

$$D_w = \sum_{i=1}^{n} a_i D_i, \quad a_i \in [0, 1].$$

But if country i gives a different weight to the damages of the rest of the world,

$$D_i = \omega \sum_{t=0}^{\infty} \frac{D_{it}}{(1+r)^t} + (1 - \omega) \sum_{j \neq i}^{n} a_j \left[\sum_{t=0}^{\infty} \frac{D_{jt}}{(1+r)^t}\right], \quad \omega \in [0, 1].$$

For a more detailed presentation of differences among countries regarding distributional weights, see Table 3. For additional information, see Anthoff and Tol (2010) and OECD (2018).

Table 3:   Distributional issues and damages from climate change.

SCC principle	Interpretation	Weight attached to the well-being of citizens abroad	Equity weight	Discount rate
Sovereignty	A country does not consider impacts elsewhere: damage to people abroad has "no standing".	No: $\omega = 1$	—	$r = \rho + \eta g_h$
Altruism	A country considers impacts elsewhere: to the extent that its citizens care about those abroad but not as much as about themselves.	Yes: depending on extent of altruism — i.e., $0.5 < \omega \leq 1$	$a = (Y_h/Y_f)^\eta$	$r = \rho + \eta g_f$
Cooperation	A country behaves as a global decision-maker would, i.e., it adopts the SCC that would maximize global welfare.	Yes: $\omega = 0.5$	$a = 1$	$r = \rho + \eta g_f$
Good neighbor	A country considers impacts elsewhere and cares about those abroad as it would do citizens within its domestic borders but allows for income differences.	Yes: $\omega = 0.5$	$a = (Y_h/Y_f)^\eta$	$r = \rho + \eta g_f$
Equity weighting	Equity weighting that the global decision-maker would adopt on the basis of differences in income (or consumption) per capita between countries.	Yes: $\omega = 0.5$	$a = (Y_w/Y_f)^\eta$	$r = \rho + \eta g_f$
Compensation	A country considers that it has a duty or requirement to compensate (nominally) damages that it causes beyond its borders. Compensation refers to how this damage is valued by those in the victim countries.	Yes: $0 < \omega < 1$	$a = 1$	$r = \rho + \eta g_h$

Notes: SCC: social cost of carbon, w: world, f: foreign, h: home.

3.2. Benefits Transfer

Benefits transfer (BT) can be defined as the transfer of existing estimates of non-market values to a new study which is different from the study for which the values were originally estimated (Boyle and Bergstrom, 1992).

Desvousges *et al.* (1998) provide two definitions for BT:

- **Broader concept**: The use of existing information designed for one specific context (original context) to address policy questions in another context (transfer context).
- **Narrower concept**: The use of values of a good estimated in one site (the "study site") as a proxy for values of the (same) good in another site (the "policy site"). This is the type of BT most commonly used in CBA.

3.2.1. *BT methods*

BT methods can be divided into four categories: (1) unit (naïve) BT, (2) adjusted unit BT, (3) value function transfer, and (4) meta-analytic function transfer:

(1) Unit BT involves estimating the value of an ecosystem service at a specific policy site. This estimation is done by multiplying the average unit value, which is determined at a study site, by the quantity of the ecosystem service present at the policy site. Unit values are typically expressed either as values per household or values per unit of area. When values are expressed per household, aggregation is based on the population that holds values for the particular ecosystem being considered. On the other hand, when values are expressed per unit of area, aggregation is done based on the area of the ecosystem.

(2) Adjusted unit transfer involves making simple adjustments to the transferred unit values to account for differences in characteristics between the study site and the policy site. Common adjustments include accounting for income differences and differences in price levels over time or between sites.

(3) Value or demand function transfer methods utilize functions that are estimated through various valuation approaches, such as travel cost, hedonic pricing, contingent valuation, or choice modeling. These functions are estimated for a study site and then combined with information on the values of explanatory variables to transfer values to the policy site.

By plugging the values of the explanatory variables of the policy site into the value function, a transferred value is calculated that better reflects the characteristics of the policy site.

(4) Meta-analytic function transfer involves using a value function that is estimated from multiple study results. This value function is combined with information on the values of the explanatory variables specific to the policy site in order to estimate values for this site. Unlike the value function derived from a single study, the meta-analytic function incorporates a broader range of site characteristics (e.g., socioeconomic and physical attributes) and study characteristics (e.g., valuation method) that cannot be captured by a single primary valuation study.

3.2.1.1. *Transfer methods: Unit or unadjusted (or naïve) WTP transfer*

The procedure utilized in this context involves borrowing an estimation of WTP from the study site (S) and applying it to the policy site (P). Typically, the estimation remains unadjusted, resulting in

$$\text{WTP}_S = \text{WTP}_P.$$

- Various unit values can be transferred, with mean or median measures being the most common choices.
- Mean values are well suited for CBA studies as they enable straightforward conversion into overall benefit estimates. For example, by multiplying the mean (average) WTP by the affected population, one can calculate the aggregate benefits.
- Factors that may differ between the study and policy sites and which impact WTP include the following:

o Socioeconomic and demographic characteristics of the populations involved, such as income, education level, and age.
o Physical characteristics of both the study and policy sites, including the environmental services provided by the good in question. For instance, in the case of a forest, it could involve factors like recreational opportunities in general and hiking or camping in particular.
o Changes in the provision of the valued good between the study and policy sites. For instance, the value derived from studies involving minor improvements in air quality may not apply to a policy entailing a substantial change in size of the area under consideration.
o Disparities in market conditions and the presence of market power.
o Temporal changes, which may involve shifts in valuations over time due to factors such as increasing incomes or diminishing availability of tropical forests.

Generally speaking, there is limited evidence supporting the assumption that unadjusted value transfer is applicable in practical scenarios.

3.2.1.2. *Adjusted methods: Efficient benefits transfer*

Efficient benefits transfer involves transferring economic or environmental values from one policy or study site to another. To ensure a successful benefits transfer, the following conditions should ideally hold:

Relevance: The policy and study sites should be relevant to each other in terms of their characteristics and context. They should share similar socioeconomic, demographic, and environmental attributes. The transfer is more likely to be accurate if the sites are comparable.

Transferability: The benefits being transferred should be transferable between the sites. This means that the underlying factors that determine the value should be consistent across the sites. For example, if the benefits being transferred are related to water quality, it is essential that the water quality indicators and conditions are similar between the sites.

Data availability: Sufficient and reliable data should be available for both the policy and study sites. This includes data on the environmental, economic, and social aspects relevant to the benefits being transferred. The data should be collected using similar methods and standards for comparability.

Compatibility: The policy and study sites should have compatible policy and institutional frameworks. The policy instruments, regulations, and governance structures should be similar enough to ensure that the transferred benefits can be effectively implemented and managed in the new context.

Adjustments: In some cases, adjustments may be necessary to account for any differences between the sites. This could involve scaling the benefits based on the disparities in site characteristics or applying statistical or econometric techniques to estimate the transferability accurately.

The WTP transfer with adjustment can be calculated as shown below:

- A widely used formula for adjusted transfer is

$$\text{WTP}_P = \text{WTP}_S (Y_P / Y_S)^e,$$

  where Y is the income per capita, WTP is the willingness to pay, and e is the income elasticity of the WTP. This latter term is an estimate of how the WTP for the (non-market) good in question varies with changes in income.
- According to this expression, if e is assumed to be equal to one, then the ratio of WTP at sites S and P is equivalent to the ratio of per capita incomes at the two sites. That is,

$$\text{WTP}_P / \text{WTP}_S = Y_P / Y_S.$$

An example of the consumer surplus transfer for recreational activities, provided by Rosenberger and Loomis (2001), is

$$\text{CS}_P = \frac{\text{CS}_S}{\Delta d_S}(d_1 \cdot N_1 - d_0 \cdot N_0),$$

where CS_P is the consumer surplus estimate for evaluating management or policy impacts on recreation, CS_S is the consumer surplus gain measure reported in the literature (the study case), d_i is the amount of recreation use in activity days before ($i = 0$) and after ($i = 1$) the management or policy action, N_i is the number of people participating in the recreation activity before ($i = 0$) and after ($i = 1$) the management or policy action, and Δd_S is the measured change in recreation participation or affected resource in the literature providing CS_S.

3.2.1.3. *Function transfer methods*

It is known that WTP at the study site is a function of a range of physical features of the site and its use, as well as the socioeconomic (and demographic) characteristics of the population at the site. This information can be used to transfer value from the study site to the policy site.

Following OECD (2018), let $\text{WTP}_S = f(A, B, C, Y)$, where A, B, C are additional and significant explanatory factors affecting WTP (in addition to Y) at site S. Then WTP_P can be estimated using the coefficients from this equation in combination with the values of A, B, C, Y at site P, i.e., $\text{WTP}_P = f(A_P, B_P, C_P, Y_P)$:

$$\text{WTP}_S = a_0 + a_1 A + a_2 B + a_3 C + a_4 Y,$$

$$\text{WTP}_P = a_0 + a_1 A_P + a_2 B_P + a_3 C_P + a_4 Y_P.$$

Assume that the explanatory factors are income, age, and educational attainment and that WTP_S increases with income and educational attainment but decreases with age. In this transfer approach, the entire benefit function would be transferred, with specific numerical values for the parameters, as follows:

$$\Rightarrow \text{WTP}_P = 3 + 0.5 Y_P - 0.3 \text{AGE}_P + 2.2 \text{EDUC}_P.$$

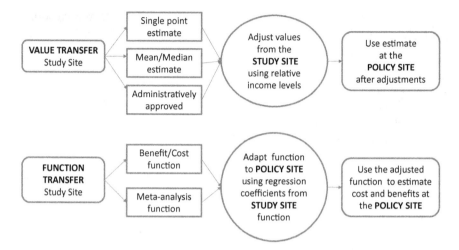

Figure 2:   Benefits transfer methods.

Another example of a transfer function (OECD, 2018) is

$$\text{WTP} = a_1 + a_2\text{TYPE\_OF\_SITE} + a_3\text{SIZE\_OF\_CHANGE}$$
$$+ a_4\text{VISITOR\_NUMBERS} + a_5\text{NON\_USERS}$$
$$+ a_6\text{INCOME} + a_7\text{ELICITATION\_FORMAT} + a_8\text{YEAR}.$$

The processes associated with value transfer and function transfer are illustrated in Figure 2.

3.2.2.   Challenges in BT methods

3.2.2.1.   Transfer errors

There are three types of errors that could affect the accuracy of benefits transfers: measurement error, generalization error, and publication selection bias.

(1) *Measurement error* in valuation estimates may result from weak methodologies or unreliable data. This type of error is also associated with the assumptions made by researchers conducting the primary research and can result from the many judgments,

technical assumptions, and decisions which they are required to make.

(2) *Generalization error* occurs when a measure of value is transferred from a study site to a policy site that has differences that are not taken into account. These could be differences in the characteristics of the population (e.g., income or education), differences in the characteristics of the environmental good, and so on.

(3) *Publication selection bias* occurs when the publication process through which valuation results are disseminated leads to a body of knowledge that is skewed to certain types of results and that does not meet the information needs of value transfer practitioners.

3.2.2.2. *Aggregation of transferred values*

Aggregation refers to the use of unit values obtained by a certain method to extend the valuation to the population or the area of the policy site. When values are expressed per beneficiary, aggregation requires the multiplication of the WTP per individual, by the number of individuals at the policy site. When values are expressed per unit area (e.g., hectare), aggregation requires the multiplication of the unit per hectare value WTP by the total area of the policy site. From the analyst's point of view, this requires the correct estimation, at the policy site, of the number of individuals who exhibit WTP for the specific environmental good, or the area that corresponds to the environmental good under valuation.

Aggregation can also refer to the summing up of the different ecosystem services provided by the same environmental good or the same services provided by a set of different environmental goods. In this type of aggregation, there are two stages: first, service aggregation and then aggregation over individuals or area. Extreme care should be taken in order to avoid double counting, which could lead to unrealistically large numbers. When system services are aggregated, independence between services is required. Correlation between services will lead to biased results.

3.2.2.3. *The spatial scale*

Characterization of the spatial scale at which services extend is also important. For example, a forest can provide *in situ* recreational services, at a regional scale, *ex situ* downstream flood control, and at a global *ex situ* scale, climate regulation through carbon sequestration. The scale at which aggregation will be implemented is important for the correct benefits transfer.

For global *ex situ* values, the number of beneficiaries who are located away from the environmental good, but who received its services, should be taken into account.

3.2.2.4. *Other challenges*

- Benefits transfer and aggregation based on unit values should take into account distributional issues, if the benefits or costs at the policy site accrue to different income or social groups. The distributional weights introduced in earlier sections could be used in such a case.
- When the benefits of an environmental good are extended to individuals in distant locations at the policy site, spatial discounting — which indicates that unit benefits are reduced with distance, in a way analogous to temporal discounting — might be necessary.

3.2.2.5. *Transfer reliability*

To test the reliability of BT between two sites, S and P, the direction of transfer is reversed and the original study site S is treated as policy site P, while the original policy site P is treated as study site S. Then the transferred estimate for the original study site is compared to the original own estimate of the study site. The transfer error is calculated as

$$\text{Transfer error} = \frac{(\text{transferred estimate} - \text{own-study estimate})}{\text{own-study estimate}} \times 100.$$

3.2.3. *Meta analysis*

In the context of benefits transfer, meta-regression analysis is a statistical technique used to estimate the economic value or benefits of a specific attribute or environmental good in a new location by utilizing information from existing studies conducted in different locations. BT is a method used when it is not feasible or practical to conduct new studies to estimate the value of a particular attribute or benefit in a specific context.

- Meta-regression analysis in BT involves combining data from multiple studies that have estimated the economic value of a specific attribute or benefit (such as clean water, biodiversity, or recreational opportunities) in different locations. The goal is to identify the relationship between the economic value and the attributes of the studies, such as study site characteristics, socioeconomic factors, or methodological choices.
- The meta-regression analysis model is of the basic form:

$$y_i = \alpha + \beta^T x_i + \varepsilon_i,$$

where i indexes each observation, y is the dependent variable (WTP for some non-market commodity or some set of services provided by the environmental good), α and β are parameters to be estimated and are, respectively, the intercept and slope coefficients for the model, x is a matrix of explanatory variables including methodology, site, and activity characteristics, and ε is the classical error term with zero mean and variance σ^2 (see Rosenberger and Loomis (2001) for more details).

- By conducting a meta-regression analysis, researchers can examine how different study characteristics influence the estimated economic values across the included studies. The analysis can help identify which attributes or factors are significant in determining the economic value and quantify their effect. This information can then be used to transfer the economic values from the existing study site to a new policy site with similar characteristics, for which no primary valuation study exists.

- Meta-regression analysis in BT is based on the assumption that the relationship between the attributes of the studies and the estimated economic values is consistent across study and policy sites.

- The success of BT using meta-regression analysis depends on the availability and quality of existing studies, the comparability of study and policy sites, and the validity of the underlying assumptions. However, when conducted carefully and with appropriate consideration of uncertainties, meta-regression analysis can be a useful tool for transferring economic values and informing policy and decision-making processes.

In summary, taking into account the distribution of costs and benefits across different social groups distinguished by their income, couples CBA — whose main objective is efficiency — with social considerations. In this way, we move toward a social CBA.

The distributional considerations are also used to incorporate the necessary adjustments when benefits transfer methods are used to transfer costs and benefits estimated for one site to another site. The distributional impacts and the benefits transfer methods discussed in this chapter provide a basis for bringing CBA closer to social objectives and offering flexibility when external factors restrict the full on-site valuation of environmental costs and benefits in a CBA study.

References

Anthoff, D., Tol, R. (2010). On international equity weights and national decision making on climate change. *Journal of Environmental Economics and Management*, 60(1), 14–20.

Boyle, K. J., Bergstrom, J. C. (1992). Benefit transfer studies: Myths, pragmatism, and idealism. *Water Resources Research*, 28, 657–663.

Desvousges, W. H., Johnson, F. R., Banzhaf, H. S. (1998). *Environmental Policy Analysis with Limited Information: Principles and Applications of the Transfer Method*. Cheltenham, UK: Edward Elgar Publishing.

OECD (2018). *Cost-Benefit Analysis and the Environment: Further Developments and Policy Use*. Paris: OECD Publishing.

Pearce, D. (2003). The social cost of carbon and its policy implications. *Oxford Review of Economic Policy*, 19, 362–384.

Pearce, D., Atkinson, G., Mourato, S. (2006). *Cost–Benefit Analysis and the Environment: Recent Development*. Paris: OECD Publishing.

Rosenberger, R., Loomis, J. (2001). *Benefit Transfer of Outdoor Recreation Use Values*. Fort Collins, CO: USDA, Forest Service.

Chapter 4

Cost–Benefit Analysis: Risk Assessment

4.1. Risk Assessment in CBA

Risk assessment is associated with uncertainties regarding the parameter values which are used to estimate the flows of costs and benefits.

As set out in Article 101 (Information necessary for the approval of a major project) of the EU Regulation No. 1303/2013, a risk assessment must be included in the CBA of a major project if it seeks co-financing from the EU. The recommended steps for assessing the project risks are as follows:

- Sensitivity analysis;
- Probabilistic risk analysis;
- Qualitative risk analysis;
- Risk prevention and mitigation.

4.2. Sensitivity Analysis

Sensitivity analysis is a way of assessing the risk of an investment project by evaluating how responsive the NPV, the IRR or the B/C ratio — the "evaluation criteria" — of the project are to changes in the variables from which it has been calculated. It analyzes the risks of investment projects, by changing the values of forecasted variables, using two methods:

- Method 1: Each project variable that is used in the calculation of the net cash flow is in turn changed by a set amount, say 5%, and the evaluation criteria are recalculated. Only one variable is changed at a time.
- Method 2: The amounts by which each project variable would have to change to make the NPV become zero are determined. Again, only one variable is changed at a time. Thus, method 2 entails finding the values of particular variables which give the project a **Breakeven NPV** of zero. Similar calculations can be performed for the critical values $i = r$, $B/C = 1$.

4.2.1. *Stages of sensitivity analysis*

- Identification of those variables which will have significant impacts on the NPV, if their future values vary around the forecast values.
  - The variables having significant impacts on the evaluation criteria are known as **sensitive variables or critical variables**.
  - Variables are considered critical if a variation of $\pm1\%$ of the value adopted in the base case gives rise to a variation of more than 1% in the value of the NPV.
- The variables are ranked in the order of their monetary impact on the NPV.
- The most sensitive variables are further investigated by management.

4.2.2. *Terminology within the analysis*

- Sensitivity and breakeven analyses are also known as: "scenario analysis" and "what-if analysis".
- Point values of forecasts are known as: "optimistic", "most likely", and "pessimistic". Respective calculated NPVs are known as: "best case", "base case" and "worst case".

- Breakeven variables give a "breakeven" value of zero to the NPV for the project, or an IRR equal to the cost of capital, or a B/C ratio equal to one.

4.2.3. *Selection criteria for variables in the analysis*

- Degree of management control.
- Management's confidence in the forecasts.
- Amount of management experience in assessing projects.
- Use of intrinsic rather than extrinsic (exogenous) variables wherever possible, because extrinsic variables are more problematic.
- Time and cost of analysis.

Table 1 provides an example of how sensitivity analysis is implemented. Table 1a provides an example of a cash flow, while Table 1b shows the output of the sensitivity analysis corresponding to this cash flow. Figures 1 and 2 provide a graphical representation of the solution. Figure 1 shows the solution as a spider graph, while Figure 2 shows the solution as a tornado graph.

Table 1a: Sensitivity analysis — cash flow.

YEAR	1	2	3	4	5	6	7
Inv Cost	-1000	-1500	0	0	0	0	0
Rev A	0	0	1300	1950	2600	2600	2600
Rev B	0	0	3500	5250	7000	7000	7000
Oper Cost A	0	0	1250	1875	2500	2500	2500
Oper Cost B	0	0	3000	4500	6000	6000	6000
Depr year 0	0	0	100	100	100	100	100
Depr year 1	0	0	100	100	100	100	100
Prof Bef Tax	0	0	350	625	900	900	900
Tax @40%	0	0	140	250	360	360	360
Prof After Tax	0	0	210	375	540	540	540
Add Deprec	0	0	410	575	740	740	740
Mainten	0	0	0	0	0	0	0
Scrap val	0	0	0	0	0	0	0
Cash Flow	-1000	-1500	620	950	1280	1280	1280
Net Benefit	0	0	1920	2900	3880	3880	3880
NPV@11%	€4,321.92						
IRR	35%						
Cumul CF	-100	-250	-207	-150.5	-80.5	-10.5	59.5
YEAR	1	2	3	4	5	6	7

The cash flow shown is restricted to seven years for better exposition. The values for NPV, IRR and Cumulative CF correspond to the full cash flow.

Table 1b: Sensitivity analysis — output.

Input Variable	Corresponding Input Value			Input Value as % of Base			NPV@11% Output Value			Swing
	Low Output	Base Case	High Output	Low %	Base %	High %	Low	Base	High	
Price B	30	35	40	85.7%	100.0%	114.3%	−2,045.27€	4,321.92€	10,689.11€	12,734.38€
VarCos B	35	30	25	116.7%	100.0%	83.3%	−2,045.27€	4,321.92€	10,689.11€	12,734.38€
VarCos A	30	25	20	120.0%	100.0%	80.0%	1,138.32€	4,321.92€	7,505.51€	6,367.19€
Price A	22	26	30	84.6%	100.0%	115.4%	1,775.04€	4,321.92€	6,868.79€	5,093.75€
QuantB	150	200	250	75.0%	100.0%	125.0%	2,730.12€	4,321.92€	5,913.72€	3,183.60€
InvCost y1	1200	1000	800	120.0%	100.0%	80.0%	4,141.74€	4,321.92€	4,502.10€	360.36€
InvCost y2	1700	1500	1300	113.3%	100.0%	86.7%	4,159.59€	4,321.92€	4,484.24€	324.65€
QuantA	80	100	120	80.0%	100.0%	120.0%	4,194.57€	4,321.92€	4,449.26€	254.69€

Input Variable	Corresponding Input Value			Input Value as % of Base			B/C Ratio Output Value			Swing
	Low Output	Base Case	High Output	Low %	Base %	High %	Low	Base	High	
VarCos B	35	30	25	116.7%	100.0%	83.3%	0.976334488	1.08686885	1.225626458	0.24929197
Price B	30	35	40	85.7%	100.0%	114.3%	0.97365523	1.08686885	1.20008247	0.22642724
VarCos A	30	25	20	120.0%	100.0%	80.0%	1.028640777	1.08686885	1.152084689	0.123443912
Price A	22	26	30	84.6%	100.0%	115.4%	1.041583402	1.08686885	1.132154298	0.090570896
QuantB	150	200	250	75.0%	100.0%	125.0%	1.070545515	1.08686885	1.098452935	0.027907421
InvCost y1	1200	1000	800	120.0%	100.0%	80.0%	1.082706393	1.08686885	1.091063435	0.008357042
InvCost y2	1700	1500	1300	113.3%	100.0%	86.7%	1.083117465	1.08686885	1.090646311	0.007528846
QuantA	120	100	80	120.0%	100.0%	80.0%	1.084357891	1.08686885	1.089681141	0.00532325

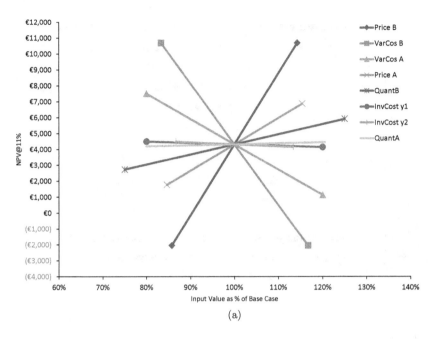

(a)

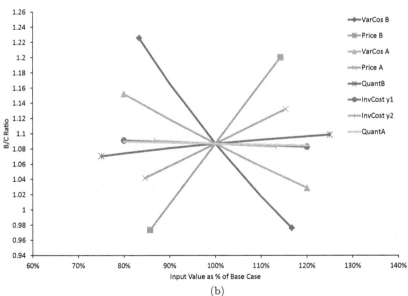

(b)

Figure 1: Spider graph.

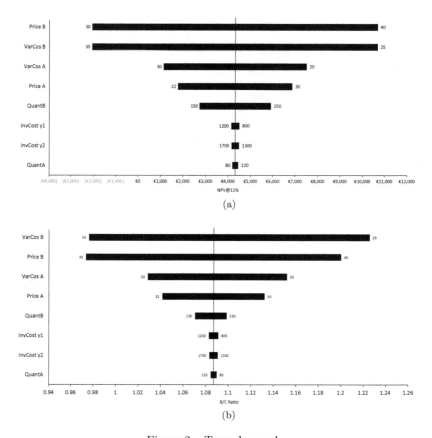

Figure 2:   Tornado graph.

The critical variables in Figure 1 correspond to lines which are steep and which extend below zero for the NPV or below 1 for the B/C ratio. In Figure 2, the critical variables are shown by the bars that extend below zero for the NPV and below 1 for the B/C ratio.

4.3.   Monte Carlo Simulations

Monte Carlo simulations entail the use of probability distributions for stochastic variables which are used in the calculation of the net cash flow and then repeated calculations of the CBA evaluation criteria (NPV, IRR, B/C ratio) for random choices of values for these variables.

4.3.1. *Procedure*

- Simulation allows the repeated solution of an evaluation model in order to calculate CBA criteria.
- Each solution randomly selects parameter values (e.g., unit prices, unit costs) from predetermined probability distributions.
- All solutions are summarized into an overall distribution of NPV or IRR or B/C ratio values.
- This distribution shows management how risky the project is.
- The specific stages of a simulation are illustrated in Sections 4.3.3 and 4.3.4.

4.3.2. *Simulation terminology*

- The treatment of risk by using simulation is known as **stochastic modeling**.
- Other names for our term "Simulation", are "Risk Analysis", "Venture Analysis", "Risk Simulation", "Monte Carlo Simulation".
- The name **Monte Carlo Simulation** helps visualization of repeated spins of the roulette wheel, creating the selected values.
- Each execution of the model is known as a "replication" or "iteration".

4.3.3. *Probability distributions of forecast variables*

The probability density functions of the most common distributions used in Monte Carlo simulations are shown in Figure 3.

4.3.4. *Input–output*

The stages of a Monte Carlo simulation are shown in Figure 4.

- First, parameter values are selected randomly from input distributions.
- Then this specific set of parameters is used in iteration calculations to estimate NPV, IRR or B/C ratio.
- Then the estimated NPV, IRR, B/C are combined into an output distribution.
- Each replication is unique.

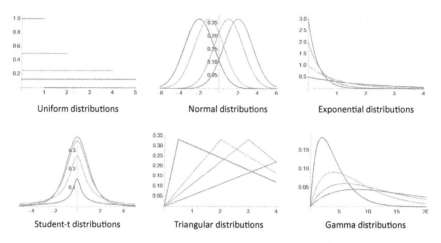

Figure 3:   Probability density functions used in Monte Carlo simulations.

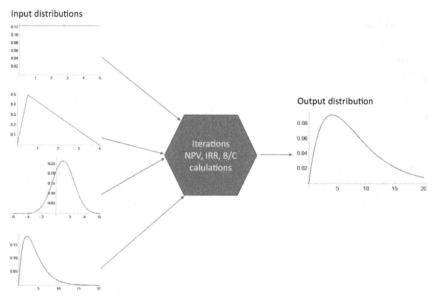

Figure 4:   The stages of a Monte Carlo simulation.

- The automated process is driven by a random number generator.
- Excel add-ons such as '@Risk' and 'Insight' can be used to streamline the process.
- About 1000–2000 replications should give a good picture of the project's risk.

4.3.4.1. *Using the output*

The output of Monte Carlo simulations can help the management to view and assess the risk associated with the project. More specifically, management can:

- Calculate the probability of generating an NPV between two given values.
- Calculate the probability of loss given by the area to the left of a zero NPV in the cumulative distribution graph (see Figures 6 and 8).
- Construct confidence intervals.

The output of representative Monte Carlo simulations corresponding to the cash flow of Table 1a is shown in Figures 5–8.

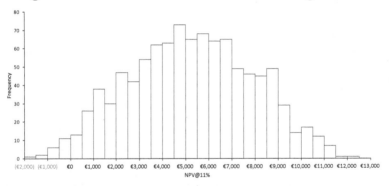

Figure 5:   Monte Carlo simulations: NPV histogram, 1000 iterations.

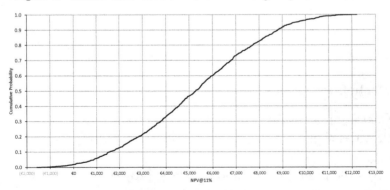

Figure 6:   Monte Carlo simulations: NPV Cumulative distribution, 1000 iterations, which shows the probability that the NPV is below a given value. For example, Pr(NPV < 6000 = 60%).

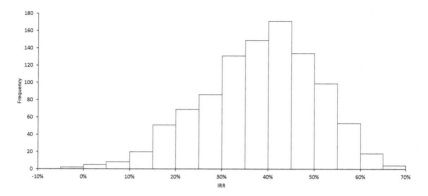

Figure 7: Monte Carlo simulations: IRR histogram, 1000 iterations.

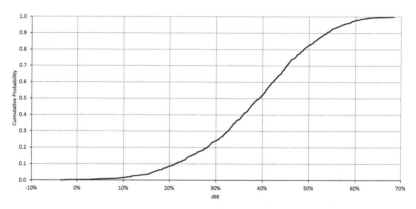

Figure 8: Monte Carlo simulations: IRR Cumulative distribution, 1000 iterations, which shows the probability that the IRR is below a given value. For example, $\Pr(\text{IRR} < 20\% = 9\%)$.

4.3.5. *Benefits and costs of simulation*

A Monte Carlo simulation:

- Focuses on a detailed definition and analysis of risk.
- Provides sophisticated analysis and clearly portrays the risk of a project.
- Gives the probability of a loss-making project.
- Allows simultaneous analysis of all variables.

However, the simulation:

- Requires a significant forecasting effort.
- Can be difficult to set up for computation.
- May produce output that can sometimes be difficult to interpret.

4.4. Qualitative Risk Analysis

Qualitative risk analysis does not explicitly quantify the risk assessment, but can provide useful information to management. The qualitative risk analysis should include the following elements (see European Commission (2015) for more details):

- A list of adverse events to which the project is exposed and which might negatively affect the cash flows of the project.
- A risk matrix for each adverse event indicating the probability of occurrence (Table 2) and the severity of the event (Table 3).
- A risk matrix produced by combining Tables 2 and 3 that determines risk level (Table 4).
- An interpretation of the risk matrix including the assessment of acceptable levels of risk.
- A description of mitigation and/or prevention measures for the main risks, indicating who is responsible for the applicable measures to reduce risk exposure, when they are considered necessary (Table 5).

Table 2: Probability of occurrence.

A. Very unlikely (0–10% probability)

B. Unlikely (10–33% probability)

C. About as likely as not (33–66% probability)

D. Likely (66–90% probability)

E. Very likely (90–100% probability)

Source: European Commission, 2015, *Guide to Cost Benefit Analysis of Investment Projects.*

Table 3:   Risk severity.

Risk severity classification	
Rating	Meaning
I	No relevant effect on social welfare, even without remedial actions.
II	Minor loss of the social welfare generated by the project, minimally affecting the project long run effects. However, remedial or corrective actions are needed.
III	*Moderate*: Social welfare loss generated by the project, mostly financial damage, even in the medium-long run. Remedial actions may correct the problem.
IV	*Critical*: High social welfare loss generated by the project; the occurrence of the risk causes a loss of the primary function(s) of the project. Remedial actions, even large in scope, are not enough to avoid serious damage.
V	*Catastrophic*: Project failure that may result in serious or even total loss of the project functions. Main project effects in medium-long term do not materialize.

Source: European Commission, 2015, *Guide to Cost Benefit Analysis of Investment Projects*.

Table 4:   Risk level.

The risk level is the combination of Probability and Severity (P*S). Four risk levels can be defined as follows with the associated shades:

Risk level	Shade	Severity / Probability	I	II	III	IV	V
Low		A	Low	Low	Low	Low	Moderate
Moderate		B	Low	Low	Moderate	Moderate	High
High		C	Low	Moderate	Moderate	High	High
Unacceptable		D	Low	Moderate	High	Very high	Very high
		E	Moderate	High	Very high	Very high	Very high

Source: European Commission, 2015, *Guide to Cost Benefit Analysis of Investment Projects*.

Table 5: Risk mitigation.

Risk prevention matrix. Example

Adverse event	Variable	Causes	Effect	Timing	Effect on cash flows	Probability (P)	Severity (S)	Risk level	Prevention and/or mitigation measures	Residual risk
Construction delays	Investment cost	Low contractor capacity	Delay in service starting	Medium	Delay in establishing a positive cash flow including benefits materialization	C	III	Moderate	Set up of a Project Implementation Unit to be assisted by technical assistance for project management during implementation.	Low
Project cost overrun	Investment cost	Inadequate design cost estimates	Investment costs higher than expected	Short	Higher (social) costs in the first phase of the project	D	V	Very high	The design of the project must be revised.	Moderate
Landslides	Not applicable	Inadequate site investigation	Interruption of the service	Long	Extra costs to rehabilitate the service	A	III	Low	Close monitoring	Low

(*Continued*)

Table 5: (*Continued*)

Adverse event	Variable	Causes	Effect	Timing	Effect on cash flows	Probability (P)	Severity (S)	Risk level	Prevention and/or mitigation measures	Residual risk
Delayed obtainment of permits	Not applicable	Low political commitment; Mismanagement of the licensing procedures process	Delay in commencement of works	Short	Delay in establishing a positive cash flow including benefits materialization	A	II	Low	Close monitoring	Low
Public opposition	Not applicable	Inadequate market strategy; Underestimation of threats	Demand lower than expected	Medium	Lower revenues and social benefits	C	V	High	Early definition of an appropriate social plan; Awareness-raising activities and campaigns to raise the level of social acceptance	Moderate

Source: European Commission, 2015, *Guide to Cost Benefit Analysis of Investment Projects.*

The application of the approaches described in this chapter can provide useful information about the risk involved in the calculation of a project's cash flow. Sensitivity analysis provides information about the impact of specific variables on the evaluation criteria, while the Monte Carlo approach gives an overall picture of the associated risks and allows the calculation of confidence intervals for evaluation criteria, and the probability they will not fall below a certain value. The qualitative analysis can be used as a stand-alone method or as a complement to the other two. The risk prevention matrix could be very useful for the correct management of the project.

Reference

European Commission (2015). *Guide to Cost Benefit Analysis of Investment Projects*, European Union.

Part 2

Ecosystem Services

Chapter 5

Total Economic Value

5.1. Economic Values and the Environment

The total economic value (TEV) of any change in well-being due to a project or policy associated with environmental goods and/or services is the aggregate of all types of values generated by these goods and/or services. This aggregate is determined by the net sum of all the relevant willingness-to-pay (WTP) for the environmental goods and services and the corresponding willingness-to-accept (WTA) for potential loss or deterioration of such goods and services. For more details, see Chapter 1, Section 1.2.

The environment is considered to generate value in four ways (Hanley *et al.*, 2000; Hanley and Barbier, 2009), by acting as a

- supplier of material and energy inputs such as minerals, fossil fuels, water and timber to production and fish biomass to consumption,
- "waste sink" for the residuals of both production and consumption, such as emissions from fossil fuel burning,
- direct source of amenity and quality of life for people, for example, when people go mountaineering or bird watching, and
- provider of vital basic life supporting services, such as global climate regulation, nutrient cycling, and water cycling.

5.2. Missing Markets

Missing markets — due to the absence of a complete and enforceable system of property rights for environmental resources — means that in many cases, environmental values are not revealed by the market. Missing markets imply negative environmental externalities and market failure which need to be corrected by environmental regulation:

- In the case of environmental resources, market prices often cannot guide us in the estimations of WTP or WTA. This creates a need to focus on methods of estimating non-market environmental values. There are direct and indirect environmental values.
- Let U be a utility function and F_1 be a production function for market good X_1 which could be an agricultural good produced by labor L, capital K, and water of quality W. Then,

$$U = U(X_1, \ldots, X_n, Z_1, \ldots, Z_m, W), \quad Q_{X_1} = F_1(L, K, W),$$

where X is market-valued goods, Q_{X_1} is output of good X_1, and Z is environmental goods.
- The direct impact of change in water quality on utility can be defined as

$$dU = \frac{\partial U}{\partial W} dW.$$

An indirect valuation of the impact of a change in water quality can be obtained from

$$dQ_{X_1} = \frac{\partial F_1}{\partial W} dW.$$

5.3. Total Economic Value by Types

Total economic value has two major constituents:

- *Use value* is the economic value that people derive from the direct or indirect use of an environmental resource. It is the value that people place on the benefits that they receive from the resource, such as food or timber, or the recreational opportunities that they enjoy from ecosystems. The potential future uses of the environment are referred to as option value.

- **Non-use value** is the economic value that people derive from the mere existence of an environmental resource, even if they never use it directly or indirectly. It is the value that people place on the knowledge that the resource exists, or the desire to preserve it for others, or the desire to pass it on to future generations.

Use value and non-use value are both important considerations in environmental decision-making. Use value is often easier to quantify than non-use value, but non-use value can be significant in some cases. For example, the non-use value of a popular tourist destination can be a major economic driver for the region. An illustration of the components that comprise total economic value (see Pearce *et al.*, 2006) is shown in Figure 1.

5.3.1. *TEV: Components and valuation techniques*

Figure 2 shows the various techniques that are best suited to measure the different components of TEV. See Pearce *et al.* (2006) for more details. The use of alternative approaches for measurement is necessary, mainly because of missing markets for non-use values for environmental goods and services.

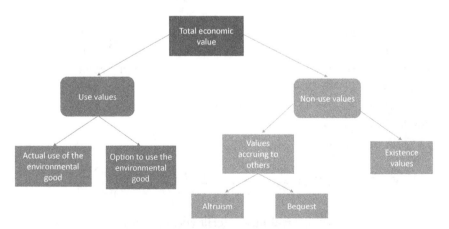

Figure 1: Components of total economic value.

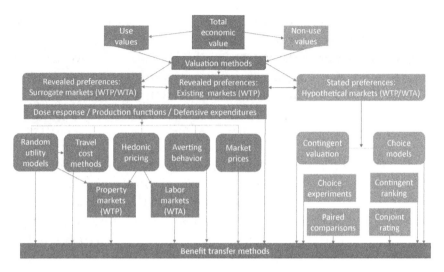

Figure 2:   Components of total economic value, and their valuation techniques.

5.3.2.   *TEV and cost–benefit analysis*

Total economic value is a crucial component in any environmental cost–benefit analysis. Suppose the annual TEV generated by an environmental system has been calculated to be

$$\text{TEV}_1, \text{TEV}_2, \dots, \text{TEV}_T.$$

The annual flow can be interpreted as the flow of ecosystem services.

A conservation project will guarantee that the flow of the TEV will remain for the next T years. The conservation project will cost C_0 and can be completed within a year. There will be no other costs (e.g., operation or maintenance). Without the project, the flow of the TEV will be zero.

The project will go ahead if

$$\text{NPV}(r) = -C_0 + \frac{\text{TEV}_1}{(1+r)} + \frac{\text{TEV}_2}{(1+r)^2} + \cdots + \frac{\text{TEV}_T}{(1+r)^T} > 0$$

or any of the other evaluation criteria presented in Chapter 1, Section 1.1.7 are satisfied.

In this set up, the discount rate r can be estimated by the methods described in Chapter 2 and risk assessment can be conducted using the methods described in Chapter 4 regarding the parameters used to estimate the flow $TEV_1, TEV_2, \ldots, TEV_T$.

If the question is: How much is the justifiable cost for conserving the ecosystem? Then the answer is

$$C_0 = \frac{TEV_1}{(1+r)} + \frac{TEV_2}{(1+r)^2} + \cdots + \frac{TEV_T}{(1+r)^T}.$$

5.4. Quasi-Option Values

5.4.1. *Defining option values*

- **Environmental option value** refers to the value or benefit derived from the existence or preservation of natural resources and ecosystems. It recognizes the non-market values associated with environmental goods and services, such as biodiversity, clean air and water, carbon sequestration, and cultural or aesthetic appreciation. Environmental option value highlights the potential future benefits that can be obtained from the environment and emphasizes the importance of considering these values in decision-making processes.
- **Environmental quasi-option value**, also known as quasi-option value of the environment, is a concept used in environmental economics. It represents the value associated with the flexibility or option to make future decisions regarding the use, conversion, or preservation of natural resources or the environment. It recognizes that there is uncertainty and irreversibility in environmental decision-making, and having the option to adapt or change decisions based on new information or changing circumstances can be valuable. Environmental quasi-option value considers the potential benefits that may arise from future environmental choices and actions.
- **Real option value**, also known as the option value or flexibility value, refers to the value associated with having the right, but not the obligation, to make decisions or take actions related to tangible

assets, projects, or investments. It is a concept used in finance and investment analysis. Real option value recognizes the additional value that arises from the flexibility to respond to changing market conditions, new information, or unexpected events. It takes into account the potential upside or downside opportunities that can be captured by exercising the option.

5.4.2. *The value of flexibility*

Following Dixit and Pindyck's (1994) example, a firm is trying to decide whether to undertake an irreversible investment with cost = 1750 that will produce one item per year forever. The current price of the item is 250 but next year it will change. With probability p, it will increase to 350, and with probability $(1 - p)$, it will be reduced to 150. Let $p = 0.5$. The cash flow for this investment is shown in Figure 3.

The expected net present value of this investment undertaken now, $t = 0$, at a risk free discount rate $r = 0.12$, with $p = 0.5$, is

$$\text{NPV}(0) = -1750 + 250 + \sum_{t=1}^{\infty} \frac{p350 + (1 - p)150}{1.12^t} = 583.33.$$

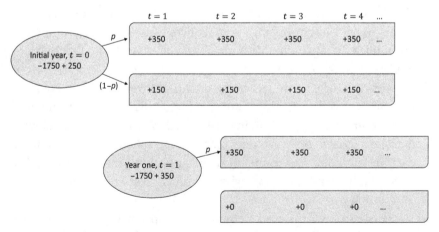

Figure 3: Cash flow for an investment with uncertainty, irreversibility, and flexible starting time.

If we wait for a year, the price uncertainty will be resolved and the investment will be undertaken only if the high price of $p = 350$ emerges. The present value now of undertaking the investment after a year, at $t = 1$, is

$$\text{NPV}(0/1) = p \left[-1750 + 350 + \sum_{t=1}^{\infty} \frac{350}{(1.12)^t} \right] \frac{1}{1.12} = 677.08.$$

The value of the "flexibility option" is $677.08 - 583.33 = 88.75$. We would be willing to pay 88.75 more for a flexible investment that can be undertaken now or a year from now.

- Consider the irreversible decision to develop a forest now, or wait for a year when new information will resolve uncertainty about the benefits of preservation.
- This involves the notion of quasi-option value (QOV), which was introduced and developed by Arrow and Fisher (1974) and Henry (1974). QOV is the value of information gained by delaying a decision to commit to some irreversible action.

5.5. Environmental Quasi-Option Value

5.5.1. *An example of quasi-option value*

QOV is complex and can be difficult to understand. Pearce *et al.* (2006) provide an example that helps clarify the concept. The example involves a forested area which could either be preserved or converted to agriculture:

- Two time periods are considered: the current period designated 0 and a future period designated 1. If the forest is converted in period 0 (now), it cannot be preserved in the future (period 1) because conversion is irreversible. If, on the other hand, it is preserved now, then there is an option to either preserve or convert in period 1.
- It is assumed that benefits from agriculture are deterministic, while benefits from preservation in the future (period 1) are stochastic. Thus by converting now, we obtain the certain agricultural

benefits, D_0 and D_1. By preserving now, we have a certain conservation value, V_0, plus a stochastic conservation value V_1. Future preservation value could be either high, with probability p, or low with probability $(1-p)$. The two possible future preservation values are denoted by $V_{1,\text{high}}$ and $V_{1,\text{low}}$, respectively.

- If the forest is preserved now (period 0), then the expected value of preservation benefits in both periods is

$$\text{EP} = V_0 + pV_{1,\text{high}} + (1 - p)V_{1,\text{low}}. \tag{1}$$

- If the forest is converted in period 0, the expected value of agricultural benefits will be

$$\text{ED} = D_0 + D_1. \tag{2}$$

- If the decision to preserve or develop has to be taken now, then (1) and (2) should be compared. The decision to develop the forest will be taken if

$$\text{ED} > \text{EP}, \quad \text{or} \quad [D_0 + D_1] > [V_0 + pV_{1,\text{high}} + (1 - p)V_{1,\text{low}}].$$

5.5.2. *Postponing an irreversible decision*

Continuing the example from Section 5.5.1 (Pearce *et al.*, 2006), assume that the irreversible decision to convert can be postponed until future period 1. Assume further that the uncertain preservation values and the certain agricultural value in future period 1 satisfy $V_{1,\text{high}} > D_1$ and $D_1 > V_{1,\text{low}}$. Then the expected value of waiting (EW) is defined as

$$V_{1,\text{high}} > D_1 > V_{1,\text{low}} : \text{EW} = V_0 + pV_{1,\text{high}} + (1 - p)D_1.$$

- "Conventional" cost–benefit analysis will choose development if $\text{ED} > \text{EP}$.
- The "options" will choose development if the stricter rule, $\text{ED} > \text{EW}$, is satisfied.
- EW and EP differ by an amount $E_{\max}(D_1 - V_1, 0)$.
- EP understates the "true" value of preservation by the amount $E_{\max}(D_1 - V_1, 0)$.

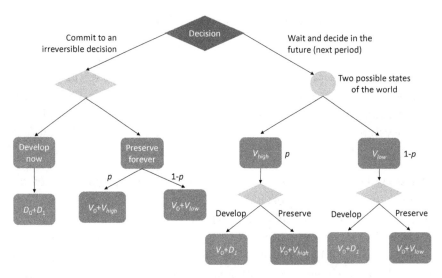

Figure 4: The decision-making process.

- Then $QOV = \mathrm{EW} - \max(\mathrm{ED}, \mathrm{EP})$. The decision-making process is illustrated in Figure 4, adapted from OECD (2018).

QOV is not a separate category of economic value. Rather it is the difference between the net benefits of making an optimal decision and one that is not optimal because it ignores the gains that may be made by delaying a decision and learning during the period of delay.

Usually, QOV arises in the context of irreversibility, but it can only emerge if there is uncertainty which can be resolved by learning. If the potential to learn is not there, QOV cannot arise.

5.6. Preservation vs Conversion

Preservation versus conversion is a central issue in the management of ecosystem services. Preservation refers to the protection of natural ecosystems and their services from human activity. It can be achieved through policies such as protected area designation, habitat restoration, and sustainable management practices. In contrast, conversion refers to the transformation of natural ecosystems into human-dominated landscapes, such as agriculture, urbanization, or mining, to meet human needs. However, it often comes at the cost of ecosystem services and biodiversity loss.

To balance these competing interests, ecosystem management approaches such as sustainable use, integrated conservation, and landscape approaches have been developed that attempt to reconcile conservation and development goals and promote the sustainable use of ecosystem services. Consider a hypothetical scenario where a forest ecosystem provides both timber and carbon sequestration services.

Preservation: If the forest is preserved, it can continue to provide carbon sequestration services by absorbing and storing carbon dioxide from the atmosphere, which helps mitigate climate change. In addition, the forest can provide a habitat for wildlife, recreational opportunities, and other cultural services. However, in this case, there would be no revenue from the forest, since it would not be harvested for timber.

Conversion: On the other hand, if the forest is converted to a timber plantation, it can provide timber and generate income for the landowner. However, the carbon sequestration capacity of the forest would be reduced, as young plantations typically store less carbon than mature forests. Additionally, there would be loss of wildlife habitat, recreational, and other cultural services. Moreover, the plantation may require the use of pesticides and fertilizers, which could have negative impacts on soil and water quality.

The relevant theory is developed in the following sections. Figure 5 presents a simple case of optimal preservation/conversion obtained by equating marginal costs with marginal benefits.

Note that if marginal benefits from preservation are very high, corresponding to MB_{P2}, then the whole landscape should be preserved.

5.6.1. *Optimal one-time conversion time*

To define the optimal time to convert when the decision is whether to fully convert or not, we follow Barbier (2008). The optimal conversion time t^* maximizes the sum of development benefits R and benefits

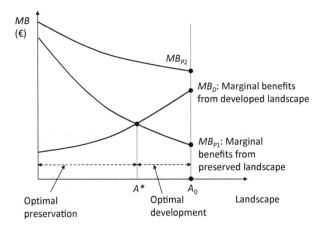

Figure 5: Optimal preservation and development.

from ecosystem services $B(u)$ before conversion, or t^* solves

$$\max_t [R(t)e^{-rt} + \int_0^t e^{-ru}B(u)du].$$

Then the optimal development time is determined as

$$e^{-rt}[R'(t) - rR(t) + B(t)] = 0 \Rightarrow R'(t) + B(t) = rR(t).$$

$R'(t) + B(t)$ represents the gain from delaying development one period, where $R' = \frac{dR}{dt}$. It includes the increase in rental value of developed land plus the additional ecosystem benefits during that period of delay.

The term $rR(t)$ represents the cost of delaying development. The value of the land, if sold in period t, could be invested to earn interest. The average interest rate on other assets in the economy is clearly key to the opportunity cost of delaying development another period. A higher interest rate means that it is costly to delay, whereas the lower interest rate has the opposite effect.

5.6.2. *Continuous transformation*

Assume that we have an area of size A_0 where species live. At each instant of time, part $u(t)$ of the area is transformed into a state that can produce direct economic benefits (e.g., deforestation that leads to agricultural production). Then the area remaining which can provide ecosystem services is

$$A(t) = A_0 - \int_0^t u(\tau)d\tau \quad \text{or} \quad \dot{A}(t) = -u(t), \quad A(0) = A_0.$$

The net flow of benefits generated by the transformed (developed) area can be written as

$$F(A(t), u(t)) = f(A_0 - A(t)) - C(u(t)),$$
$$f' \geq 0, \quad f'' < 0, \quad C' > 0, \quad C'' \geq 0,$$

where $C(u(t))$ denotes convex transformation costs.

The benefits of the undeveloped area are $B(A(t))$, $B' \geq 0$, $B'' < 0$. The problem for a regulator that seeks to decide how much of the initial area should be developed becomes

$$\max_{u(t)} \int_0^\infty e^{-rt}[f(A_0 - A(t)) - C(u(t)) + B(A(t))]dt,$$

subject to

$$\dot{A}(t) = -u(t), \quad A(0) = A_0, \quad u(t) \geq 0, \quad 0 \leq A(t) \leq A_0.$$

The current value Hamiltonian for this problem, disregarding, for the time being, the pure state constraint, is

$$H = [f(A_0 - A(t)) - C(u(t)) + B(A(t))] - \lambda(t)u(t),$$

with optimality conditions:

$$C'(u(t)) \leq -\lambda(t), \quad u(t) \geq 0, \quad u(t) = h(\lambda(t))$$

for interior solution $u(t) > 0$, $h' < 0$,

$$\dot{\lambda}(t) = r\lambda(t) + f'(A_0 - A(t)) - B'(A(t)),$$
$$\dot{A}(t) = -h(\lambda(t)),$$

with transversality condition $\lim_{t \to \infty} e^{-rt}\lambda(t)A(t) = 0$.

A steady state, dropping t for simplicity, which determines the optimal amount A^* to be developed is characterized by

$$\lambda^* : 0 = -h(\lambda^*), \quad A^* : \lambda^* = \frac{B'(A^*) - f'(A_0 - A^*)}{r}, \quad A^* \geq 0.$$

The Jacobian of the Hamiltonian system is

$$J = \begin{bmatrix} r & -f'' - B'' \\ -h' & 0 \end{bmatrix}, \quad \det J < 0.$$

The steady state has the saddle point property which means that for any initial size of the landscape, the regulator can choose an optimal development path that would lead to a steady state.

5.7. Ecosystem Services

The Millennium Ecosystem Assessment (MA) and The Economics of Ecosystems and Biodiversity (TEEB) are two major global initiatives focused on understanding and valuing the world's ecosystem services. Biodiversity refers to the variety of life on Earth, including the number of species, genetic diversity, and the diversity of ecosystems, while ecosystems are complex communities of living and non-living components that interact with each other and with their environment.

The Millennium Ecosystem Assessment (2005) is a landmark international study that assessed the state of the world's ecosystems and the services they provide to human well-being. It examined the impacts of ecosystem change on human well-being and provided a comprehensive scientific basis for ecosystem management and policy-making.

TEEB was launched in 2007 when the environment ministers from the governments of Brazil, Canada, China, France, Germany, India, Italy, Japan, Mexico, Russia, South Africa, the United Kingdom, and the United States agreed to initiate the process of analyzing the global economic benefit of biological diversity, and the costs of the loss of biodiversity and the failure to take protective measures versus the costs of effective conservation.

The outcome of that decision led to *The Economics of Ecosystems and Biodiversity*, a series of reports that aim to show how economic concepts and tools can help incorporate the values of nature into decision-making at all levels. Its aim is to provide decision-makers with tools and information to make informed choices about the use of natural resources, emphasizing the need to integrate the value of natural capital into decision-making processes.

The analysis of TEEB (2010) builds on extensive work with regard to biodiversity and the value of ecosystem services over the last decades. Its findings have been used to inform policy decisions at the local, national and international levels. The TEEB study builds on the MA by providing a more comprehensive economic analysis of the value of ecosystem services, including the benefits that are not typically captured in traditional economic analyses, such as cultural and spiritual values.

5.7.1. *Ecosystems*

An *ecosystem* is "a dynamic complex of plant, animal and microorganism communities and their non-living environment interacting as a functional unit" (Article 2, Convention on Biological Diversity). Each ecosystem contains complex relationships between living (biotic) and non-living (abiotic) components (resources), sunlight, air, water, minerals, and nutrients. The quantity (e.g., biomass and productivity), quality, and diversity of species (richness, rarity, and uniqueness) each play an important role in a given ecosystem. The functioning of an ecosystem often hinges on a number of species or groups of species that perform certain functions (e.g., pollination, grazing, predation, and nitrogen fixing).

5.7.2. *Ecosystems as assets*

An asset is something, tangible or intangible, that can generate a flow of benefits over its lifetime. In economics, a tangible asset is a stock of produced capital (e.g., buildings, machinery, and infrastructure), while an intangible asset is human capital (e.g., knowledge, skills, and health). Since ecosystems, which are tangible, can provide a flow of benefits over their lifetime, they can be regarded as assets. In this sense, Nature is considered as **natural capital**:

- The value of an asset is determined by the present value of goods and services it provides over its lifetime. Thus the value of a fishery, for example, is the value of the fish that it can produce over its lifetime. Likewise, the environmental value of a forest, in terms of climate change, is the carbon sequestered by the forest over its lifetime. In general, the value of an ecosystem is the present value of the flow of services that it provides. The value of these services is determined in the context of TEV.
- The lifetime of an ecosystem could be indefinite if it is able to regenerate. The value of an underground aquifer, for example, is the flow of irrigation water provided and the potential benefits from supporting ecosystems.
- The social value of a unit of an asset is called its *accounting* or *shadow price* and represents its value to society.
- The accounting price of an asset is not necessarily the same as its market price, if the asset is associated with positive or negative externalities. An asset might not even have a market price if markets for its services are missing.

5.7.3. *What are ecosystem services?*

Broadly defined, **ecosystem services** "are the benefits people obtain from ecosystems" (Millennium Ecosystem Assessment, 2005, p. 53). These include provisioning services (e.g., food, fiber, fuel, and water), regulating services (benefits obtained from ecosystem processes that regulate, e.g., climate, floods, disease, waste, and water quality), cultural services (e.g., recreation, aesthetic enjoyment, tourism, and spiritual and ethical values), and supporting services necessary for the production of all other ecosystem services (e.g., soil formation, photosynthesis, and nutrient cycling) (see Table 1). The relationship between the types of ecosystem services shown in Table 1 and the types of total economic value depicted in Figure 1 is presented in Table 2.

Table 1:   A typology of ecosystem services.

Provisioning services	Regulating services
Examples	*Examples*
• Food, such as fish, game, and fruit	• Air quality regulation
• Water	• Climate regulation
• Raw materials, such as timber, biofuels, fodder, fertilizer, and plant oils	• Moderation of extreme events, such as storm protection and flood prevention
• Genetic resources, including crop-improvement genes and health care	• Carbon sequestration and storage
	• Regulation of water flows (e.g., natural drainage, irrigation, and drought prevention)
• Medicinal resources (e.g., biochemical products, models, and test organisms)	• Waste treatment
• Energy (hydropower and biomass fuels)	• Erosion prevention
	• Maintenance of soil fertility
• Ornamental resources, such as artisan work, decorative plants, pet animals, fashion, and jewelry	• Pollination
	• Biological control (e.g., pest and disease control)

Cultural and amenity services	Supporting or habitat services
Examples	*Examples*
• Aesthetic experiences that enhance life quality	• Habitat provision for species, including provision of food, water, and shelter
• Recreational activities, such as hiking, camping, fishing, and birdwatching	• Maintenance of life cycles of migratory species, including birds, fish, mammals, and insects
• Inspiration for creativity and artistic expression	
• Cultural and/or spiritual experience	• Maintenance of genetic diversity, especially in gene pool protection
• Opportunities for tourism	• Nutrient cycling
• Information for cognitive development	• Soil formation
• Opportunities for education and learning about natural systems and the environment	

Table 2: Economic values associated with ecosystem services.

	Components of total economic value			
Ecosystem services	Direct use values (production, consumption)	Indirect use values (resilience)	Option values (potential future values)	Non-use values (the intrinsic value of Nature)
Provisioning	*		*	
Regulating	*		*	*
Cultural	*	*	*	
Supporting	*	*	*	*

Ecosystem functions refer to the biological, physical, and chemical processes that occur within an ecosystem, such as photosynthesis, nutrient cycling, and carbon sequestration (see Table 3). *Ecosystem processes* are the various interactions and exchanges that occur within and between ecosystems, such as the movement of nutrients from the land to the sea or the exchange of carbon dioxide and oxygen between plants and animals (Table 3). See Barbier (2008) for more information.

The concept of ecosystem services highlights the importance of the natural environment and recognizes that human well-being is closely interconnected with the health and functioning of ecosystems. Understanding and valuing ecosystem services are crucial for sustainable resource management and conservation efforts. Although the value of ecosystem services can be subjective and can vary across different societies, cultures, and individuals, sustainable management of ecosystems requires a holistic approach that considers and balances the multiple ecosystem services and their diverse values.

Human well-being and the economy are supported by ecosystem services as well as biodiversity. Ecosystem services are critical for human well-being, as they provide the resources and conditions necessary for human survival and development. Some examples of these services are provided in Tables 1 and 3. However, human activities such as deforestation, overfishing, and pollution can degrade

Table 3: Some examples of ecosystem functions and the ecosystem services they provide.

Ecosystem function	Ecosystem process	Examples of ecosystem services
Climate regulation	The capacity of ecosystems to regulate the Earth's climate by absorbing and releasing greenhouse gasses, such as carbon dioxide and methane, from the atmosphere	• Stabilizing weather patterns (e.g., temperature and precipitation) • Buffering against extreme weather events
Carbon sequestration	The process by which carbon dioxide is removed from the atmosphere and stored in carbon sinks such as forests, soil, and oceans	• Mitigating climate change • Enhancing soil structure, water holding capacity, and nutrient availability
Water regulation	The capacity of ecosystems to regulate the quantity and quality of water	• Water storage and purification • Flood mitigation
Niche and refuge	Provision of suitable living space for wild plants and animals	• Maintenance of biodiversity • Maintenance of beneficial species
Waste treatment	The natural processes by which ecosystems break down and recycle organic and inorganic matter	• Controlling the spread of diseases • Breaking down organic matter and creating new soil
Photosynthesis	The process by which plants, algae, and some bacteria convert carbon dioxide and water into organic compounds, such as glucose, using energy from sunlight	• Oxygen production • Ecosystem productivity • Habitat creation • Erosion prevention
Pollination	The transfer of pollen from one flower to another, by pollinators such as bees, butterflies, and birds	• Enabling the reproduction of many plant species and other organisms
Soil formation	The process by which soil is formed through the accumulation of organic matter, the breakdown of rocks, and the action of microorganisms	• Maintenance of productivity on arable land
Nutrient cycling	The cycling of nutrients, such as nitrogen, phosphorus, and carbon, through the biotic and abiotic components of ecosystems	• Essential for the growth and development of plants and animals
Gas regulation	The exchange and regulation of gasses, such as carbon dioxide, oxygen, and methane, between the atmosphere and the biosphere	• Maintaining the balance of greenhouse gasses, which are responsible for regulating the temperature of the Earth • Regulating the water cycle

ecosystems and reduce the benefits they provide. This can have negative impacts on human well-being, such as reduced access to clean water and food, increased risk of flooding and drought, and loss of cultural and recreational values.

Therefore, it is important to protect and conserve ecosystems and biodiversity to ensure the continued provision of ecosystem services and to support human well-being. This can be achieved through sustainable management practices, such as reducing pollution, protecting biodiversity, and using natural resources in a responsible and sustainable way.

The complex role of ecosystem services is illustrated in Figure 6 which also provides a link between ecosystem services, human well-being, and the United Nations sustainable development goals (SDGs). A detailed presentation of the SDGs is provided in Chapter 14, Section 14.4.

Given that ecosystem services are associated with missing markets and externalities, it is well known that competitive markets cannot produce the socially optimal outcomes. Thus, markets fail in the socially optimal provision of ecosystem services and appropriate

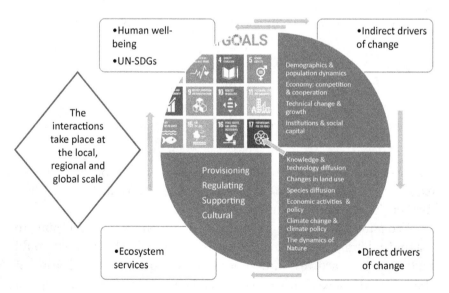

Figure 6: Ecosystem services, human well-being, and UN-SDGs.

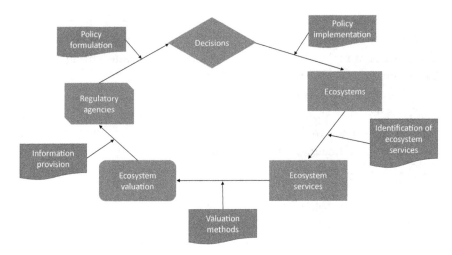

Figure 7:   Designing policy for ecosystem management.

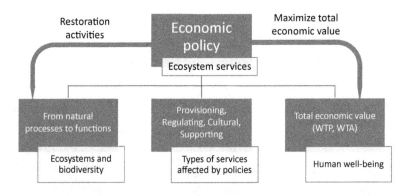

Figure 8:   Economic policy, restoration activities, and total economic value.

management policies should be designed and implemented. An example of such a process is presented graphically in Figure 7. For further details, see Daily *et al.* (2009).

Economic policy for ecosystem management should aim to maximize human well-being. Economic policies in this context could be directed toward restoration activities or toward maximization of the TEV associated with ecosystems. The way in which this type of policy could be structured is presented in Figure 8.

5.7.4. *Ecosystem services, natural capital, and biodiversity*

Ecosystem services and biodiversity are important to human well-being because they contribute to different elements of TEV, which comprises use values (including direct use such as resource use, recreation, and indirect use from regulating services) and the value people place on protecting nature for future use (option values), and non-use values, e.g., or for ethical reasons (bequest and existence values). The economic importance of most of these values can be measured in monetary terms, with varying degrees of accuracy, using various approaches.

Ecosystems are collections of all species living in a particular area together with the physical and chemical environment they live in. The stocks of these organisms should be regarded as capital stocks as should the stocks of resources such as water, minerals, and natural gas. This is **natural capital**. Ecosystem services are generated by these stocks of natural capital.

Biodiversity plays an important role in the provision of many of the services we receive from natural capital.

Ecosystems can be described, in principle, as nonlinear dynamical systems of different stocks of natural capital (e.g., grasslands, woodlands, and freshwater):

$$\frac{dS_1}{dt} = F_1(S_1, \ldots, S_n, B),$$
$$\ldots$$
$$\frac{dS_n}{dt} = F_n(S_1, \ldots, S_n, B).$$

The dynamic system above shows that the growth rates of the different stocks of natural capital in the ecosystem depend on own stock and the stocks of resources and other species which characterize competition/facilitation among species. Biodiversity B measured by an appropriate metric — species richness, Shannon index, or Simpson index — affects the evolution of the different stocks of natural capital and the services they generate. The structure of the dynamical system is illustrated in Figure 9.

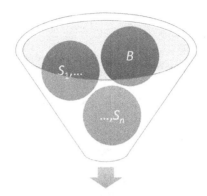

Supporting, Provisioning, Regulating, Cultural Ecosystem Services

Figure 9:   Stocks of natural capital, biodiversity, and ecosystem services.

This chapter provided a description of total economic value and the services provided by ecosystems. The methods for valuing these services are presented in Chapter 6.

References

Arrow, K. J., Fisher, A. C. (1974). Environmental preservation, uncertainty, and irreversibility. *The Quarterly Journal of Economics*, 88(2), 312–319.

Barbier, E. (2008). Ecosystems as natural assets. *Foundations and Trends in Microeconomics*, 4, 611–681.

Daily, G., Polasky, S., Goldstein, J., Kareiva, P. M., *et al.* (2009). Ecosystem services in decision making: Time to deliver. *Frontiers in Ecology and the Environment*, 7, 21–28. Reprinted in TEEB, 2010.

Dixit, A. K. Pindyck, R. S. (1994). *Investment under Uncertainty*. Princeton, NJ: Princeton University Press.

Hanley, N., Barbier, E. (2009). *Pricing Nature: Cost–Benefit Analysis and Environmental Policy*. Cheltenham, UK: Edward Elgar Publishing.

Hanley, N., Shogren, J., White, B. (2000). *An Introduction to Environmental Economics*. Oxford, UK: Oxford University Press.

Henry, C. (1974). Option values in the economics of irreplaceable assets. *The Review of Economic Studies*, 41(5), 89–104.

Millennium Ecosystem Assessment (2005). *Ecosystems and Human Well-being: Synthesis*. Washington, DC: Island Press.

OECD (2018). *Cost–Benefit Analysis and the Environment: Further Developments and Policy Use.* Paris: OECD Publishing.

Pearce, D., Atkinson, G., Mourato, S. (2006). *Cost–Benefit Analysis and the Environment: Recent Developments.* Paris: OECD Publishing.

TEEB (2010). *The Economics of Ecosystems and Biodiversity. Ecological and Economic Foundations*, P. Kumar (ed.). London and Washington: Earthscan.

Chapter 6

Valuation of Ecosystem Services

6.1. Approaches to Valuation

Chapter 5 described ecosystem services and discussed the reasons why the valuation of these services, in monetary terms, is desirable. This chapter provides an introduction to the valuation of these ecosystem services.

As analyzed in TEEB (2010), there are two well-differentiated paradigms for valuation:

- *Biophysical methods* use a "cost of production" approach, as did some value theories in classical economics.
- *Preference-based methods*, which are based on willingness-to-pay and willingness-to-accept concepts, are more commonly used in economics.

Biophysical valuation is based on the cost of production approach and derives values from measurements of the physical costs of producing a given good or service. In valuing ecosystem services and biodiversity, this approach would consider the physical costs of maintaining a given ecological state. Biophysical methods, shown in Figure 1, are generally more useful for the valuation of natural capital stocks than for valuation at the margin of flows of ecosystem services.

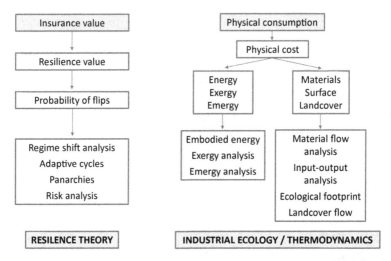

Figure 1:   Biophysical approaches to estimating the value of ecosystem services.

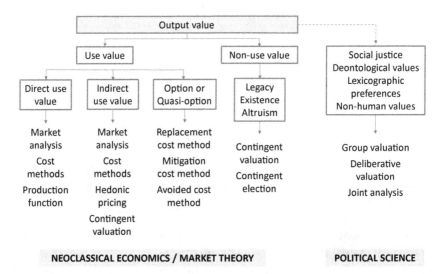

Figure 2:   Preference-based approaches to estimating the value of ecosystem services.

In contrast, preference-based methods of valuation, shown in Figure 2, rely on models of human behavior and assume that values arise from the subjective preferences of individuals. These methods assume that ecosystem values can be measured in monetary terms, thus providing a method of comparing the trade-offs involved in alternative uses of ecosystems. For a more detailed analysis, see TEEB (2010, Chapter 5).

6.1.1. *Direct market valuation*

Direct market valuation involves estimating the value of ecosystem services by observing and analyzing actual market transactions that involve those services. There are three main approaches to direct market valuation: market price-based, cost-based, and production function-based approaches:

- *Market price-based approaches* are used to value provisioning services, which are the products or services that ecosystems provide directly to humans. The market price-based approach estimates the value of a provisioning service by multiplying the price of the product or service by the marginal product of the ecosystem service. The marginal product is the additional amount of the product that is produced by a small change in the ecosystem service. It is the most commonly used approach because it is based on actual market transactions.
- *Cost-based approaches* estimate the value of ecosystem services by estimating the costs that would be incurred if the services were to be lost or degraded. For example, if a wetland is not providing flood control, then the cost-based approach would estimate the cost of building levees or other infrastructure to provide flood control.
- *Production function-based (PF) approaches* estimate the value of ecosystem services by estimating how much a given ecosystem service contributes to the production of another service or commodity that is traded on an existing market. For example, a PF approach could be used to estimate the value of pollination services by estimating how much pollination services increase crop yields.

The PF approach is a two-step approach. In the first step, the contribution of the ecosystem service to the production of the other service or commodity is estimated. In the second step, the value of the other service or commodity is estimated.

6.1.1.1. *Limitations of direct market valuation*

While direct market valuation has certain advantages — e.g., the use of actual market transactions, accurate and objective estimates, and the ability to capture both use and non-use values — it also has some limitations. These include:

Missing or incomplete markets: Many ecosystem services do not have well-functioning markets, making it difficult to directly observe transactions and prices. For instance, services like air and water purification provided by ecosystems often lack clear market mechanisms.

Externalities: Ecosystem services often involve positive or negative externalities, where the benefits or costs extend beyond the direct participants in a transaction. For example, the value of wetlands for flood control benefits neighboring communities, but this value might not be directly captured in market transactions.

Public goods: Many ecosystem services, such as biodiversity-related services, have public goods characteristics — non-excludability and non-rivalry — which means that individuals cannot be excluded from using them, and one person's use does not diminish their availability to others. Public goods therefore often lead to *free rider* problems, where individuals may not be willing to pay for the service, since they can benefit without contributing. Competitive markets cannot provide the socially desirable level of public goods.

Market failures: In addition to missing markets, externalities, and public goods, markets may fail to capture the true value of ecosystem services due to other factors such as asymmetric information, ambiguity, and unequal distribution of costs and benefits.

Existence value and altruistic preferences: Some ecosystem services have value simply because people know they exist, even if they do not directly use them. For instance, people might value the existence of a pristine forest for aesthetic or biodiversity reasons. Direct market valuation is unable to capture such existence values or altruistic preferences. (See Chapter 5, Section 5.3 for more details.)

Temporal and spatial variations: Ecosystem services often vary in their availability over time and across different locations. Market prices might not accurately reflect these variations, making it challenging to accurately estimate their value.

Substitutability and complementarity: Ecosystem services can be interconnected and interdependent. For example, a wetland might provide both water purification and habitats for wildlife. Direct market valuation could be unable to account for these complex relationships.

6.1.2. *Revealed preferences*

Revealed preference techniques are based on the idea that people's preferences are revealed by their choices. These techniques are used to value ecosystem services by observing people's choices in existing markets that are related to the ecosystem service. The two main methods within this approach are as follows:

- The *travel cost method* is used to value recreational ecosystem services. It estimates the value of a recreational site by measuring the cost that people incur to travel to and use the site.
- The *hedonic pricing approach* is used to value ecosystem services that are associated with marketed commodities. It estimates the value of an ecosystem service by measuring the difference in price between two commodities that differ in the level of the ecosystem service.

  For example, the hedonic pricing approach could be used to estimate the value of ecosystem services related to a house, based on its characteristics, such as its proximity to a park. The method uses statistical analysis to determine how much more expensive a house is for every additional kilometer closer it is to the park. For example, a house that is 1 km closer to a park may be worth

10,000€ more than a house that is 1 km farther from the park. Thus the value of ecosystem services associated with 1 km proximity to the park is 10,000€ for this house.

Revealed preference methods are presented in greater detail in Chapter 7.

6.1.3. *Stated preferences*

Stated preference approaches simulate a market for ecosystem services by asking people how much they would be willing to pay for changes in the provision of ecosystem services. These approaches can be used to estimate both use and non-use values of ecosystems, and they can be used when no market exists for the ecosystem service. Researchers often turn to stated preference techniques to estimate the value of ecosystem services that are not well-suited to direct market valuation or the revealed preference methods discussed above.

The main types of stated preference techniques are the following:

- *Contingent valuation* asks people how much they would be willing to pay to increase or enhance the provision of an ecosystem service. Alternatively, it can ask people how much they would be willing to accept for the loss or degradation of an ecosystem service.
- *Choice modeling* asks people to choose between two or more alternatives that differ in the provision of ecosystem services. The choices that people make can be used to estimate their preferences for different levels of ecosystem services.
- *Group valuation* combines stated preference techniques with elements of deliberative processes from political science. It involves bringing together a group of people to discuss the value of an ecosystem service and to make a collective decision about how much they would be willing to pay for it.

Stated preference methods are presented in greater detail in Chapter 9.

6.2. Methods of Valuation

Ecosystem services are valued using revealed and stated preferences when direct market valuation is not possible. Depending on the specific problem and availability of data, a wide variety of different methods can be used.

Valuation methods and values are shown in Table 1, and specific valuation methods and some examples of their applications are presented in Tables 2 and 3. For more information on the main economic methods for mapping and assessment of ecosystem services, see Brander *et al.* (2018). Table 4 provides examples of monetary valuations of ecosystem services from forests.

Among its many uses, valuation of ecosystem services is essential in order to quantify the importance of ecosystem services to human well-being, especially the well-being of the poorer income groups.

Table 1: Valuation methods and values.

Approach		Method	Value
Market valuation	Price-based	Market prices	Direct and indirect use
		Avoided cost	Direct and indirect use
	Cost-based	Replacement cost	Direct and indirect use
		Mitigation/Restoration cost	Direct and indirect use
	Production-based	Production function approach	Indirect use
		Factor income	Indirect use
Revealed preferences		Travel cost method	Direct and indirect use
		Hedonic pricing	Direct and indirect use
Stated preferences		Contingent valuation	Use and non-use
		Choice modeling/ Conjoint analysis/ Contingent ranking	Use and non-use
		Deliberative group value	Use and non-use

Table 2:　A brief description of valuation methods for ecosystem services and some examples of applications.

Valuation method	Acronym	Brief description	Examples of applications
Choice modeling (Discrete choice experiment, Conjoint analysis)	CE	Estimates the value people place on different attributes of a product or service by presenting them with a set of hypothetical alternatives and asking them to choose their preferred option. By varying the attributes and levels of the alternatives, researchers can determine the relative importance and trade-offs that people make in their choices.	• A study seeks to estimate the value people place on improved water quality in a river system. Respondents are presented with hypothetical scenarios that describe different levels of improvement in water quality and asked to choose which scenario they prefer. • A national park is considering different fee structures for visitors. Respondents are presented with different fee structures that vary in terms of the level of fees charged and the use of funds and asked to choose which fee structure they prefer.
Contingent valuation	CV	Individuals state their willingness to pay (WTP) for a good or their willingness to accept (WTA) payment for something that is taken away.	• A survey asks people how much they would be willing to pay for the preservation of a historical landmark. • Nearby residents are asked how much compensation they would need to be willing to accept the loss of a forested area in order to construct a new highway.

Damage cost avoided	DC	Estimates the value of ecosystem services by calculating the costs that would be incurred if those services were lost or damaged, and then subtracting those costs from the value of the services.	• A city estimates the economic value of urban trees in reducing air pollution by quantifying the avoided health costs associated with improved air quality. • A study estimates the value of coral reefs in reducing damages from coastal erosion and storms by comparing the costs of erosion and storm damage in areas with and without healthy coral reef ecosystems.
Defensive expenditure	DE	Estimates the value of ecosystem services by looking at how much people spend to avoid or mitigate the negative effects of environmental damage or degradation.	• The cost of building sea walls or other flood protection measures to protect coastal properties from sea-level rise or storm surges. • Paying for bottled water or home filtration systems to avoid contaminated water sources due to pollution. • The cost of pesticide or herbicide application in agriculture to reduce crop damage or loss from pests or weeds.
Group valuation (Participatory valuation)	GV	Involves working with local communities to identify and assess the value of ecosystem services, incorporating their traditional knowledge and perspectives in the valuation process.	• A local community participates in a valuation process to identify the economic value of medicinal plants found in their traditional lands. • Local fishermen work with researchers to assess the value of a healthy mangrove ecosystem for their livelihoods and the surrounding community.

(Continued)

Table 2:   (*Continued*)

Valuation method	Acronym	Brief description	Examples of applications
Hedonic pricing	HP	Estimates the value of a good or service based on the prices of similar goods or services that differ in terms of one or more characteristics, such as location, quality, or amenities.	• The value of scenic views can be estimated by comparing the prices of properties that have different views, such as waterfront versus non-waterfront properties. • The value of air quality can be estimated by looking at the difference in housing prices between areas with different levels of pollution. • Real estate prices can be used to estimate the value of proximity to a park or other natural area, as properties that are closer to these areas often command higher prices.
Input–output modeling	IO	Estimates the economic impacts of changes in demand or supply for goods and services. It shows how changes in one sector of the economy can affect other sectors by tracing the flow of goods, services, and income between different industries.	• The economic value of timber production from forests can be estimated by tracing the flow of timber sales revenue through the regional or national economy, accounting for the direct and indirect impacts of the timber industry on economic activity. • The economic value of pollination services provided by bees and other pollinators can be estimated by tracing the flow of agricultural production through the regional or national economy, accounting for the direct and indirect impacts of pollinators on crop yields and related economic activity.

Market prices (Gross revenue)	MP	Estimates the value of ecosystem services based on the market prices of the goods and services that depend on these ecosystem services, such as timber, crops, or fisheries.	• The economic value of tourism can be estimated by looking at the market prices of different types of tourism activities (such as guided tours or recreational activities) and the revenue generated by the tourism industry. • The economic value of carbon sequestration can be estimated by looking at the market prices of carbon credits or offsets that companies purchase to offset their carbon emissions.
Net factor income (Residual value, Resource rent)	FI	Estimates the economic value of ecosystem services by subtracting the costs associated with producing and maintaining those services from the revenue generated by their use. The resulting net value represents the economic surplus or rent generated by the ecosystem service.	• The economic value of oil drilling in a region can be estimated by subtracting the costs of extracting the oil (such as drilling, transport, and refining) and the environmental damage caused by the activity from the revenue generated by selling the oil. The resulting net value represents the resource rent or surplus generated by the oil industry. • The economic value of grazing on public lands can be estimated by subtracting the costs of managing and maintaining the lands from the revenue generated by the grazing activity. The resulting net value represents the resource rent or surplus generated by the grazing activity.

(Continued)

Table 2: (*Continued*)

Valuation method	Acronym	Brief description	Examples of applications
Opportunity cost	OC	Estimates the economic value of ecosystem services by considering the cost of foregone alternatives. It measures the value of an ecosystem service as the value of the next best use of the land or resources if the ecosystem service was not provided.	• The economic value of protecting a coral reef can be estimated by considering the cost of foregone fishing or tourism revenue if the coral reef was destroyed. • The economic value of conserving a watershed can be estimated by considering the cost of foregone hydropower or agricultural uses of the water if the watershed was degraded or polluted. • The economic value of a wetland can be estimated by considering the value of foregone agriculture if the wetland was converted to agricultural use.
Production function	PF	Estimates the economic value of ecosystem services by analyzing their contribution to the production of goods and services in the economy. It measures the value of an ecosystem service as the increase in economic output resulting from its provision.	• The economic value of nutrient cycling services provided by soil microorganisms can be estimated by analyzing the increase in agricultural productivity resulting from the presence of healthy soil ecosystems. • The economic value of biodiversity in pharmaceutical research and development can be estimated by analyzing the potential increase in profits resulting from the discovery of new medicines derived from natural sources.

| Public pricing | PP | Estimates the value of a good or service by observing the prices that consumers are willing to pay for it in public markets. This method assumes that the market price reflects the value that consumers place on the good or service. | • Carbon pricing assigns a monetary value to the carbon emissions generated by economic activities. By putting a price on carbon, governments can incentivize companies to reduce their emissions and invest in low-carbon technologies.
 • Water pricing assigns a monetary value to the use of freshwater resources. By pricing water, governments can encourage users to conserve this vital ecosystem service and allocate water resources more efficiently. |
| Replacement cost | RC | Estimates the value of an ecosystem service by determining the cost of replacing the service using artificial means. This method is based on the assumption that the value of the ecosystem service is equal to the cost of replacing it. | • A company wants to assess the value of a wetland it plans to destroy to build a new factory. The replacement cost method would estimate the cost of creating a new wetland with similar characteristics as the destroyed one.
 • A government agency wants to assess the economic value of a park that was damaged by a landslide. The replacement cost method would estimate the cost of replacing the park with a new one at a location nearby. |

(Continued)

Table 2: (*Continued*)

Valuation method	Acronym	Brief description	Examples of applications
Restoration cost	RT	Estimates the economic value of restoring a damaged or degraded natural resource by determining the costs of restoring the resource to its original state. It takes into account both the direct and indirect costs associated with the restoration process.	• In the case of a wildfire, restoration cost would include the cost of replanting trees and restoring the vegetation. • In the case of a mining project, restoration cost would include the cost of restoring the affected area to its pre-mining condition, including the re-establishment of vegetation and the rehabilitation of any waterways or ecosystems that were impacted by the mining activity.
Travel cost	TC	Estimates the economic value of a recreational site by analyzing the travel costs incurred by visitors to reach the site. The analysis uses the relationship between travel cost and the number of visits to estimate the economic value of the site.	• Estimating the economic value of a ski resort by analyzing the travel costs incurred by skiers to reach the resort and the number of ski trips taken to the resort. • Estimating the economic value of a hiking trail by analyzing the travel costs incurred by hikers to reach the trail and the number of visits to the trail.

| Value transfer (Benefits transfer) | VT | Estimates the economic value of ecosystem services in one location based on data from similar studies conducted in other locations. It transfers the value estimates from one study site to another location with similar ecological and socioeconomic conditions. | • The economic value of a conservation program for a rare or endangered species in one location can be estimated based on the value estimates from similar conservation programs conducted in other locations with similar species and ecological characteristics. |
| | | | • The economic value of improved air quality resulting from a proposed emission reduction policy in one city can be estimated based on the value estimates from similar emission reduction policies implemented in other cities with similar air quality conditions and socioeconomic characteristics. |

Table 3:   Economic valuation methods with some examples from the literature.

Approach	Method	Examples	References
Market valuation	Market price	• This study examined the feasibility and reliability of value estimates of the market price method by applying it to the Gubi Dam area in Bauchi State, Nigeria.	• Adeyemi, A., Dukku, S., Gambo, M., Ufere, K. (2013). The market price method and economic valuation of biodiversity in Bauchi State, Nigeria. *International Journal of Economic Development Research and Invest-ment*, 3.
	Cost-based Avoided cost	• Measures based on avoided costs were used to provide an estimate of the cost-effectiveness of public programs aimed at achieving healthier and more environmentally sustainable diets.	• Springmann, M., Godfray, H. C. J., Rayner, M., Scarborough, P. (2016). Analysis and valuation of the health and climate change cobenefits of dietary change. *PNAS*, 113, 4146–4151.
		• This study proposes a methodology based on the estimation of shadow prices for the pollutants removed in a treatment process, which represents the environmental benefit (avoided cost) associated with undischarged pollution.	• Hernández-Sancho, F., Molinos-Senante, M., Sala-Garrido, R. (2010). Economic valuation of environmental benefits from wastewater treatment processes: An empirical approach for Spain. *Science of the Total Environment*, 408, 953–957.

Replacement cost	• The economic value of the protective function for homogeneous zones in mountain forests was estimated by applying the replacement cost method to an Italian alpine forest.
	• Using the replacement cost method, this study quantified the direct consumptive value of aquatic species and sites for indigenous subsistence in three Australian tropical river catchments.
Mitigation/ Restoration cost	• The benefits from a restoration project (e.g., flood regulation and biodiversity) were compared with the associated costs.
	• This study presents a detailed economic analysis of an urban drain restoration project in Perth, Western Australia.
Notaro, S., Paletto, A. (2012). The economic valuation of natural hazards mountain forests: An approach based on the replacement cost method. *Journal of Forest Economics*, 18, 318–328.
Jackson, S., Finn, M., Scheepers, K. (2014). The use of replacement cost method to assess and manage the impacts of water resource development on Australian indigenous customary economies. *Journal of Environmental Management*, 135, 100–109.
Brouwer, R., Sheremet, O. (2017). The economic value of river restoration. *Water Resources and Economics*, 17, 1–8.
Polyakov, M., Fogarty, J., Zhang, F., Pandit, R., Pannell, D. J. (2017). The value of restoring urban drains to living streams. *Water Resources and Economics*, 17, 42–55.

(Continued)

Table 3: (*Continued*)

Approach	Method	Examples	References
	Production function/ Factor income	• Using cereal production in the Czech Republic as a case study, this study employed the production function valuation method to assess the economic value of green water as a factor of production.	• Grammatikopoulou, I., Sylla, M., Zoumides, C. (2020). Economic evaluation of green water in cereal crop production: A production function approach. *Water Resources and Economics*, 29, 100148.
		• This study used a health production function approach to conduct an objective assessment of the health damages incurred by urban households in Delhi, India.	• Dasgupta, P. (2004). Valuing health damages from water pollution in urban Delhi, India: A health production function approach. *Environment and Development Economics*, 9, 83–106.
Revealed preferences	Travel cost method	• A travel cost random utility model was used to estimate the value of recreational ecosystem services provided by more than 170 outdoor sites located on the island of Maui.	• Fezzi, C., Ford, D. J., Oleson, K. L. L. (2023). The economic value of coral reefs: Climate change impacts and spatial targeting of restoration measures. *Ecological Economics*, 203, 107628.
		• The value of Kakum National Park in Ghana to recreationers was assessed, by adopting the simple formulation of the individual travel cost method.	• Twerefou, D. K., Ababio, D. K. A. (2012). An economic valuation of the Kakum National Park: An individual travel cost approach. *African Journal of Environmental Science and Technology*, 6.

Hedonic pricing method	• Hedonic pricing models were used to develop real estate pricing models for two mid-size cities in the south of Brazil.	• Poeta, S., Gerhardt, T., Stumpf Gonzalez, M. (2019). Hedonic price analysis of single-family housing. *Revista Ingeniería de Construcción*, 34.
	• The monetary value associated with waterfronts was estimated using the hedonic pricing method and real estate sales data for the coastal cities of Mobile and Daphne in Alabama, USA.	• Dahal, R. P., Grala, R. K., Gordon, J. S., Munn, I. A., Petrolia, D. R., Cummings, J. R. (2019). A hedonic pricing method to estimate the value of waterfronts in the Gulf of Mexico. *Urban Forestry & Urban Greening*, 41, 185–194.
Stated preference	• This study employed the contingent valuation method to evaluate the WTP of residents in a region in Western Greece for the addition of renewable energy in electricity generation.	• Paravantis, J. A., Stigka, E., Mihalakakou, G., Michalena, E., *et al.* (2018). Social acceptance of renewable energy projects: A contingent valuation investigation in Western Greece. *Renewable Energy*, 123, 639–651.
Contingent valuation method (CVM)	• This study reports the results of a survey using the contingent valuation method of the willingness of Japanese households to pay more, in the form of a flat monthly surcharge, for renewable energy.	• Nomura, N., Akai, M. (2004). Willingness to pay for green electricity in Japan as estimated through contingent valuation method. *Applied Energy*, 78, 453–463.

(Continued)

Table 3: *(Continued)*

Approach	Method	Examples	References
	Choice modeling	• Choice experiments were used to investigate the willingness to pay of a sample of residents of Bath, England, for a hypothetical program that promotes the production of renewable energy.	• Longo, A., Markandya, A., Petrucci, M. (2008). The internalization of externalities in the production of electricity: Willingness to pay for the attributes of a policy for renewable energy. *Ecological Economics*, 67, 140–152.
		• A choice modeling experiment was used to examine whether subsistence level/indigenous people living on the banks of the Amazon River place a value on the preservation of ecosystems independent of direct impacts of environmental change.	• Casey, J. F., Kahn, J. R., Rivas, A. A. (2008). Willingness to accept compensation for the environmental risks of oil transport on the Amazon: A choice modeling experiment. *Ecological Economics*, 67, 552–559.
	Group valuation	• This study used qualitative research with four in-depth discussion groups to determine the most highly valued open spaces in the city.	• Burgess, J., Harrison, C. M., Limb, M. (1988). People, parks and the urban green: A study of popular meanings and values for open spaces in the city. *Urban Studies*, 25, 455–473.
		• This study reports on a deliberative non-monetary valuation process designed to address the value of peatland ecosystem services in Southern Finland.	• Saarikoski, H., Mustajoki, J. (2021). Valuation through deliberation — Citizens' panels on peatland ecosystem services in Finland. *Ecological Economics*, 183, 106955.

Table 4: Some estimated values of ecosystem services (ES) from forests.

Ecosystem service	Value	Source
Water purification	This study aimed to estimate the economic value of forest water purification ecosystem services in Costa Rica. It found that the estimated value of water purification service provided by Costa Rican forests is US$ 9.5 per hectare per year. Depending on the discount rate, this results in a net present value of water purification service ranging between US$ 315.4 and US$ 113.9 per hectare.	Piaggio, M., Siikamäki, J. (2021). The value of forest water purification ecosystem services in Costa Rica. *Science of the Total Environment*, 789, 147952.
Various ES	Evidence presented in this study suggests that total net value of benefits (i.e., value of services minus disservices) provided by the Nagarhole National Park in Karnataka, India ranges between US$ 13 and 148 million per annum or US$ 203 and 2,294 per hectare per annum using alternate valuation methods.	Ninan, K. N., Kontoleon, A. (2016). Valuing forest ecosystem services and disservices — Case study of a protected area in India. *Ecosystem Services*, 20, 1–14.
Carbon sequestration	This study aimed to estimate the economic value of carbon storage and sequestration provided by Lobeke National Park, a protected area located in southeast Cameroon. The value of the service of carbon sequestration was estimated to be over US$ 1,434 billion.	Zapfack, L., Noiha, N. V., Tabue, M. R. B. (2016). Economic estimation of carbon storage and sequestration as ecosystem services of protected areas: A case study of Lobeke National Park. *Journal of Tropical Forest Science*, 406–415.

(Continued)

Table 4: *(Continued)*

Ecosystem service	Value	Source
Various ES	The TEV value of forest ecosystem services in Malaysia in 2016, including direct use values (timber, recreation), indirect use values (carbon sequestration, watershed services), and non-use value (conservation), was estimated at Malaysian RM 13 billion.	Nitanan, K. M., Shuib, A., Sridar, R., Kunjuraman, V., Zaiton, S., Herman, M. A. (2020). The total economic value of forest ecosystem services in the tropical forests of Malaysia. *International Forestry Review*, 22, 485–503.
Various ES	The overall average value estimate for the regulating and cultural ecosystem services (e.g., provision of habitat for species, carbon sequestration, water regulation, recreation, and ecotourism) provided by the Amazon rainforest to local populations and communities in Brazil was found to be US$ 410 per hectare per year with a standard error of 123.	Brouwer, R., Pinto, R., Dugstad, A., Navrud, S. (2022). The economic value of the Brazilian Amazon rainforest ecosystem services: A meta-analysis of the Brazilian literature. *PloS One*, 17, e0268425.

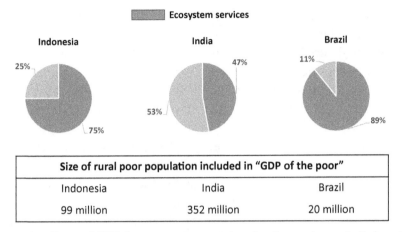

Figure 3: Share of GDP from ecosystem services for the rural poor in Indonesia, India, and Brazil.

Data source: TEEB (2010).

Their contribution to the livelihoods of poor rural households is significant, and therefore conserving ecosystems could play an important role in poverty reduction, which is the United Nations sustainable development goal #1 (see also Chapter 14, Section 14.4).

As noted by TEEB (2010), it has been estimated that ecosystem services and other non-market goods account for between 47% and 89% of the effective GDP or total source of livelihood of rural and forest-dwelling poor households (the so-called 'GDP of the poor'). Figure 3 shows the percentage of the GDP of the rural poor that is derived from ecosystem services in Indonesia, India, and Brazil.

6.3. Issues in the Valuation of Ecosystem Services

The valuation of ecosystem services is a complex and multidisciplinary endeavor. In this context, some of the important issues and challenges include the following:

- **Conceptual and definition issues**: Defining and categorizing ecosystem services can be challenging due to the diverse range of services that ecosystems provide and the complexity of their interactions. Different stakeholders might have varying perspectives on what constitutes an ecosystem service.

- **Cultural, social, and ethical issues**: The value of ecosystem services can vary across cultures, communities, and regions. Different societies place different levels of importance on various services, and cultural and ethical values might not always align with economic valuation approaches.

- **Scale and spatial variability**: Ecosystem services are often location-specific and can vary in value across different spatial scales. Valuation needs to account for these variations, but accurately assessing values at different scales can be challenging.

- **Temporal dynamics**: Ecosystem services can change over time due to natural processes, human activities, and environmental changes, so valuation should consider the dynamic nature of services and their values over time.

- **Uncertainty**: There is often uncertainty associated with both the ecological processes that provide ecosystem services and the economic models used to value them. This uncertainty can affect the accuracy of valuation estimates.

- **Data limitations**: Availability of data on ecosystem characteristics, human preferences, and economic behaviors can be limited and inconsistent, particularly in developing regions.

- **Double counting and substitutability**: Ecosystem services are often interconnected, and the alteration of one service might affect others. Valuation methods need to account for potential double counting of benefits and the substitutability or complementarity of services.

- **Equity and distributional concerns**: The benefits of ecosystem services might not be distributed equally among different social and economic groups, so valuation should consider equity issues to avoid exacerbating existing inequalities.

- **Policy implications**: Valuation of ecosystem services has policy implications, and decisions based on these valuations can affect resource management, conservation efforts, and development projects. The accuracy of valuations can influence the effectiveness of policy decisions.

6.3.1.   *The value of an ecosystem and the price of natural capital*

Efficient policy design requires valuation of the natural capital that generates ecosystem services, as well as the valuation of an ecosystem as a whole, in terms of the specific types of values that it generates. Thus, the value of an ecosystem is the aggregate value of the services it produces. It is defined as the discounted sum of the flow of the values of all services VS_t provided by the ecosystem which have been valued using the methods described in Table 2, discounted at the social discount rate r. Formally,

$$\text{Value}_0 = \sum_{t=0}^{\infty} \frac{VS_t}{(1+r)^t}.$$

If there are (approximately efficient) markets for the services generated by a stock of natural capital, then the market price is a good proxy, especially for direct use values.

If markets are missing or if they are heavily distorted, we need accounting or shadow prices. An *accounting price* for a natural stock is defined as the change in the total value of ecosystem services caused by a marginal change in the stock associated with the specific service. An example, shown in Figure 4, is a lake of value V_1 (oligotrophic) and V_2 (eutrophic) and with stock of phosphorus S_t. It is assumed

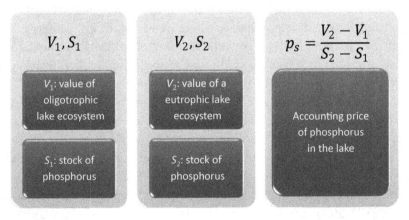

Figure 4:   Approximating an accounting price for phosphorus stock in a lake.

that $S_2 > S_1$, $V_2 < V_1$, indicating that the accounting price for the stock of phosphorus is negative. That is, an increase in the stock of phosphorus in the lake represents a cost.

6.4. Valuation Databases

The need to value ecosystem services has generated a very large number of valuation studies. Valuation databases collect the information from these studies and present them in a compact and uniform way in order to facilitate research and policy design.

The TEEB database (van der Ploeg and de Groot, 2010) contains over 1,300 data points from 267 case studies on monetary values of ecosystem services across 11 biomes and was updated in 2010. All 22 ecosystem services identified in the TEEB study were taken into account. It contains original values in monetary units organized by service and biome. Table 5 provides an indication of the extensive scope of the data included in the TEEB database.

The Ecosystem Services Valuation Database (ESVD) (de Groot *et al.*, 2020) is a follow-up to the original TEEB database. The ESVD 2020 database contains 4,042 value records (three times as many as the original TEEB database) based on 693 studies and increased the number of publications in the repository to 3,783 (14 times more than the TEEB repository).

The ESVD also added additional variables, including additional information on study site location, size, and condition. Moreover, in addition to the TEEB ecosystem services classification, the ESVD values are also linked to the Common International Classification of Ecosystem Services (CICES) V5.1.

A biome is a large geographical area that is characterized by a distinct set of plant and animal communities that are adapted to a specific climate, soil type, and topography. Biomes are generally classified based on the dominant vegetation type and the physical environment, but different studies can have classifications that vary. The original TEEB database uses 12 main types of biomes while the ESVD 2020 database uses the 16 categories listed in Table 6.

Table 5:   Summary of range and types of data available in the TEEB database.

Publication

- **Reference**: The full citation for the reference
- **Publication year**
- **Publication type**: Whether the publication is, e.g., an article, a report, or a book
- **Peer-reviewed publication**: Whether or not the publication was peer-reviewed

Ecological Information

- **Biome/ecosystem type**: Each study is classified according to the TEEB classification of different biome/ecosystem types
- **Ecosystem**: Each study is classified according to the TEEB classification of ecosystems per biome
- **Ecosystem services**: Each study is classified according to the TEEB subclassification of ecosystem services (ES)
- **Service area**: The area (in hectares) for which the ES was estimated (as indicated in the publication)

Economic Information

- **Valuation method**: The TEEB classification of valuation methods is used for the value in each study
- **Economic value**: The economic value as presented in the publication
- **Discount rate and years**: Included when stock, PV, and NPV are available in the publication
- **Unit**: The monetary unit used in the publication (e.g., EUR/ha or USD/ha/yr)
- **Currency**: The currency used in the publication
- **Year of value**: The year of validation of the value in the publication

Location Information

- **Location name**: A description of the location of the case study
- **Country**: Selected from the country/territory list
- **Location coordinates**: Latitude and longitude coordinates in WGS datum
- **Scale of the case study**: For example, local ecosystem, province, country, or world
- **Protected status**: Classification of the level of protection in the study area (unprotected, partially protected, completely protected, or unknown)

Table 6:   Classification of biomes used in the ESVD 2020 database.

Biome	Ecosystem	
Open sea/ ocean	• Shelf sea/neritic zone • Deep sea/abyssal zone	• Pelagic zone (up to 200 m deep) • Other (sea/ocean)
Coral reefs	• Barrier reefs • Atolls • Fringing reefs	• Patch reefs • Other (coral reefs)
Coastal systems (including wetlands)	• Sand dunes, beaches, rocky shores • Tidal marshes • Salt marshes • Mangroves • Lagoons • Estuaries	• Unvegetated sediment • Shellfish reefs • Seagrass beds • Kelp forests • Other (coastal systems)
Inland wetlands	• Swamps, marshes • Peatland, non-forested • Peatland, forested • Peatland, tropical • Peatland, boreal	• Wetlands, forested (on alluvial soils) • Wetlands, groundwater-dependent • Floodplains • Other (inland wetlands)
Rivers and lakes	• Rivers • Lakes, freshwater • Lakes, saltwater	• Human-made water bodies • Other (rivers and lakes)
Tropical forests	• Tropical rain forest • Tropical dry forest	• Tropical cloud forests • Other (tropical forests)
Temperate forests	• Temperate rain or evergreen forest • Temperate deciduous forest	• Boreal/coniferous forest ('Taiga') • Other (temperate forests)
Woodland and Shrubland	• Tropical woodland and shrubland • Mediterranean woodland and shrubland • Temperate woodland and shrubland	• Heathland • Other (woodland and shrubland)

Table 6: (*Continued*)

Biome	Ecosystem	
Grassland/ Rangeland	• Savanna • Tropical grasslands • Temperate grasslands	• Steppe (dry, cold grassland) • Other (grassland)
Desert	• True desert (sand/rock/ salt) • Semi-desert	• Other (desert)
Tundra	• Alpine tundra • Arctic tundra	• Other (tundra)
High mountain and polar systems	• High mountain — forest • High mountain — grassland • High mountain — snow and ice	• Polar • Other (high mountains and polar)
Inland un- or sparsely vegetated	• Underground systems • Inland rock formations	• Other (inland un- or sparsely vegetated)
Cultivated areas	• Cropland (arable land) • Pastures • Orchards/agro-forestry • Plantations	• Rice paddies, etc. • Aquaculture • Small landscape elements • Other (cultivated areas)
Urban green and blue infrastructure	• Urban parks and forests • Lawns, sports fields, golf courses • Urban lakes, ponds, wetlands	• Cultivated areas • (Street) trees and shrubs • Other (urban green-blue)
Other		

Tables 7 and 8 provide some examples of the value of various ecosystem services in selected biomes, taken from the ESVD 2020 database.

Table 7:   Values of selected *provisioning and regulating* ecosystem services per biome.

Biome	Food	Water	Air quality regulation	Climate regulation	Moderation of extreme events	Waste treatment
Open sea and ocean	43	—	—	69	—	28,190
Coral reefs	6,231	—	—	—	15,312	61,013
Coastal systems	9,892	5,172	15	262	12,730	36,556
Mangroves	6,717	10,496	1,323	1,698	16,960	4,079
Inland wetlands	6,030	1,934	34	150	13,320	2,043
Rivers and lakes	2,288	9,198	—	251	18	50,760
Tropical forests	602	47,869	309	658	108	12
Temperate forests	4	—	1,593	481	6	—
Woodland and shrubland	8	—	7	89	—	—
Grassland	—	313	8	73	—	—
High mountain and polar systems	2,448	58	—	190	419	—
Cultivated areas	510	604	10	10	993	40
Urban green-blue	—	—	9,416	1,722	—	—

Ecosystem service
Mean standardized value in International\$/hectare/year (2020 price levels)

Data source: de Groot *et al.* (2020).

Table 8: Values of selected *supporting* and *cultural* ecosystem services per biome.

Biome	Ecosystem service Mean standardized value in International$/hectare/year (2020 price levels)					
	Life cycle maintenance of migratory species	Maintenance of genetic diversity	Aesthetic information	Opportunities for recreation and tourism	Inspiration for culture, art, and design	Information for cognitive development
Open sea and ocean	—	—	—	2,473	—	—
Coral reefs	—	—	1,200	14,057	244	90
Coastal systems	375	165	268	7,694	145	5,683
Mangroves	1,658	6,645	334	4,366	3,890	1,429
Inland wetlands	1,886	3,427	59	2,660	114	120
Rivers and lakes	803	17,987	2,276	13,633	310	116
Tropical forests	19	7	—	52,789	5	—
Temperate forests	—	—	35	281	196	147
Woodland and shrubland	—	—	38	124	214	214
Grassland	—	—	—	92	284	147
High mountain and polar systems	—	—	—	167	—	—
Cultivated areas	—	—	395	3,101	16	—
Urban green-blue	—	—	—	—	—	—

Notes: Additional ecosystem services included in the ESVD but not shown in Tables 7–8 are Raw materials, Genetic resources, Medicinal resources, Ornamental resources, Regulation of water flows, Erosion prevention, Maintenance of soil fertility, Pollination, Biological control, Spiritual experience, and Existence and bequest values. There are additional biomes that are not included in Tables 7–8.
Data source: de Groot *et al.* (2020).

The ESVD database (de Groot *et al.*, 2020) contains a wealth of information on the economic value of ecosystem services. It can be used in a variety of ways, including:

Research: The database can be used as a resource for researchers interested in studying ecosystem services and their economic value. Researchers can use the database to identify knowledge gaps, evaluate the quality of existing studies, and develop new models for estimating the economic value of ecosystem services.

Education: The database can be used as an educational tool to teach students and the public about the importance of ecosystem services and their economic value.

Policy-making: The database provides information which can be used to inform policy-making related to ecosystem management, land-use planning, and natural resource management. For example, policy-makers can use the database to assess the economic benefits and costs of different policy options and make more informed decisions that balance economic development with environmental conservation.

Collaboration: The database can be used to facilitate collaboration between researchers, policy-makers, and other stakeholders interested in ecosystem services. It can thus lead to more effective decision-making and better conservation outcomes. The database contains extensive data on the economic value of ecosystem services, including estimates of the value of different services in different regions of the world.

Tables 9–13 provide just a few examples that illustrate the very rich variety of data contained in the ESVD.

De Groot *et al.* (2012) provide an overview of the monetary value of ecosystem services of 10 main biomes based on 665 data points. Data from their analysis indicates that the total value of ecosystem services that can potentially be provided ranges from 491 Int\$/hectare/year for open oceans to 25,000 Int\$/hectare/year for inland wetlands to over 350,000 Int\$/hectare/year for coral reefs.

Table 9: Examples of selected subsets of data available from the ESVD for the biomes: Open sea and ocean, Coral reefs, and Coastal systems.

Biome	Ecosystem	Country/Region of study	Valuation method	Value	Currency ISO code	Value year	Reference
Open sea/ ocean	Shelf sea/ neritic zone	United Kingdom	TC	2500000	GBP	2013	Ruiz-Frau, A., Hinz, H., Edward-Jones, G., Kaiser, M. J. (2013). Spatially explicit economic assessment of cultural ecosystem services: Non-extractive recreational uses of the coastal environment related to marine biodiversity.
Open sea/ ocean	Shelf sea	South Africa, Republic of	CV	0.64	USD	2001	Turpie, J. K. (2003). The existence value of biodiversity in South Africa: How interest, experience, knowledge, income and perceived level of threat influence local willingness to pay. *Ecological Economics*, 46(2), 199–216.
Coral reefs	Barrier	Taiwan	CV	4500000	USD	2018	Maynard, N., *et al.* (2019). Using Internet surveys to estimate visitors' willingness to pay for coral reef conservation in the Kentin National Park, Taiwan.

(*Continued*)

Table 9: (*Continued*)

Biome	Ecosystem	Country of study	Valuation method	Value	Currency ISO code	Value year	Reference
Coral reefs	Other	Madagascar, Republic of	CE	56.78	MGA	2013	Oleson, K. L. L., *et al.* (2015). Cultural bequest values for ecosystem service flows among indigenous fishers: A discrete choice experiment validated with mixed methods.
Coral reefs	Fringing	Thailand, Kingdom of	CV	13870000	THB	2014	Piriyapada, S., Wang, E. (2015). Modeling willingness to pay for coastal tourism resource protection in Ko Chang Marine National Park, Thailand.
Coral reefs	Barrier, Atoll Fringing	Philippines, Republic of	MP	20740000	USD	2016	Tamayo, N. C. A., *et al.* (2018). National Estimates of Values of Philippine Reefs' Ecosystem Services.
Coastal systems	Mangroves	Bangladesh, People's Republic of	FI	6400000	BDT	2012	Chow, J. (2015). Spatially explicit evaluation of local extractive benefits from mangrove plantations in Bangladesh. *Journal of Sustainable Forestry,* 34(6–7), 651–681.

Coastal systems	Lagoons	Spain, Kingdom of	CV	43326181	EUR	2013	Velasco, A. M. *et al.* (2018). Ecosystem services and main environmental risks in a coastal lagoon (Mar Menor, Murcia, SE Spain): The public perception.
Coastal systems	Mangrove	Brazil	CE	475000000	BRL	2010	de Rezende, C. E., Kahn, J. R., Passareli, L., Vásquez, W. F. (2015). An economic valuation of mangrove restoration in Brazil. *Ecological Economics*, 120, 296–302.
Coastal systems	Mangrove	Vietnam, Socialist Republic of	CV	712300000	VND	2016	Pham, T. D., Kaida, N., Yoshino, K., Nguyen, X. H., Nguyen, H. T., Bui, D. T. (2018). Willingness to pay for mangrove restoration in the context of climate change in the Cat Ba biosphere reserve, Vietnam. *Ocean & Coastal Management*, 163.

Notes: TC: Travel cost. CV: Contingent valuation. CE: Choice modeling (Discrete choice Experiment; Conjoint analysis). MP: Market prices (Gross revenue). FI: Net factor income (Residual value; Resource rent).

Data source: Ecosystem Services Valuation Database (ESVD), Version June 2020.

Table 10: Examples of selected subsets of data available from the ESVD for the biomes: Inland wetlands, Rivers and lakes, and Tropical forests.

Biome	Ecosystem	Country	Valuation method	Value in Int\$/ hectare/year	Value year	Reference
Inland wetlands	Swamps, marshes	Indonesia, Republic of	MP	9639.016342	2012	Hanafi, I., Fitrianto, A., Arsyad, L. F., Setiawan, B. (2014). Economic-ecological values of non-tidal swamp ecosystem: Case study in Tapin District, Kalimantan, Indonesia. *Modern Applied Science*, 8(1), 97.
Inland wetlands	Peatland (non-forested)	United Kingdom	CE	322.1306064	2018	Glenk, K., Martin-Ortega, J. (2018). The economics of peatland restoration. *Journal of Environmental Economics and Policy*, 7(4), 345–362.
Rivers and lakes	Human-made water bodies	Nepal, State of	DE	11415.42975	2015	Baral, S., *et al.* (2016). A total economic valuation of wetland ecosystem services: An evidence from Jagadishpur Ramsar site, Nepal. *The Scientific World Journal*, 2016, 9, Article ID 2605609.

Rivers and lakes	Lakes, freshwater	China, People's Republic of	RC	60.34541271	2015	Li, T., Gao, X. (2016). Ecosystem services valuation of lakeside wetland park beside Chaohu Lake in China. *Water*, 8(7), 301.
Tropical forests	Tropical rain forest	Malaysia	DC	14.60029955	2018	Brander L., Tai B., Crossman, N., Hong Yeo, B. (2018). Natural capital valuation using primary data research methods in Baleh, Sarawak Heart of Borneo Project. WWF-Malaysia Project Report.
Tropical forests	Tropical cloud forest	Ethiopia, Federal Democratic Republic of	CV	25.4999176	2016	Getachew, T. (2018). Estimating willingness to pay for forest ecosystem conservation. The case of Wof-Washa Forest, North Shewa Zone, Amhara National Regional State, Ethiopia. *Journal of Resources Development and Management*, 46.
Tropical forests	Tropical rain forest	Costa Rica, Republic of	PF	506.5565187	2011	Ricketts, T. H., Lonsdorf, E. (2013). Mapping the margin: Comparing marginal values of tropical forest remnants for pollination services. *Ecological Applications*, 23(5), 1113–1123.

Notes: MP: Market prices (Gross revenue). CE: Choice modeling (Discrete choice Experiment; Conjoint analysis). DE: Defensive expenditure. RC: Replacement cost. DC: Damage cost avoided. CV: Contingent valuation. PF: Production function.
Data source: Ecosystem Services Valuation Database (ESVD), Version June 2020.

Table 11: Examples of selected subsets of data available from the ESVD for the biomes: Temperate forests, Woodland and shrubland, and Grass-/Rangeland.

Biome	Ecosystem	Country ISO code	Value year	Ecosystem service (text description from study)	Value in Int$/ hectare/year	Type of beneficiaries	Reference
Temperate forest	Temperate deciduous forest	GBR	2013	Timber	79.34672346	Forest industry	White, C., Dunscombe, R., Dvarskas, A., Eves, C., Finisdore, J., Kieboom, E., Maclean, I., Obst, C., Rowcroft, P. Silcock, P. (2015). Developing ecosystem accounts for protected areas in England and Scotland: The Borders Summary Report.
Woodland and shrubland	Mediterranean wood- and shrubland	ITA	2010	Animal genetic resources (Maremmana cattle)	—	Citizens	Zander, K. K., Signorello, G., De Salvo, M., Gandini, G., Drucker, A. G. (2013). Assessing the total economic value of threatened livestock breeds in Italy: Implications for conservation policy. *Ecological Economics*, 93, 219–229.
Woodland and shrubland	Heathland	GBR	2016	Biodiversity conservation	—	National	Czajkowski, M., Hanley, N., LaRiviere, J. (2016). Controlling for the effects of information in a public goods discrete choice modeling.

Biome	Sub-type	Country	Year	Ecosystem service	Value	Beneficiary	Reference
Grass-/Rangeland	Other (grassland)	USA	2010	Removal of air pollutants (NO2)	1.120578209	General public	Gopalakrishnan, V., Hirabayashi, S., Ziv, G., Bakshi, B. R. (2018). Air quality and human health impacts of grasslands and shrublands in the United States. *Atmospheric Environment*, 182, 193–199.
Grass-/Rangeland	Savanna	ZAF	2016	Grazing (monetary flow account)	637.3718582	Local farmers	Mudavanhu, S., Blignaut, J., Stegmann, N., Barnes, G., Prinsloo, W., Tuckett, A. (2017). The economic value of ecosystem goods and services: The case of Mogale's Gate Biodiversity Centre, South Africa. *Ecosystem Services*, 26, 127–136.
Grass-/Rangeland	Tropical grasslands	BRA	2012	Conservation of the park	13.75687293	Visitors, tourists	Resende, F. M., Fernandes, G. W., Andrade, D. C., Néder, H. D. (2017). Economic valuation of the ecosystem services provided by a protected area in the Brazilian Cerrado: Application of the contingent valuation method. *Brazilian Journal of Biology*, 77(4), 762–773.

Notes: GBR: United Kingdom of Great Britain and Northern Ireland. ITA: Italy, Italian Republic. USA: United States of America. ZAF: South Africa, Republic of. BRA: Brazil, Federative Republic of.

Data source: Ecosystem Services Valuation Database (ESVD), Version June 2020.

Table 12: Examples of selected subsets of data available from the ESVD for the biomes: Desert, Tundra, and High mountain and polar systems.

Biome	Ecosystem	Country	Site area	Site area spatial unit	Location name	References
Desert	True desert (sand/rock/salt)	Chile, Republic of	457.08	km²	Llanos de Challe National Park, Atacama desert	Cerda, C., Fuentes, J. P., de la Maza, C. L., Louit, C., Araos, A. (2018). Assessing visitors' preferences for ecosystem features in a desert biodiversity hotspot. *Environmental Conservation*, 45(1), 75–82.
Tundra	Arctic tundra	United States of America	78000	km²	Arctic National Wildlife Refuge	Turner, A. C., Young, M. A., McClung, M. R., Moran, M. D. (2020). Comprehensive valuation of the ecosystem services of the Arctic National Wildlife Refuge. bioRxiv.
High mountain and polar systems	High mountain — forest	Italy, Italian Republic	73600	ha	Fiemme and Fassa Valleys	Häyhä, T., Franzese, P. P., Paletto, A., Fath, B. D. (2015). Assessing, valuing, and mapping ecosystem services in Alpine forests. *Ecosystem Services*, 14, 12–23.

High mountain and polar systems	High mountain — forest	Austria, Republic of	1880	ha	Leiblachtal	Paletto, A., Geitner, C., Grilli, G., Hastik, R., Pastorella, F., García, L. R. (2015). Mapping the value of ecosystem services: A case study from the Austrian Alps. *Annals of Forest Research*, 58(1), 157–175.
High mountain and polar systems	High mountain — forest	Nepal, State of	15900	ha	Shivapuri-Nagarjun National Park in Nepal.	Peh, K. S. H., Thapa, I., Basnyat, M., Balmford, A., Bhattarai, G. P., Bradbury, R. B., ... Hughes, F. M. (2016). Synergies between biodiversity conservation and ecosystem service provision: Lessons on integrated ecosystem service valuation from a Himalayan protected area, Nepal. *Ecosystem Services*, 22, 359–369.

Data source: Ecosystem Services Valuation Database (ESVD), Version June 2020.

Table 13: Examples of selected subsets of data available from the ESVD for the biomes: Inland un- or sparsely vegetated, Cultivated areas, Urban green and blue infrastructure, and Other.

Biome	Ecosystem	Country	Ecosystem service (text description from study)	TEEB ES 1	Value	Currency ISO Code	References
Inland un- or sparsely vegetated	Underground systems	Thailand, Kingdom of	Biocontrol of rice pests ... by the wrinkle-lipped bat ...	Biological control	1213997	USD	Wanger, T. C., Darras, K., Bumrungsri, S., Tscharntke, T., Klein, A. M. (2014). Bat pest control contributes to food security in Thailand. *Biological Conservation*, 171, 220–223.
Cultivated areas	Orchards/agro-forestry	Netherlands, Kingdom of the, and Belgium, Kingdom of	Biological Pest Control	Biological control	1495.34	EUR	Daniels, S., Witters, N., Beliën, T., Vrancken, K., Vangronsveld, J., Van Passel, S. (2017). Monetary valuation of natural predators for biological pest control in pear production. *Ecological Economics*, 134, 160–173.
Cultivated areas	All types of cultivated ecosystems (excl. aquaculture)	Czech Republic	Pollination	Pollination	2935	EUR	Leonhardt, S. D., Gallai, N., Garibaldi, L. A., Kuhlmann, M., Klein, A. M. (2013). Economic gain, stability of pollination and bee diversity decrease from southern to northern Europe. *Basic and Applied Ecology*, 14(6), 461–471.

Cultivated areas	Cropland (arable land)	Ireland	Insect pollination	Pollination	5084533	EUR	Stanley, D. A., Gunning, D., Stout, J. C. (2013). Pollinators and pollination of oilseed rape crops (Brassica napus L.) in Ireland: Ecological and economic incentives for pollinator conservation. *Journal of Insect Conservation,* 17(6), 1181–1189.
Urban green and blue infrastructure	Urban lakes, ponds, wetlands	Spain, Kingdom of	Value of wetland for recreational functions	Opportunities for recreation and tourism	3.38	EUR	Alfranca, O. (2011). Economic valuation of a created wetland fed with treated wastewater located in a peri-urban park in Catalonia, Spain. *Water Science and Technology* 63.5 (2011): 891–898
Urban green and blue infrastructure	Urban parks and forests	United Kingdom	Amenity, Recreation	Aesthetic information	23.14	GBP	Andrews, B., Ferrini, S., Bateman, I. (2017). Good parks–bad parks: The influence of perceptions of location on WTP and preference motives for urban parks. *Journal of Environmental Economics and Policy,* 6(2), 204–224.

(Continued)

Table 13: (*Continued*)

Biome	Ecosystem	Country	Ecosystem service (text description from study)	TEEB ES 1	Value	Currency ISO Code	References
Urban green and blue infrastructure	Urban parks and forests (Street) trees and shrubs	United Kingdom	Climate regulation — carbon sequestration	Climate regulation	461400	GBP	Doik, A., *et al.* (2016). Valuing the urban trees in Bridgend County Borough.
Urban green and blue infrastructure	Urban parks and forests (Street) trees and shrubs	United Kingdom	Health benefits of trees removing PM2.5	Air quality regulation	1053338	GBP	Eftec and Centre for Ecology and Hydrology (2019). Pollution removal by vegetation.
Urban green and blue infrastructure	Urban lakes, ponds, wetlands	United Kingdom	Angling	Opportunities for recreation and tourism	5000000	GBP	Peirson, G., *et al.* (2001). Economic evaluation of inland fisheries in England and Wales.
Other	N/A	Czech Republic	Crop genetic resources (including oil crops..., legumes..., vegetables, potatoes, and cereals...)	Genetic resources	2.2	USD	Tyack, N., Ščasný, M. (2018). Social valuation of genebank activities: Assessing public demand for genetic resource conservation in the Czech Republic. *Sustainability*, 10(11), 3997.

| Other | N/A | Nepal, State of | (*ex situ*) conservation of rice landraces in gene bank | Genetic resources | 84000000 | USD | Poudel, D., Johnsen, F. H. (2009). Valuation of crop genetic resources in Kaski, Nepal: Farmers' willingness to pay for rice landraces conservation. *Journal of Environmental Management*, 90(1), 483–491. |

Note: TEEB ES 1: The first TEEB ecosystem service that is the subject of the value observation.
Data source: Ecosystem Services Valuation Database (ESVD), Version June 2020.

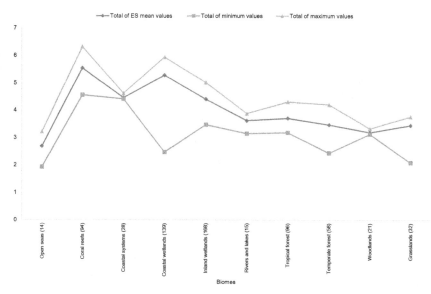

Figure 5: The mean, minimum, and maximum value of ecosystem services per biome, in logarithmic scale.

Notes: Number of studies for each biome in parentheses on the horizontal axis. The biomes Desert and Polar Regions were excluded from the analysis in de Groot *et al.* (2012) because of the small number of value data points. The biomes Cultivated Land and Urban Areas were excluded because they are human-dominated systems.

Data source: de Groot *et al.* (2012).

Figure 5 shows the mean, minimum, and maximum values of ecosystem services associated with the ten biomes. The original values expressed in Int$/hectare/year have been transformed into a logarithmic scale for presentation purposes. A small distance between the three values could be interpreted as a sign of relatively less uncertainty and potentially more accuracy in the estimation. (For the original values, see de Groot *et al.* (2012)).

The authors emphasize that most of the monetary value of ecosystem services is outside the market and best considered as non-tradable public benefits. The authors state the following: "The continued over-exploitation of ecosystems thus comes at the expense of the livelihood of the poor and future generations. Given that many of the positive externalities of ecosystems are lost or strongly reduced after land use conversion, better accounting for the public goods and services provided by ecosystems is crucial to improve decision-making and institutions for biodiversity conservation and sustainable ecosystem management" (de Groot *et al.*, 2012, p. 50).

This chapter provided a summary description of the approaches used in the valuation of ecosystem approaches. It also explained the importance of valuation databases in this context and presented some examples of the wide range of data they provide.

References

Brander, L. M., van Beukering, P., Balzan, M., *et al.* (2018). Report on economic mapping and assessment methods for ecosystem services. Deliverable D3.2 EU Horizon 2020 ESMERALDA Project, Grant agreement No. 642007.

de Groot, R., Brander, L., Solomonides, S. (2020). Update of global ecosystem service valuation database (ESVD). FSD report No. 2020-06, Wageningen, The Netherlands.

de Groot, R., Brander, L., van der Ploeg, S., Costanza, R., Bernard, F., *et al.* (2012). Global estimates of the value of ecosystems and their services in monetary units. *Ecosystem Services*, 1, 50–61.

TEEB (2010). *The Economics of Ecosystems and Biodiversity. Ecological and Economic Foundations*, P. Kumar (ed.). London and Washington: Earthscan.

Van der Ploeg, S., de Groot, R. S. (2010). *The TEEB Valuation Database — A Searchable Database of 1310 Estimates of Monetary Values of Ecosystem Services*. Wageningen, The Netherlands: Foundation for Sustainable Development.

Chapter 7

Revealed Preference Methods

7.1. An Overview

Revealed preference methods (RPMs), which were introduced in Chapter 6, draw statistical inferences on values from actual choices people make within markets (see, e.g., Boyle, 2003). RPMs can be used in environmental economics to reveal values for non-market goods which are embedded in observed prices of market goods. The main revealed preference methods — travel cost, hedonic pricing, averting behavior, and defensive expenditure — share the common feature of using market information and/or behavior to infer the economic value of an associated non-market impact:

- The unifying characteristic of RPMs is that they rely on individuals' observed choices and behavior in real-world market settings to infer their preferences and valuations (OECD, 2018). These methods are based on the idea that individuals reveal their preferences through their actual purchasing decisions and consumption patterns. RPMs can be contrasted with stated preference methods which ask people how they would hypothetically value changes in the provision of non-market goods.
- RPMs can be applied in a variety of contexts:
  o The travel cost method, for example, is a popular RPM used to estimate the recreational value of natural areas, parks, and

other environmental resources by analyzing the travel costs individuals incur to visit these sites.

○ Hedonic pricing, another commonly used RPM, estimates the value of specific environmental attributes (e.g., air quality or green spaces) on property prices. By analyzing real estate market data, economists can determine how changes in environmental quality or amenities affect property values, allowing for the estimation of the implicit value of those environmental attributes.

○ Averting behavior and defensive expenditures analysis focuses on the costs individuals incur to avoid or mitigate environmental damages or hazards. For instance, it can be applied to estimate the economic value of reducing pollution to avoid negative health effects or the cost of avoiding environmental risks.

7.2. The Travel Cost Method

7.2.1. *Conceptual issues*

The travel cost method (TCM) uses people's actual behavior to infer their preferences. In this case, the behavior that is being observed is the amount of money and time that a person is willing to spend to travel to a recreational site. The site is an unpriced good for which the market is missing, but other goods and services used to reach the site and have the recreational experience are market goods with prices. Thus, the TCM uses observed choices of traveling to a recreational area to value, in an indirect way, the site itself:

• The TCM is based on the idea that the cost of travel is a proxy for the value of the recreational area people visit. They are only willing to pay for something that they value, and the cost of travel, both in terms of money spent to make the trip and the time spent to reach the site, is a measure of how much value people place on the recreational site.

• To estimate the value of a recreational area using the TCM, two pieces of information are needed:

- ○ **The number of trips**: This tells us how much a person values the recreational area. The more trips people take, the more they value the area.
- ○ **The cost of travel**: This tells us the price a person is willing to pay to visit the area. The higher the cost of travel, the less people are willing to visit the area, which means the area is less valuable. The travel cost should include both traditional transportation costs (e.g., cost of fuel and depreciation of the vehicle) and the value of time required to reach the area. Time is a scarce resource with an opportunity cost, and so the more time that is required to reach an area, the lower is the demand for trips for given traveling costs and similar site characteristics.

By combining these two pieces of information, we can estimate the value of the recreational area to people. This information can be used to make decisions about how to manage the area and how to allocate resources to other recreational areas.

- The TCM estimates the value of a recreational area using transportation costs and the value of time. One of the key assumptions of the TCM is that the value of time in leisure can be approximated by the wage rate. However, this assumption is not always accurate, as people cannot always choose the number of hours they work.
- Empirical work suggests that time spent traveling is valued at somewhere between a third and a half of the wage rate. This means that the TCM may underestimate the value of a recreational area, as it does not fully account for the opportunity cost of time.
- Another assumption of the TCM is that the value of a recreational area is independent of other factors, such as the availability of alternative leisure activities or the quality of the area. However, these factors can also influence people's willingness to visit a recreational area.
- As a result of these assumptions, the TCM can only estimate use values or the value of a recreational area to people who actually visit it. It cannot estimate non-use values or the value of a recreational area to people who do not visit it.

Overall, the TCM is a useful tool for estimating the value of recreational areas. However, it is important to be aware of its limitations when interpreting the results. Some of these limitations are discussed in Section 7.2.4.

7.2.2. *The zonal travel cost model*

The zonal travel cost model is a variant of the travel cost method that accounts for the geographic distribution of visitors and their travel costs within different zones or regions surrounding a recreational site (see Figure 1). The regression equation for the zonal model (Hanley and Barbier, 2009, p. 81) can be written as

$$V_{zj} = V(\mathrm{TC}_{zj}, \mathrm{Pop}_z, S_z), \quad z = 1, \ldots, Z$$

where V_{zj} are visits from zone z to site j, TC_{zj} is the generalized travel cost from zone z to site j, Pop_z is the population of zone z, and S_z are socioeconomic variables such as income averaged for each

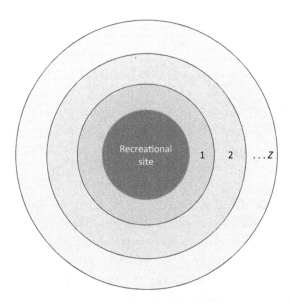

Figure 1:   The zonal model.

zone z. The dependent variable is often expressed as (V_{zj}/Pop_z) or trips to site j per capita.

7.2.2.1. *An example of the zonal travel cost model*

As a simple example, imagine that a park is visited only by residents of two cities: one 50 miles away and the other 200 miles away. Roundtrip travel costs from the two cities are $20 and $80, respectively, and it is known that people from the nearer city average eight trips per year while people from the farther city average four trips per year. If the park charges no admission fee, the only cost of visiting is the travel cost, and the data provide two points on the demand curve for the park. Assuming that the demand curve is linear, we have the diagram shown in Figure 2.

The annual value of the park to a person living at its entrance (who would face zero travel cost per visit) would be their consumer surplus at a price of zero. This is equal to the entire area under the demand curve, which is $500. The annual value of the park to a person living in the nearer of the two cities would be the consumer surplus associated with a price of $20 and a quantity of eight visits or $320. The annual value of the park to a person living in the farther

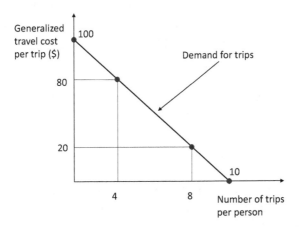

Figure 2: Valuation of visits to a park.

of the two cities would be the consumer surplus associated with a price of \$80 and a quantity of four visits or \$40.

The demand for a specific recreation site in a linear form (e.g., Parsons, 2003) can be specified as

$$V_z = \beta_0 + \beta_1 \mathrm{TC}_z + \beta_2 \mathrm{TC}_o + \beta_3 Y + \beta_4 S_z,$$

where TC_o is travel cost to other competing recreational sites and Y is income. Once the demand function for the zonal model has been estimated, the gains in consumer surplus can be estimated by standard methods.

For a general demand for visits $f(\mathrm{TC}_z, \mathrm{TC}_o, Y, S_z)$, the aggregate consumer surplus CS for a given travel cost level TC_{z1} is

$$CS = \int_{\mathrm{TC}_{z1}}^{\mathrm{TC}_{choke}} f(\mathrm{TC}_z, \mathrm{TC}_o, Y, S_z) d\mathrm{TC}_z,$$

where TC_{choke} is the choke travel cost price.

7.2.2.2. *Estimation of the zonal travel cost model*

The zonal travel cost model uses the number of visits per year as its dependent variable. This kind of data is known as count data, and for such data, it is not appropriate to use standard ordinary least squares (OLS) regression to estimate the zonal travel cost model. Instead, a Poisson or negative binomial regression model should be used (Hanley and Barbier, 2009):

- Poisson regression is a statistical model that is used to model count data that can only take on integer values in a given period of time, such as the number of visitors to a recreational site, the number of wildfires in an area, or the number of accidents that occur in a city.

  Poisson regression assumes that the mean and variance of the dependent variable are equal. This means that the probability of observing a certain number of events is proportional to the mean of the distribution. For example, if the mean number of customers who visit a recreation site in a month is 1,000, then the probability of observing 1,000 visitors, 900 visitors, or 1,100 visitors is the same for all.

- Poisson regression can be used to answer a variety of questions about count data. For example, it could be used to:

  - **Identify the factors that influence the number of events that occur.** For example, Poisson regression could be used to identify the factors (e.g., temperature or precipitation) that influence the number of wildfires of a certain size in a year.
  - **Predict the number of events that will occur in the future.** For example, Poisson regression could be used to predict the number of wildfires of a certain size in a year given the evolution of climate change.

- Poisson regression is a powerful tool for analyzing count data, but the Poisson model does not always fit the data perfectly. In some cases, the variance of the data may be greater than the mean, in which case a negative binomial regression model may be more appropriate.
- The main advantages of using Poisson regression are that it is (1) a relatively simple model to understand and interpret, (2) relatively easy to estimate using statistical software, and (3) a very flexible model and can be used to model a variety of count data.
- The main disadvantages are (1) the assumption that the mean and variance of the dependent variable are equal, which may not always be true in real data, and (2) the fact that the Poisson model is not as powerful as some other models for count data, such as negative binomial regression.
- Negative binomial regression is a generalization of Poisson regression that relaxes this assumption and allows the variance to be greater than the mean. This makes negative binomial regression a more flexible model than Poisson regression, and it is often used when the data are over-dispersed.
- Over-dispersion occurs when the variance of the data is greater than the mean. This can happen for a variety of reasons, such as when there is a small number of very large values in the data. When the data are over-dispersed, Poisson regression will not fit

the data well. In this case, negative binomial regression is a more appropriate model:

- o Some of the advantages of using negative binomial regression are that it is (1) a more flexible model than Poisson regression and can be used to model data that are over-dispersed, (2) relatively easy to estimate using statistical software, and (3) a very powerful model and can be used to model a variety of count data. However, the negative binomial model is more complex than the Poisson model and can be more difficult to interpret.

- If under-dispersion occurs (i.e., the variance is less than the mean), then generalized Poisson regression can be used. If the data have a large number of zeros because the event (e.g., a wildfire or a visit) did not happen in a given region or period, then "zero inflated" Poisson or negative binomial regression could be used.
- **LIMDEP** and **STATA** are statistical software packages that can be used to estimate both Poisson and negative binomial regression models.
- Box 1 provides a simplified example of a zonal travel cost model estimation for Lake Gahar in Iran.

Box 1: An example of a simple travel cost model

Kheyri *et al.* (2020) estimated the economic value of the Gahar Lake resort in western Iran using the zonal travel cost method. Gahar Lake enjoys features such as diverse natural landscapes, high diversity of wildlife species, diverse flora, and the existence of rare and endangered animal species. It holds extensive potential for the development of the tourism industry.

Using the map of Iran and considering the resort as the center, eight concentric circles (zones) were drawn at fixed distances of 150 km to cover the entire country. Questionnaires were distributed to 380 tourists by the simple random sampling method

---

Box 1. (*Continued*)

based on the appropriate spatiotemporal distributions during the visiting seasons. The study estimated the number of visits to the site from each zone within a specified time frame, the average cost of access from each zone to the resort, and the average distance of the resort from each of the zones. In addition, visitors were divided into five age groups, six levels of educational achievement, and six income groups based on monthly income.

The recreational value of Gahar Lake was calculated based on the demand function. The regression equation of this function was calculated as follows:

$$VR = -9.88 - 1.41\text{TC} - 0.000751S + 2.62I - 3.12A + 2.49E,$$

where VR is the number of visitors per 1,000 zonal population, TC is the total cost, S is the distance, I is the average monthly income, A is the age of the visitors, and E is their educational level. By replacing the mean value of each variable and taking an integral from the equation, which is the same as the area under the demand curve, the value of the resort was estimated to be US$ 84.538 per visitor and US$ 1,986,657.163 per year.

Data source: Kheyri *et al.* (2020).

7.2.3. *The random utility choice model*

- In the traditional approach to determining the use value of a recreational site, some of the typical questions that were asked include:
  - How many times have you visited this site in the past year?
  - How far did you travel to get here?
  - How long did you spend at the site?
  - How long was the trip from your starting point to the site?
  - What were your reasons for visiting the site?
  - How much did you spend on travel, entrance fees, and other expenses?

- How would you rate the quality of the recreational experience at the site?
- Would you be willing to pay more to visit the site?
- If the site were closed, how much would you miss it?

- The random utility choice model (RUCM) is a more recent approach to the determination of recreational values that extends the traditional approach. It is a tool that can be used to understand how people choose which recreation sites to visit from a set of potential substitutes. The RUCM is based on the idea that people choose the site that offers them the most value, taking into account factors such as the cost of visiting, the quality of the amenities, the distance to the site, and their socioeconomic characteristics.
- The RUCM is a discrete choice model, which means that it assumes that people choose one site to visit from a set of possible sites.
- The RUCM can be used to estimate the value of different recreation attributes, based on the cost of visiting a site or the quality of the amenities at a site. This is a way to approximate the use value of the site. The model can also be used to predict how changes in recreation attributes will affect the number of people who visit a site.

  For example, if the cost of visiting a site increases, the RUCM can be used to predict how many fewer people will visit that site. It can also be used to estimate how much people are willing to pay to visit a site with better amenities and to inform decision-makers about the management of recreational resources, such as the setting of fees or the provision of amenities.
- In the RUCM, the deterministic part of utility is usually assumed to be a linear function of site characteristics or

$$V_{ij} = \beta_0 + \beta_1 X_{j1} + \beta_2 X_{j2} + \cdots + \beta_n X_{jn} + \lambda(Y_i - p_{ij}), \qquad (1)$$

where X_{jk}, $k = 1, \ldots, n$, represent the attributes of site j as shown, for example, in Table 1 where $j = 3$ and $k = 2$, Y_i is individual i's income, and p_{ij} represents the travel costs of visiting site j for individual i. Using the conditional logit model (see Hanley and Barbier, 2009), the probability that site j will be chosen over all

Table 1: The random utility choice model. An example.

	Visits in past year	Round trip travel cost, € per trip	Possibility of swimming at site (1 = yes, 0 = no)	Unevenness of terrain (5 = very, 1 = little)
Carlos				
Visits to site A	1	60	1	1
Visits to site B	4	20	0	3
Visits to site C	3	30	1	2
Roberto				
Visits to site A	2	20	1	1
Visits to site B	0	8	0	4
Visits to site C	3	10	1	2

other sites in choice set C for individual i is given by

$$\pi_i(j) = \frac{\exp(V_{ij})}{\sum_{j \in C} \exp(V_{ij})}. \tag{2}$$

- Suppose that one of the sites in the choice set is shut down, that is, change from 0 to 1. Then the change in utility for the representative individual is given by

$$\text{CS} = -\frac{1}{\lambda} \left[\ln \left(\sum_{j \in C} \exp(V_{j0}) \right) - \ln \left(\sum_{j \in C} \exp(V_{j1}) \right) \right].$$

- Utility changes resulting from a change in an attribute are converted into money-metric by dividing the corresponding coefficient of the attribute by the marginal utility of income λ.
- Equation (2) can be estimated using STATA or LIMDEP and can provide the values for the β parameters from equation (1). The sign of these parameters indicates how a change in site attributes could influence site choice (for example, whether an increase in perceived hiking difficulty will attract more or fewer visits to the site, other things being equal).

7.2.4. Problems with the travel cost method

- *Valuing time*: The TCM is used to estimate the non-market value of recreational sites by analyzing the costs (expenses and time) that individuals incur to visit these sites. Thus, one crucial factor is understanding how people value their time spent traveling to these recreational sites. People have different time preferences, and their WTP for visiting a site is affected by how much they value their time. However, accurately determining the value of time can be complex and subjective (see Czajkowski *et al.* (2019) for an in-depth discussion of the problem), and it poses challenges for researchers and policy-makers trying to measure the true economic value of these sites.
- *Combining decisions over how often to go with where to go*: The TCM must simultaneously consider two interrelated decisions made by individuals: (1) how often they choose to visit a recreational site and (2) which specific site(s) they select for their recreational activities. Researchers need to understand visitors' decision-making processes regarding both the frequency of visits and the choice of site in order to estimate the economic value of each recreational site accurately.
- *Defining the choice set*: The choice set represents all the feasible alternatives that individuals consider when making decisions about how to spend their time and resources on recreational activities. It directly impacts the estimation of the non-market value of a recreational site. However, if the choice set is not appropriately defined or if some feasible options are missing, the estimates derived from the travel cost analysis might be biased or inaccurate.
- *How to measure site characteristics*: Site characteristics can be diverse and may include natural features, recreational amenities, accessibility, environmental quality, and other factors that contribute to the overall appeal and enjoyment of the site. They are essential components of the travel cost analysis, as they play a significant role in determining the demand for and value of the recreational site. It can be challenging to accurately quantify

and value these attributes for many reasons, such as subjectivity of perceptions, data collection, the dynamic nature of the site characteristics, and others.

- *Preference heterogeneity*: Different individuals or visitor groups may have varying levels of interest in a particular recreational site and may derive different levels of utility or satisfaction from the same experience, depending on, for example, individual preferences, demographics, and recreational objectives. This poses a challenge in the TCM because researchers must accurately account for these variations in preferences when estimating the non-market value of a recreational site.
- *Crowding and congestion*: Challenges arise when estimating the economic value of a recreational site that experiences high levels of visitor use. Crowding and congestion can have both positive and negative effects on visitors' experiences and, consequently, influence their decisions to visit the site and their willingness to pay for the recreational activity.

7.3. The Hedonic Price Method

7.3.1. *Conceptual issues*

The hedonic price method (HPM) is an economic valuation technique used to estimate the implicit or non-market value of specific attributes or characteristics of a good or service. It is often employed to assess the economic value of intangible or non-priced factors that contribute to the overall utility or desirability of a product.

In the context of environmental economics, the HPM is commonly used to estimate the value of various environmental amenities or features, such as air quality, proximity to parks, access to natural landscapes, or noise levels, among others. The method assumes that the price of a good or service in the market is a reflection of the sum of its observable and unobservable characteristics. Therefore, by analyzing market data and prices, researchers can identify the implicit value of specific attributes.

The HPM follows certain steps:

(1) *Data collection*: Researchers gather data on the prices and quantities of the product (e.g., housing, rental properties, or consumer goods) and the characteristics associated with each unit or observation.
(2) *Regression analysis*: Using statistical techniques, researchers perform regression analysis to identify the relationship between the observed prices (dependent variable) and the various attributes of the product (independent variables). The attributes could include environmental factors, location, property size, number of bedrooms, and other relevant features.
(3) *Estimation of implicit prices*: Through the regression analysis, researchers can estimate the implicit prices of the attributes by measuring the impact of each characteristic on the observed prices. For example, they can determine how much consumers are willing to pay for better air quality or proximity to a park.
(4) *Economic valuation*: The implicit prices provide a monetary value for each attribute, representing how much consumers value those characteristics. These estimated values can then be used to calculate the total economic value of the environmental amenity or feature under consideration.

The HPM has wide-ranging applications. Some examples include the following:

- **Real estate**: Hedonic price models are often used to estimate the value of houses. The characteristics that are typically included in the models for houses include the size of the house, the number of bedrooms and bathrooms, the lot size, the location, and the quality of the construction.
- **Environmental amenities**: Hedonic price models are used to estimate the value of environmental amenities, such as proximity to a park or a clean water source. The characteristics that are typically included in the models for environmental amenities include the distance to the amenity, the quality of the amenity, and the type of amenity.

- **Education**: Hedonic price models have also been used to estimate the value of education. The characteristics that are typically included in the models for education include the quality of the school, the size of the school, and the location of the school.
- **Health care**: Hedonic price models are also used to estimate the value of health care. The characteristics that are typically included in the models for health care include the quality of care, the type of care, and the location where care is provided.

Hedonic methods are especially useful when market prices do not directly reflect the value of certain factors and can provide valuable insights for policy-makers and businesses in understanding the economic significance of non-market goods and services.

7.3.2. *The characteristics theory of value*

The characteristics theory of value states that the value of a good or service is determined as a function of the values of its individual characteristics. The idea is that consumers have preferences for different characteristics, and the value of a good or service is determined by how well it satisfies those preferences.

The value of a unit in a given commodity class, such as a house i, with value approximated by the price of the house, p_{hi}, is a function of a vector of characteristics:

$$Z_i : p_{hi} = f(Z_i), Z_i = (z_1, \ldots, z_j, \ldots, z_n). \tag{3}$$

The implicit price of a characteristic in the characteristics theory of value is the amount of money that consumers are willing to pay for a unit increase in the characteristic. Thus, the implicit price of a characteristic z_j in the vector Z_i is the derivative $\partial p_{hi}/\partial z_i$ from (3). The implicit price can be regarded as the average WTP.

The implicit price for a characteristic can be used to understand how consumers value different characteristics. It can also be used to predict how consumers will respond to changes in the characteristics of goods and services.

Consumers will bid an amount $B_j[z_j(\cdot)]$ for an increase in the characteristic, depending on the value to them of that characteristic (e.g., better air quality, less noise, or better views). In market equilibrium, every consumer will be in a position where the marginal bid, $\partial B_j/\partial z_j$, is equal to the implicit price (that is, marginal cost) of the characteristic.

Thus, the implicit price of "proximity to a park" — which can be regarded as an approximation of the value of air quality — is the amount of money that consumers are willing to pay for a unit increase in air quality. This can be used to estimate the marginal willingness to pay (MWTP) for air quality, which is the additional amount of money that consumers are willing to pay for a small increase in air quality. In this context, house prices should reflect the capitalized value of environmental quality to the homeowner.

7.3.3. *A hedonic price equation*

A hedonic price equation can be used to determine implicit prices. In general, this equation takes the form

$$p_h = p(S_i, N_j, Q_k) + \varepsilon.$$

In this hedonic equation, house prices (p_h) within a city might depend on site characteristics (S_i), such as the size of the house and the number of rooms; neighborhood characteristics (N_j), such as the proximity to transportation systems and the quality of schools in the area; and environmental quality variables (Q_k), such as noise levels and air quality (as shown in Figure 3a).

An example of a hedonic price equation for house prices that depends on house characteristics, neighborhood characteristics, and environmental quality is

$$P = \beta_0 + \beta_1 * \text{HOUSE\_SIZE} + \beta_2 * \text{BEDROOMS}$$
$$+ \beta_3 * \text{BATHROOMS} + \beta_4 * \text{LOT\_SIZE}$$
$$+ \beta_5 * \text{CLOSE\_TO\_PARK} + \beta_6 * \text{AIR\_QUALITY}$$
$$+ \beta_7 * \text{NEIGHBORHOOD\_RATING}$$
$$+ \beta_8 * \text{SCHOOL\_QUALITY}.$$

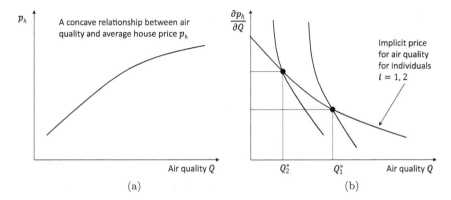

Figure 3: (a) Air quality vs house prices. (b) Implicit price for air quality.

In this equation, P is the price of the house, HOUSE_SIZE is the house size in square meters, BEDROOMS is the number of bedrooms, BATHROOMS is the number of bathrooms, LOT_SIZE is the area in square meters of the lot, CLOSE_TO_PARK is a dummy variable that indicates whether the house is close to a park, AIR_QUALITY is a measure of the air quality in the area, NEIGHBORHOOD_RATING is a measure of the quality of the neighborhood, and SCHOOL_QUALITY is a measure of the quality of the schools in the area. The coefficients $\beta_0, \beta_1, \beta_2, \beta_3, \beta_4, \beta_5, \beta_6, \beta_7$, and β_8 can be estimated using a regression analysis of a dataset of houses. The coefficients can then be used to estimate the value of each characteristic.

The coefficients β_6 and β_7 can be interpreted as the implicit prices of air quality and neighborhood quality. This means that the price of a house increases by β_6 for each unit increase in air quality and by β_7 for each unit increase in neighborhood quality.

For example, if the coefficient β_6 is 1,000€ and the coefficient β_7 is 2,000€, then a house with one unit higher air quality and one unit higher neighborhood quality would be worth 3,000€ more than a similar house with one unit lower air quality and one unit lower neighborhood quality.

Another example is provided by Bjørner *et al.* (2003), who found a significant relationship between noise levels generated by traffic in

Copenhagen and house prices in that city, with house prices declining by 0.49% per decibel increase.

In Figure 3(b), the two steeper curves reflect the marginal valuation curves of individuals 1 and 2, who maximize utility by choosing air quality. The path of the utility-maximizing choices of individuals defines the implicit price for the air quality curve.

7.3.4. *Calculating the value of environmental quality*

Consider a linear hedonic price equation that was estimated on houses in a city using particulate concentrations as one of the environmental attributes. The coefficient on particulates was found to be -500, with a standard error of 150. This means that a one-unit increase in particulates would reduce house prices by an average of 500€. A 10% reduction in particulates to $27 \, \mu g/m^3$ would increase house prices by an average of 1500€. The average aggregate value of the reduction is the sum of the increases in house prices in the city.

An example of estimating implicit prices is given in Box 2.

Box 2: Non-market values and implicit prices

Applying a cost–benefit framework to environmental policy is not easy. Although some costs are easy to assess, others are more challenging to determine. But estimating the benefits can be even more challenging. This is because estimating the benefits of an environmental policy requires knowing how the condition of the environment will be changed by the policy and then placing a value on the change in condition. This can be particularly difficult when values are not reflected in market prices — the so-called "non-market" values.

Baker and Ruting (2014) undertook a study on behalf of Australia's Productivity Commission to explore several non-market valuation methods and their potential for improving environmental policy. They assessed the validity and reliability of various non-market valuation methods and how best they could be

---

Box 2. (*Continued*)

used in developing environmental policy. One of the case studies that illustrates how non-market valuation has been used in Australia involves Australia's State Underground Power Program (SUPP).

In 2011, the Economic Regulation Authority (ERA) of Western Australia conducted an inquiry into the costs and benefits of the SUPP, which involves replacing existing overground power distribution infrastructure (mainly wires, poles, and transformers) with underground power supply in residential areas. The ERA commissioned a hedonic pricing study from Marsden Jacob Associates (MJA) to quantify the extent to which underground power supply increased residential property prices in the Perth metropolitan area.

The study used data on attributes from properties both with and without underground power supply, including sale price, age of property when sold, number of rooms, land area, distance from the coast, distance from Perth's central business district, and distance from certain attributes (e.g., beaches and waterways).

MJA (2011) used regression modeling to examine how the variables of interest affected house prices over a 10-year study period. The logarithm of house prices was modeled as a function of house characteristics over time (a log-linear model). Specifically,

$$P_{i,t} = \sum_{t=1}^{T} \alpha_t D_{i,t} + \beta_t X_{i,t} + \varepsilon_{i,t},$$

where $P_{i,t}$ is the logarithm of the price of house i at time t, $D_{i,t}$ takes a value of one if the house is sold in time period t and zero otherwise, $X_{i,t}$ represents house characteristics, $\varepsilon_{i,t}$ is an error term, and β is the vector of coefficients to be estimated.

The study estimated that the average implicit price of underground power was \$9,962 per property (in 2011 dollars), with a standard deviation of \$2,613 (MJA, 2011). This implicit price

(*Continued*)

Box 2. (*Continued*)

was equivalent to 1.6% of the average residential property price. It represents the incremental value of underground power (as capitalized in house prices), on average, across residential properties in Perth (including, but not limited to, those that had been covered by SUPP projects). Note that MJA (2011) recommend exercising caution when using the mean value, as the capitalized amenity value of underground power is itself an endogenous function of other housing attributes.

Information sources: Baker and Ruting (2014). *Environmental Policy Analysis: A Guide to Non-Market Valuation.* Productivity Commission Staff Working Paper, Canberra. Marsden Jacob Associates (2011). *Estimating the Capitalised Value of Underground Power in Perth.* Report prepared for the Economic Regulation Authority, Perth. ERA (Economic Regulation Authority (Western Australia)) (2011). *Inquiry into State Underground Power Program Cost Benefit Study.* Final Report, Perth.

7.3.5. *The hedonic price model and the labor market*

In the labor market, the hedonic price models can be used to estimate the value of job characteristics, such as the level of education, experience, or job amenities:

- One way of using hedonic price models in the labor market is to estimate the compensating wage differential, which is the difference in wages between two jobs that have different levels of risk or unpleasantness. For example, a job that is more dangerous may pay a higher wage to compensate workers for the increased risk.
- Hedonic price models can also be used to estimate the values of human capital, which is the knowledge, skills, and abilities that workers acquire through education, training, and experience. Such models can be used to estimate the value of human capital by measuring the impact of these factors on wages.

For example, a study by Card and Krueger (1992) used hedonic price models to estimate the value of education. The study found that an additional year of education increased wages by about 10%. This suggests that the value of education is significant and that workers are compensated for their investment in education.

- Some additional examples of how hedonic price models have been used in the labor market include using it to estimate the following:

   o the value of job amenities, such as flexible work hours or access to a gym,
   o the impact of discrimination on wages,
   o the value of on-the-job training,
   o the impact of labor market regulations on wages.

Hedonic price models are a valuable tool for studying the labor market. By estimating the value of job characteristics, the compensating wage differential, and the value of human capital, they can provide information that can be used to inform policy decisions about education, training, and workplace safety.

7.3.6. *Problems with the hedonic price method*

The HPM remains a valuable tool for estimating the economic value of non-market goods and attributes. However, researchers should be aware of its limitations and potential biases, such as the following:

Omitted variable bias: When there are additional important variables that are relevant to the price determination but are not included in the model, these omitted variables may be correlated with both the included variables and the outcome variable (the price), thus leading to misleading conclusions. For example, say we are trying to build a hedonic price model to predict the price of used cars, and we include only the car's age and mileage as predictors. We omit other relevant variables, such as the car's make, model, and the presence of air conditioning. If the omitted variables (e.g., make and model) are actually important determinants of the car's price, the effect of age and mileage on price may be confounded with the effects of the omitted variables. To address this problem, researchers need to carefully select and include all relevant variables that affect the price of the product or service being studied.

Multicollinearity: In a hedonic price model, when two or more independent variables (regressors) are highly correlated with each other, it can cause problems in the model, leading to unstable and inaccurate estimates of the relationships between the independent variables and the dependent variable (the price in the case of a hedonic price model). For example, consider a model to predict the price of smartphones based on two features: screen size and battery capacity. If these two features are highly correlated (e.g., smartphones with larger screens tend to have bigger batteries), then the model might find it difficult to differentiate their separate effects. This situation can lead to coefficients that are imprecise or have the wrong sign, making it challenging to interpret the results accurately.

Choosing the functional form: When building a hedonic price model, the choice of the form of the hedonic price function is a critical decision. The functional form represents the mathematical relationship between the price of a product or service and its characteristics. The choice of the functional form can significantly impact the model's performance, interpretability, and the accuracy of price predictions. The problem of choosing a functional form arises for a number of reasons, such as model fit, model interpretability, data structure, assumptions about linearity, and computational complexity.

Spatial auto-correlation: This is a statistical phenomenon, also known as spatial dependence, which occurs when observations in a dataset are not independent but are influenced by the values of neighboring observations in space. In the context of a hedonic price model, spatial auto-correlation arises when the prices of properties (e.g., houses and apartments) in a particular location are correlated with the prices of neighboring properties. This can be a significant problem in a hedonic price model because it violates one of the key assumptions of traditional regression analysis: the independence of observations. When spatial auto-correlation is present, the standard errors of the model's parameter estimates may be biased, leading to incorrect statistical inference and unreliable conclusions.

Causality and endogeneity: The hedonic price model assumes that changes in the price of a good are solely driven by changes in the characteristics being studied. However, it is often challenging to establish a clear cause-and-effect relationship between a specific characteristic and the price of a good. Other factors and confounding variables can influence both the characteristic and the price simultaneously, leading to biased estimates.

Selection bias: The hedonic price model relies on data from the market, which means it only captures the characteristics of goods that are traded in the market and certain non-market goods or characteristics that are not traded in the market are not included in the analysis. As a result, the method may not accurately represent the economic value of all relevant characteristics.

Market segmentation: Dividing a market or a group of potential buyers into distinct subgroups based on similar characteristics, preferences, or behavior is a process used to determine how different subsets of consumers value the various attributes or features of the product, which in turn affects their WTP different prices. This market segmentation helps businesses to better understand their customers and create products and marketing strategies that resonate with different groups. The hedonic price model complements this process by providing insights into how product characteristics influence prices and how consumers value these attributes differently, thus helping businesses make informed decisions to serve diverse market segments effectively.

Data availability and quality: Collecting comprehensive and reliable data on the characteristics of goods and their corresponding prices can be challenging, especially for non-market goods or attributes that are not explicitly valued in the market.

Heterogeneity of preferences: The hedonic price model assumes that the value of a characteristic is constant across all consumers, but in reality, preferences may differ widely based on individual tastes, needs, and expectations. Ignoring this heterogeneity can lead to inaccurate estimates of the economic value of characteristics.

Spatial and temporal variations: The hedonic price model assumes that the value of characteristics remains constant across space and time. However, the economic value of certain characteristics may vary across different locations or change over time due to changes in demand, technology, or other factors. Failure to account for such variations can affect the accuracy of the estimates.

Monocentric bias: In the context of urban studies, the hedonic price method often assumes a monocentric city, where all economic activity is concentrated in a single central location. This may not accurately represent the complexities of real-world urban structures, leading to biased estimates of the economic value of urban amenities.

7.4. Averting Behavior and Defensive Expenditures

Averting behavior and defensive expenditures are important concepts used to understand how consumers respond to certain characteristics of goods or services that might pose risks or exhibit negative aspects:

- *Averting behavior* refers to the actions taken by consumers to avoid or mitigate the negative consequences of a particular attribute or characteristic of a product or service (e.g., OECD, 2018). In the context of hedonic price models, it is often used to assess how consumers adjust their purchasing decisions based on the perceived risks associated with a certain feature or quality of a product.

  For example, suppose you are considering purchasing a house that is located near a noisy highway. The traffic noise could be perceived as a negative attribute, and to avoid or minimize the impact of the noise, you might invest in soundproofing measures or other strategies to make the property more appealing. Averting behavior takes into account the costs and efforts consumers undertake to counteract the negative aspects of a good or service.

- *Defensive expenditures* refer to the expenses incurred by consumers to protect themselves from harm or undesirable consequences arising from the consumption of a product or service. These expenses are incurred alongside the purchase of the product to reduce potential risks or negative effects associated with specific characteristics of the product.

Using the same house example, if you decide to purchase the property despite its proximity to the noisy highway, you might invest in double-glazed windows, which are more expensive but can reduce the impact of the traffic noise inside the house. These defensive expenditures are incurred to safeguard against the negative consequences of the product.

- In hedonic price models, both averting behavior and defensive expenditures are considered as factors influencing the overall valuation of a product or service. By understanding how consumers react to certain attributes, economists and analysts can more accurately estimate the economic value of these attributes and their impact on market prices. These models are especially useful in the real estate industry, environmental economics (e.g., valuing cleaner air or water), and any context where goods or services have specific characteristics that can be either attractive or unattractive to potential buyers.

7.5. Cost of Illness and Lost Output Approaches

The cost of illness and lost output approaches are two methods used in the context of hedonic price models to estimate the economic value of certain attributes, specifically related to health and productivity. These approaches are commonly employed in the field of environmental economics and public health to assess the economic impact of environmental pollution or other factors affecting human health and productivity:

- *The cost of illness approach* is used to estimate the economic burden of a particular illness or health condition on society. It involves calculating the direct and indirect costs associated with the illness, which may include medical expenses, hospitalization costs, medication costs, and other healthcare-related expenditures (e.g., Pearce *et al.*, 2006).

- In the context of hedonic price models, the cost of illness approach is used to assess how specific environmental factors or product attributes might affect human health and lead to increased medical expenditures. By analyzing data on medical costs and health outcomes, researchers can estimate the monetary value that individuals are willing to pay to avoid health risks associated with certain environmental conditions or product features. This WTP provides a basis for valuing the benefits of reducing or eliminating these risks.

  For instance, if a particular area has high levels of air pollution, the cost of illness approach might be used to estimate the economic value of cleaner air by examining how reduced pollution levels can lead to decreased medical expenses for respiratory illnesses and other health conditions.

- Hedonic price models have been used to estimate the cost of a variety of diseases, including asthma, heart disease, cancer, and diabetes. These studies have found that the cost of illness can be significant, both in terms of direct medical costs and indirect costs, such as lost productivity.

- Hedonic price models have a number of advantages as a method for estimating the cost of illness. First, they are based on actual market transactions, which makes them more reliable than other methods, such as surveys. Second, they can be used to estimate the cost of a variety of diseases, even those that are not directly observable in the market.

- However, hedonic price models also have limitations that include the fact that they can only estimate the cost of illness for those attributes that are reflected in market prices. For example, a hedonic price model would not be able to estimate the cost of pain or suffering, as these are not directly observable in the market. Another limitation is that they can be sensitive to the choice of attributes. For example, if a study only includes attributes that are easily observable, it may underestimate the true cost of illness.

- *The lost output approach*, also known as the productivity or human capital approach, aims to estimate the economic impact of reduced productivity or labor output due to illness or health-related factors. It assesses the monetary value of lost productivity caused by health problems, both in terms of absenteeism (time taken off work due to illness) and presenteeism (reduced productivity while at work due to illness).

- In the context of hedonic price models, the lost output approach can be applied to understand how certain attributes, such as environmental pollution or workplace conditions, affect the health of workers and subsequently impact their productivity. By quantifying the economic losses associated with reduced labor output, researchers can derive estimates of the value of avoiding these productivity losses.

  For example, if a factory exposes its workers to hazardous substances that cause health issues and reduce their productivity, the lost output approach can help determine the economic benefits of improving workplace conditions and avoiding these productivity losses. Studies have found that the cost of environmental degradation can be significant, both in terms of direct costs such as medical expenses and indirect costs such as lost productivity.

Both the cost of illness and lost output approaches provide valuable insights into the potential benefits of policies or interventions aimed at improving public health, reducing environmental pollution, or enhancing workplace conditions.

7.6. Exposure–Response Relationships

The calculation of the cost of illness or lost output requires knowledge of the relationship between an environmental impact (e.g., increased air or water pollution) and the health, productivity, or output effect. This can be obtained through exposure–response relationships:

- *Exposure–response relationships* measure the physical response (health and physical output) to a change in the state of the environment which can then be used to estimate the economic value from this change in terms of a variety of environmental goods and services, such as air quality and water quality. These estimates can be used to inform public policy decisions about how to protect the environment and promote economic growth.

- There are a number of different methods that can be used to estimate exposure–response relationships. One common method is to use epidemiological data to examine the relationship between exposure to an environmental pollutant and the incidence of a particular health outcome. For example, a study might examine the relationship between exposure to air pollution and the incidence of asthma.

- Another method that can be used to estimate exposure–response relationships is to use laboratory experiments. In these experiments, researchers expose animals, humans, or plants to different levels of an environmental pollutant and then measure the resulting health or productivity effects.

- Exposure–response relationships are a valuable tool for the valuation of environmental goods and services. It is important to note that these relationships are not always straightforward. In some cases, the relationship between exposure and response can be nonlinear. On the other hand, in cases of agricultural products, the relationship might be more straightforward, since the response to a change in irrigation water salinity, for example, could be measured by the change in the value of an agricultural product.

- Additionally, exposure–response relationships can be affected by a number of other factors, such as the age and health status of the individual.

It is therefore important to carefully consider all of these factors when using exposure–response relationships to estimate the economic value of environmental goods and services.

References

Baker, R., Ruting, B. (2014). *Environmental Policy Analysis: A Guide to Non-Market Valuation*, Productivity Commission Staff Working Paper, Canberra.

Bjørner, T. B., Kronbak, J., Lundhede, T. (2003). *Valuation of Noise Reduction — Comparing Results from Hedonic Pricing and Contingent Valuation*. Denmark: AKF Forlaget.

Boyle, K. J. (2003). Introduction to revealed preference methods. In P. A. Champ, K. J. Boyle, T. C. Brown (eds.), *A Primer on Nonmarket Valuation* (pp. 259–267). New York: Springer.

Card, D., Krueger, A. B. (1992). Does school quality matter? Returns to education and the characteristics of public schools in the United States. *Journal of Political Economy*, 100(1), 1–40.

Czajkowski, M., Giergiczny, M., Kronenberg, J, Englin, J. (2019). The individual travel cost method with consumer-specific values of travel time savings. *Environmental and Resource Economics*, 74, 961–984.

Hanley, N., Barbier, E. (2009). *Pricing Nature: Cost–Benefit Analysis and Environmental Policy*. Cheltenham, UK: Edward Elgar Publishing.

Kheyri, E., Morovati, M., Neshat, A., Siahati, G. (2020). Economic valuation of natural promenades in Iran using zonal travel costs method (Case study area: Gahar Lake in Lorestan Province in western Iran). *PLoS ONE*, 15, e0241396.

Marsden Jacob Associates (2011). *Estimating the Capitalised Value of Underground Power in Perth*. Report prepared for the Economic Regulation Authority, Perth.

OECD (2018). *Cost–Benefit Analysis and the Environment: Further Developments and Policy Use*. Paris: OECD Publishing.

Parsons, G. R. (2003). The travel cost model. In P. A. Champ, K. J. Boyle, T. C. Brown (eds.), *A Primer on Nonmarket Valuation* (pp. 269–329). New York: Springer.

Pearce, D., Atkinson G., Mourato S. (2006). *Cost–Benefit Analysis and the Environment: Recent Developments*. Paris: OECD Publishing.

Chapter 8

Valuing Health and Life Risks

8.1. Environmental Factors and Human Health

Degradation of the natural environment through various processes including pollution, deforestation, habitat destruction, and climate change can have significant impacts on human health. Some of these impacts are described below:

- **Air pollution** consists of chemicals or particles in the air that can harm the health of humans, animals, and plants, and which can be gasses, solid particles, or liquid droplets. Exposure to air pollutants increases people's risk of developing cardiovascular diseases, respiratory diseases, and cancers. Exposure to air pollution can also increase the risk of premature death. Recent studies suggest that the health impacts of exposure to pollution are larger than previously thought:

  ○ The World Health Organization (2022) estimates that in 2019, ambient (outdoor) air pollution was responsible for 4.2 million premature deaths worldwide.
  ○ The State of Global Air 2020 report (Health Effects Institute and Institute for Health Metrics and Evaluation, 2020) estimates that in 2019 there were 6.7 million premature deaths due to air pollution, both within the household and outdoors.

○ Lelieveld *et al.* (2019) put the estimate even higher, at 8.8 million deaths in total every year due to indoor and outdoor air pollution.

- **Climate change** is already having a number of negative impacts on human health. It threatens human health and well-being in many ways, including impacts from increased extreme weather events, wildfires, decreased air quality, and illnesses transmitted by food, water, and disease carriers such as mosquitoes and ticks. Climate change is also expected to increase the risk of food insecurity and water scarcity. Moreover, it may result in changing disease patterns and cause greater vulnerability to nervous system and respiratory diseases, diarrhea, and other illnesses.
- **Water pollution**, whether from industrial discharges, agricultural runoff, or improper waste disposal, can cause a variety of health problems. Contaminated water is a major source of waterborne diseases such as cholera, typhoid, dysentery, and hepatitis A. Also included in health effects of water pollution are gastrointestinal problems, cancer, neurological problems and reproductive problems, and increase in the risk of premature death.
- **Foodborne illnesses** can be caused by a variety of bacteria, viruses, and parasites. These pathogens can be found in contaminated food, water, or soil and can cause a variety of health problems, including diarrhea, vomiting, nausea, and fever. One example is food poisoning from *E. coli*, a type of bacteria that can be found in the environment and in foods, which can cause respiratory illnesses, urinary tract infections, and other adverse health effects. In severe cases, foodborne illnesses can be fatal.

  There are also a number of harmful microbes that live in the soil. Humans can come into contact with them by ingesting them (through contaminated food) or through inhaling them (through soil particles in the air). Tetanus and botulism are examples of diseases caused by soil-borne microbes.
- **Pesticides and chemicals exposure**: People can be exposed to pesticides through airborne drift, direct contact with treated crops, or contaminated water sources. They can be exposed to other harmful chemicals in numerous ways, such as inhalation of polluted

air, drinking contaminated water, consuming food contaminated with heavy metals and food additives, using certain household or personal care products, exposure to contaminated soil, inhaling cigarette smoke, improper disposal of hazardous materials and waste, and industrial accidents or environmental disasters that release harmful chemicals into the environment.

The adverse effects on human health range from acute poisoning to chronic respiratory illnesses, neurological disorders, cancer, and even death. Such exposure has also been linked to birth defects, developmental issues in children, and reproductive health and fertility.

- **Loss of biodiversity** can disrupt ecosystems, leading to increased interactions between humans and wildlife that can elevate the risk of zoonotic diseases, which are infections that spread from animals to humans (e.g., COVID-19 and Ebola), and alter disease patterns. Biodiversity loss can affect the food supply, thus increasing malnutrition. It can also reduce access to pharmaceuticals and traditional medicines derived from plants and animals found in natural ecosystems.

8.2. Environmental Policy and Human Health

Environmental policy can help protect human health by, for example, reducing exposure to environmental pollutants, improving water quality, and adopting measures to mitigate or adapt to climate change. Such policies can reduce premature mortality and improve health, that is, reduce morbidity. Some important examples of the impact of environmental policy on human health include the following:

- **The Clean Air Act** in the United States, which was first passed in 1963 and amended significantly in 1977 and 1990, has helped reduce air pollution and improve air quality. This has led to a decrease in the number of deaths and illnesses caused by air pollution.

- **The Safe Drinking Water Act** in the United States, enacted in 1974, has helped improve the quality of drinking water. This has led to a decrease in the number of cases of waterborne illness.
- **The Montreal Protocol**, an international agreement enacted in 1987 to reduce the production and use of ozone-depleting substances, has helped protect the ozone layer. This has led to a decrease in the number of cases of skin cancer and other health problems caused by exposure to UV radiation.
- **The European Union's Water Framework Directive** was adopted in 2000 and has helped improve water quality in rivers, lakes, and coastal waters across Europe. This has led to a decrease in the number of cases of waterborne illness.
- **The United Nations Convention on the Law of the Sea** came into force in 1994 after being ratified by 60 countries and has helped protect marine ecosystems from pollution and overfishing. It has helped improve the health of marine life, which is a source of food and income for millions of people around the world.
- **The Convention on International Trade in Endangered Species of Wild Flora and Fauna** (CITES) went into effect in 1975. It has helped protect endangered species from overexploitation and is designed to ensure that international trade in animals and plants does not threaten their survival in the wild.

Moreover, there is a category of investment programs whose objective is to reduce mortality or improve the health conditions of populations. Some examples of these programs are listed below:

- **Vaccination programs** help protect people from a variety of infectious diseases, such as COVID-19, measles, mumps, rubella, polio, and hepatitis B. These diseases can cause serious illness, disability, and death.
- **Maternal and child health programs** provide essential services to mothers and children, such as prenatal care, childbirth assistance, and immunizations. These services can help reduce the risk of death and disability for mothers and children.
- **Water and sanitation projects** provide clean water and sanitation facilities to people in developing countries. This can help

reduce the risk of waterborne diseases, such as cholera, diarrhea, and typhoid fever.

- **Malaria control programs** provide mosquito nets, insecticides, and other interventions to help prevent malaria, which is a serious mosquito-borne disease that can cause death.
- **HIV/AIDS prevention and treatment programs** provide education, counseling, and treatment services to people living with HIV/AIDS. These programs can help reduce the risk of death and disability from HIV/AIDS.

The evaluation of such programs involves a cost–benefit analysis in which benefits are the number of lives saved or the improvement of health conditions. This requires the association of monetary values with lives saved or health conditions improved.

8.3. The Value of a Statistical Life

Valuation of risks to life, that is, a *mortality risk*, associated with a certain policy — for example, an investment program — implies estimation of the WTP to obtain a mortality risk reduction or to avoid a mortality risk increase arising from a policy or project, or the WTA compensation for tolerating higher than "normal" risks. The WTP or WTA is the basis for estimating the value of a statistical life (VOSL) that measures the economic value of reducing mortality risks:

- The WTP and WTA are typically estimated using revealed preference or stated preference methods. Revealed preference methods use data on how people actually behave to infer their WTP to reduce their risk of death. For example, the wage differential between risky and non-risky jobs can be used to estimate the VOSL. Stated preference methods ask people directly how much they would be willing to pay to reduce their risk of death. This can be done through surveys or experiments.
- The VOSL is obtained by dividing the estimated risk reduction in a fatality due to the project, by the estimated WTP or WTA.

- It is important to note that the VOSL is not the value of an actual life. It is the value placed on changes in the likelihood of death, not the price someone would pay to avoid certain death. Thus, it focuses on a statistical life saved, which means that a fatality is avoided because the mortality risk faced by a group of people is reduced. So although we do not know who will die without the project, we know that a smaller number of people will die with the project than without the project (see, e.g., OECD (2018) for more details).

- The terms *statistical life* and *certain life* are often used in the context of CBA and risk assessment, particularly in fields such as health economics, environmental policy, and safety regulations. A statistical life refers to the value placed on an individual's life based on statistical probabilities and aggregate data. A certain life, on the other hand, refers to the intrinsic and individual value placed on a specific human life. An example of the difference between a statistical life and a certain life is provided in Box 1.

Box 1: Rescue after a weather disaster

The difference between a certain and a statistical life can be clarified using the following example:

A person is at high risk during an extreme weather event. If the person is not rescued by the next day, this person will die. A search and rescue effort is being considered which involves 20 rescue workers.

Due to the extreme nature of the weather event, there is a 10% probability of a fatal accident among the rescue workers. Therefore, the expected number of fatalities among the rescue workers would be

$$20 \times 0.1 = 2 \text{ fatalities.}$$

Thus, the decision to launch the rescue implies a trade-off between one certain life and two statistical lives.

8.3.1. *Risk, WTP, and the VOSL*

- In Figure 1, the downward-sloping curve shows marginal WTP as a function of mortality risk reduction. Higher risk corresponds to higher marginal WTP for its reduction. Suppose the policy measure in question reduces risk levels from P_2 to P_1 in Figure 1.
- Then, the WTP for that risk reduction is given by the standard change in consumer surplus and is equal to the area under the marginal willingness to pay (MWTP) curve between P_2 and P_1.
- MWTP may be fairly constant at low levels of risk (right side of Figure 1). Thus, small changes at low levels will have a small effect on the VOSL.
- Now consider an investment project that is expected to reduce mortality risk from 10 in 100,000 to 5 in 100,000, a change of 5 in 100,000 (Δr). Suppose that the mean WTP to secure this risk reduction is 75€. Then, the VOSL is usually computed as

$$\frac{\text{WTP}}{\Delta r} = \frac{75 \times 100,000}{5} = 1,500,000€.$$

- The WTP to reduce risks is a function of the quality of life expected in the period survived and wealth. The WTP to reduce risks is higher if the individual anticipates being in good health in the period survived, rather than in poor health. The WTP to reduce risks also increases with wealth. This is under the assumption that the marginal utility of wealth is greater if it refers to the survival of the owner of the wealth than if it is left as a bequest, and that individuals are averse to financial risk. For more details, see OECD (2018).

8.3.2. *VOSL and hedonic wage models*

The VOSL is typically estimated using the hedonic wage model, which is a statistical model that assumes that people are willing to accept a higher wage in return for a higher risk of death. The difference in wages between risky and non-risky jobs is the conceptual basis for estimating the VOSL since, other things being the same, riskier jobs should offer higher wage rates.

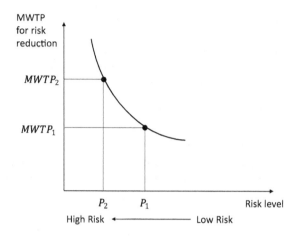

Figure 1: Willingness to pay for risk reduction.

A hedonic wage model could provide estimates of the average WTA a higher wage in exchange for a marginal increase in the probability of a job-related accidental death. A hedonic wage regression can be written as

$$\ln w_i = \beta X + r^* \gamma + \varepsilon_i,$$

where $\ln w_i$ is the natural logarithm of the ith worker's wage, r^* is the measure of risk associated with a fatal accident (possibly a vector), X is a vector of covariates, (β, γ) are coefficients to be estimated, and ε_i is the error term of the regression. The vector of covariates could include worker's socioeconomic characteristics and job characteristics, such as job satisfaction or working conditions (see, e.g., Black and Kniesner, 2003).

This model could be used to estimate the value of risk of death in a particular occupation. For example, if the coefficient γ is 0.05 for a scalar risk measure, then this means that a worker would be willing to accept a 5% higher wage in return for a job with a 1% higher risk of death.

Following Zerbe and Bellas (2006, p. 175), if a regression of hourly wage on various explanatory factors and the mortality rate (measured in fatalities per 1,000 full-time workers) yielded a coefficient of 0.55 on the fatality rate, this would suggest that as the probability of death increases by one in 1,000, the wage should increase by about $0.55/hour or, over a 2080-hour work year, about $1,144. If this marginal change in risk were applied to 1,000 workers over the course of a year, the expected impact would be one additional fatality, and the value of this one statistical life would be the product of $1,144 and 1,000, or $1,144,000.

Cropper *et al.* (2011) provide a comprehensive review of the importance of VOSL in assessing the benefits of environmental policies. They emphasize the improvements in the quality of VOSL studies in recent years, due to better data and statistical methods and improved methodology. These improvements have made VOSL studies better able to address the types of illnesses and subpopulations most likely to be affected by environmental exposures. They also point out the need for meta-analyses using the more recent and methodologically superior studies.

Robinson *et al.* (2019) provide a thorough discussion of estimates used to value mortality risk reductions in relation to health and environmental policies, which are a major determinant of the benefits of many public health and environmental policies. They point out that these values have been relatively well studied in high-income countries but less so in lower-income countries. As a result, values from wealthier countries are typically extrapolated to lower-income countries, adjusting only for income differences. This approach, however, depends on assumptions of uncertain validity, and thus the authors stress the need for more research on the value of mortality risk reductions in low and middle-income countries.

Table 1 provides some examples of the various types of VOSL studies in addition to the hedonic wage model. It also shows examples of the types of risk that were studied. Table 2 provides additional information for the same group of studies, such as the country which the study refers to and the World Bank income classification of that country. The VOSL is shown in column 4, and the gross national income per capita (GNIpc) in the country studied for the same year as the VOSL estimate is provided in column 5. As indicated by Robinson *et al.* (2019), they used GNIpc as the measure of income because it is consistently derived, is easily accessible for a

Table 1: Selected VOSL studies by type of study and risk context.

Study	Type of study	Risk context
Hoffmann *et al.* (2012)	Stated preference approach	Mortality risk reduction through clean air policy
Yusoff *et al.* (2013)	Conjoint analysis	Fatal injury among drivers and riders
Mofadal *et al.* (2015)	Contingent valuation	Pedestrian accidents
Chaturabong *et al.* (2011)	Stated preference approach	Motorcycle accidents
Tekeşin and Ara (2014)	Choice experiment	Lung cancer, other type of cancer, respiratory disease, traffic accident
Hammitt and Ibarrarán (2006)	Compensating wage differentials	Fatal and non-fatal occupational risks
Parada-Contzen *et al.* (2013)	Hedonic wage equations	Job mortality and job injury risks
Qin *et al.* (2013)	Hedonic wage regression	Job mortality risk
Benkhalifa *et al.* (2013)	Hedonic wage regression	Fatal injury in building and manufacturing industry
Rafiq and Shah (2010)	Compensating wage differentials	Job mortality risk in the manufacturing sector

large number of countries, and is a broader measure than GDP per capita.

8.3.3. *The value of a statistical life year*

The value of a statistical life year (VOSLY) is a monetary estimate of the value of one year of life in good health. It can be used in CBA to compare the costs and benefits of different health interventions:

- The VOSLY is calculated by asking people how much they would be willing to pay to reduce mortality risks in the coming year by a small amount. The results suggest that the VOSLY varies over the life cycle of people, following an inverted U-shaped curve. This means that the estimated VOSLY is highest in early adulthood,

Table 2: Selected estimates of the VOSL.

Study	Country	World Bank classification	Year of data collection	VOSL	GNIpc	VOSL/ GNIpc
Stated Preference Studies						
Hoffmann et al. (2012)	Mongolia	Lower-middle income	2010	$921,167	$6,830	134.9
Yusoff et al. (2013)	Malaysia	Upper-middle income	2006	$1,000,000	$17,160	58.3
Mofadal et al. (2015)	Sudan	Lower-middle income	2013	$60,000	$2,700	22.2
Chaturabong et al. (2011)	Thailand	Upper-middle income	2011	$504,032	$13,210	38.2
Tekeşin and Ara (2014)	Turkey	Upper-middle income	2012	$726,414	$20,480	35.5
Revealed Preference Studies						
Hammitt and Ibarrarán (2006)	Mexico	Upper-middle income	2002	$280,000	$10,290	27.2
Parada-Contzen et al. (2013)	Chile	High income	2006	$4,625,958	$13,850	334.0
Qin et al. (2013)	China	Upper-middle income	2005	$188,000	$2,900	64.8
Benkhalifa et al. (2013)	Tunisia	Lower-middle income	2002	$617,700	$5,740	107.6
Rafiq and Shah (2010)	Pakistan	Lower-middle income	2006	$1,728,978	$3,900	443.3

Notes: The VOSL are reported in international dollars based on purchasing power parity for the year in which the data were reported by the authors. Monetary estimates have not been updated for inflation and reflect different base years and so are not directly comparable. Some studies reported multiple VOSL estimates. In such cases, the VOSL here is the midpoint of the reported values.

Data source: Robinson et al. (2019).

Lectures in Applied Environmental Economics and Policy

then declines until middle age, and then increases again in later life.

- Let VOSLY$_A$ be the VOSLY of a representative individual at age A who has an expected life of T years. Then, the VOSLY can be estimated (OECD, 2018) as

$$\text{VOSLY}_A = \frac{VOSL_A}{T - A}.$$

For example, for $A = 40$, with a life expectancy of $T = 80$ and VOSL of 8 million euros, VOSLY$_{40}$ = 200,000€.

- In CBA, VOSL is regarded as more relevant for projects associated with acute deaths and "latent" deaths, while VOSLY seems to be more relevant for projects associated with chronic health effects.
- The VOSLY seems to better fit the analysis of risks associated with environmental issues than the transfer of VOSL estimates from studies of workplace accidents, which tend to affect healthy, middle-aged adults, and road accidents, which tend to affect median-age individuals (see Pearce *et al.* (2006) and Box 2).

Box 2: VOSL vs VOSLY

In their paper regarding the calculation of the damage costs of air pollution, Desaigues *et al.* (2011) advocate using the value of a statistical life year, VOSLY, to quantify the cost of air pollution mortality, rather than using the value of a statistical life, VOSL. The VOSLY evaluates the change in life expectancy due to air pollution. The damage cost, also called external cost, of a pollutant is increasingly being used by governments for the cost–benefit analysis of environmental regulations or for the determination of pollution taxes. In order to add to the extant literature on VOSLY, the authors use a contingent valuation survey, administered in nine European countries, to determine the VOSLY for the European Union.

A total sample size of 1,463 people in France, Spain, UK, Denmark, Germany, Switzerland, Czech Republic, Hungary, and

---

Box 2. (*Continued*)

Poland were asked to state their WTP for a gain in life expectancy of 3 and 6 months. The WTP of the pooled sample was regressed on income and other characteristics and used to calculate the VOSLY.

Based on the results of their survey and calculations, and after considering a number of relevant factors, Desaigues *et al.* (2011) recommend a VOSLY estimate of 40,000€ for cost–benefit analysis of air pollution policies for the European Union. With regard to confidence intervals, they argue that VOSLY is at least 25,000€ and at most 100,000€.

8.3.4. *Valuing morbidity*

- While risks associated with mortality and captured by the VOSL or the VOSLY concepts are the most important health costs in CBA, costs associated with morbidity (i.e., non-fatal health effects) might be important in CBA studies, such as the health cost of air pollution (ambient ozone or particulate matter). Morbidity valuation can be based on hospital admissions, restricted activity days, bronchitis, and lower respiratory illnesses due to air pollution (see OECD (2018) for more details).
- Pearce *et al.* (2006) link WTP to avoid certain episodes of illness, estimated by a contingent valuation study, with explanatory factors which include quality of well-being index, duration of illness in days, and socioeconomic characteristics of the population.

References

Benkhalifa, A., Ayadi, M., Lanoie, P. (2013). Estimated hedonic wage function and value of life in an African country. *Economics Bulletin*, 33(4), 3023–3031.

Black, D. A., Kniesner, T. J. (2003). On the measurement of job risk in hedonic wage models. *Journal of Risk and Uncertainty*, 27, 205–220.

Chaturabong, P., Kanitpong, K., Jiwattanakulpaisarn, P. (2011). Analysis of costs of motorcycle accidents in Thailand by willingness-to-pay method. *Transportation Research Record*, 2239, 56–63.

Cropper, M., Hammitt, J. K., Robinson, L. A. (2011). Valuing mortality risk reductions: Progress and challenges. *Annual Review of Resource Economics*, 3, 313–336.

Desaigues, B., Ami, D., Bartczak, A., Braun-Kohlová, M., Chilton, S., Czajkowski, M., *et al.* (2011). Economic valuation of air pollution mortality: A 9-country contingent valuation survey of value of a life year (VOLY). *Ecological Indicators*, 11, 902–910.

Hammitt, J. K., Ibarrarán, M. E. (2006). The economic value of fatal and nonfatal occupational risks in Mexico City using actuarial- and perceived-risk estimates. *Health Economics*, 15(12), 1329–1335.

Health Effects Institute and Institute for Health Metrics and Evaluation (2020). *State of Global Air 2020. Special Report on Global Air Exposure and its Health Impacts*. Boston, MA.

Hoffmann, S., Qin, P., Krupnick, A., Badrakh, B., Batbaatar, S., Altangerel, E., Sereeter, L. (2012). The willingness to pay for mortality risk reductions in Mongolia. *Resource and Energy Economics*, 34(4), 493–513.

Lelieveld, J., Klingmüller, K., Pozzer, A., Burnett, R. T., Haines, A., Ramanathan, V. (2019). Effects of fossil fuel and total anthropogenic emission removal on public health and climate. *PNAS*, 116(15), 7192–7197.

Mofadal, A. I. A., Kanitpong, K., Jiwattanakulpaisarn, P. (2015). Analysis of pedestrian accident costs in Sudan using the willingness-to-pay method. *Accident Analysis and Prevention*, 78, 201–211.

OECD (2018). *Cost-Benefit Analysis and the Environment: Further Developments and Policy Use*. Paris: OECD Publishing.

Parada-Contzen, M., Riquelme-Won, A., Vasquez-Lavin, F. (2013). The value of a statistical life in Chile. *Empirical Economics*, 45(3), 1073–1087.

Pearce, D., Atkinson, G., Mourato, S. (2006). *Cost–Benefit Analysis and the Environment: Recent Developments*. Paris: OECD Publishing.

Qin, X., Li, L., Liu, Y. (2013). The value of life and its regional difference in China. *China Agricultural Economic Review*, 5(3), 373–390.

Rafiq, M., Shah, M. K. (2010). The value of reduced risk of injury and deaths in Pakistan — Using actual and perceived risk estimates. *The Pakistan Development Review*, 49(4), 823–837.

Robinson, L. A., Hammitt, J. K., O'Keeffe, L. (2019). Valuing mortality risk reductions in global benefit-cost analysis. *Journal of Benefit Cost Analysis*, 10(S1), 15–50.

World Health Organization (2022). Ambient (outdoor) air pollution. https://www.who.int/news-room/fact-sheets/detail/ambient-(outdoor)-air-quality-and-health.

Tekeşin, C., Ara, S. (2014). Measuring the value of mortality risk reductions in Turkey. *International Journal of Environmental Research and Public Health*, 11(7), 6890–6922.

Yusoff, M. F. M., Mohamad, N. A., Abidin, N. Z., Nor, N. G. M., Salleh, H. (2013). The value of statistical life in fatal injury among drivers and riders in Malaysia: Conjoint analysis method. MIROS Internal Report No. 130.

Zerbe, R. O. Jr., Bellas, A. S. (2006). *A Primer for Benefit–Cost Analysis.* Cheltenham, UK: Edward Edgar Publishing.

Chapter 9

Stated Preference Approaches

9.1. Stated Preference Approaches I: Contingent Valuation Method

9.1.1. *Basic concepts*

- Modern cost–benefit analysis has been extended to the evaluation of projects, mainly environment-related projects, that include flows of costs and benefits for which markets do not exist. This is because many environmental goods and services involved in — or affected by — investment and policies do not have markets. Missing markets result in the market failing to provide the socially desirable amount of these goods and services. In terms of the environment, this means that the flow of services provided is not valued by the markets although, as we have already seen, it encompasses many values which constitute the concept of total economic value.

- If markets, that is, revealed preference methods, cannot be used in an indirect way to value these goods and services — as in the case of travel cost or hedonic pricing (see Chapter 7) — the economic value could be determined by *stated preference* methods.

- Stated preference approaches are survey-based. The objective is to elicit people's intended future behavior with respect to environmental goods and services by constructing a hypothetical market.

- The *contingent valuation method* (CVM), which is one of the main stated preference approaches, uses a questionnaire to construct the hypothetical market.
- In a CVM study, the environmental good or service is clearly defined, along with the associated institutional context. The way in which the environmental improvement (e.g., cleaning up a river) will be financed is also clearly defined. Then a random sample of people is selected and they are asked to reveal their willingness to pay (WTP) for the environmental improvement or their willingness to accept (WTA) not to have the improvement. Alternatively, people can be asked to reveal their maximum WTP to avoid a deterioration in environmental quality or loss in ecosystem services, or their minimum WTA for this deterioration or loss.
- In the CVM, the central assumption is that respondents behave as though they were in a real market. The CVM is applicable, in principle, to almost all environmental goods and services for which markets are missing and can capture all types of values: use, non-use, and option.

9.1.2. *Designing questionnaires for CVM*

A well-designed CVM questionnaire is essential for obtaining accurate and reliable estimates of WTP. The following are the key stages in designing a CVM questionnaire:

1. **Define the valuation problem**: This involves specifying the good or service to be valued, the relevant population, and the specific objectives of the valuation. For example, if you are interested in valuing the benefits of a new park, you would need to specify the location of the park, the types of activities that would be available in the park, and the target population for the survey.
2. **Construct the hypothetical market**: This includes describing the good or service, the benefits it provides, and the payment mechanism. For example, you would need to explain what the park would look like, what activities would be available, and how much it would cost to maintain the park.

3. **Elicit the monetary value**: This can be done using a variety of methods, such as open-ended questions, payment cards, or dichotomous choice questions. Open-ended questions ask respondents to state how much they would be willing to pay for the good or service. Payment cards provide respondents with a range of possible prices and ask them to indicate which price they would be willing to pay. Dichotomous choice questions ask respondents whether they would be willing to pay a certain price for the good or service. Some of the different elicitation formats are shown in Tables 1 and 2. These formats have varying strengths and weaknesses, some of which are presented in Table 3. For a more detailed analysis, see Carson and Czajkowski (2014) and Johnston *et al.* (2017).

4. **Socioeconomics**: This entails collecting information about the socioeconomic and demographic characteristics of respondents.

5. **Pretest the questionnaire**: This step is important to ensure that the questions are clear, understandable, and unbiased. The questionnaire should be pretested with a small group of people to get feedback.

6. **Administer the survey**: This can be done in person, by phone, or online.

7. **Analyze the data**: This involves using econometric techniques to estimate the WTP or the WTA of the respondents.

9.1.3. *The hypothetical scenario*

The hypothetical scenario in a CVM study is a description of the good or service being valued, the benefits it provides, the payment mechanism, and the context in which the constructed market exists. It is important to carefully design the hypothetical scenario so that it is clear, understandable, and realistic, which will motivate respondents to provide accurate and reliable estimates of their WTP. The components of the hypothetical scenario include the following:

- **Description of the good or service**: This should focus on the physical characteristics of the good or service, such as its

Table 1:   Examples of CVM elicitation formats.

"Imagine that a project is being considered to preserve and maintain the Acropolis, a world-renowned historical site that holds significant cultural and historical value. We would like to understand your willingness to pay for this preservation effort. Please answer the following questions."

Format	Description
Bidding game	"Would you pay €10 every year, through a tax surcharge, to preserve and maintain the Acropolis in the ways I have just described?"
	If Yes: Interviewer keeps increasing the bid until the respondent answers "no". Then maximum WTP is elicited.
	If No: Interviewer keeps decreasing the bid until respondent answers "yes". Then maximum WTP is elicited.
Open-ended	"What is the maximum amount that you would be prepared to pay every year, through a tax surcharge, to preserve and maintain the Acropolis in the ways I have just described?"
Payment card	"Which of the amounts listed below best describes your maximum willingness to pay every year, through a tax surcharge, to preserve and maintain the Acropolis in the ways I have just described?"

€0	€15
€1	€20
€2	€35
€4	€50
€6	€75
€8	€100
€10	> €100

Format	Description
Single-bounded dichotomous choice	"Would you pay €X every year, through a tax surcharge, to preserve and maintain the Acropolis in the ways I have just described?" (The X value is varied randomly across the sample.)
Double-bounded dichotomous choice	"Would you pay €X every year, through a tax surcharge, to preserve and maintain the Acropolis in the ways I have just described?" (The X value is varied randomly across the sample.) If Yes: "And would you pay €Y (amount higher than X)?" If No: "And would you pay €Z (amount lower than X)?"

Table 2:   Example of a payment card.

€per year	I would definitely pay (Put ✓)	I would definitely not pay (Put ✗)
1	✓	
3	✓	
5	✓	
10	✓	
15	✓	
20	✓	
25	✓	
30		
40		
50		✗
60		✗
70		✗
80		✗
90		✗
100		✗
120		✗

size, location, and amenities. For example, a new park might be described as a 100-acre park with a playground, a walking trail, and a picnic area.

- **Description of the benefits**: This should focus on the intangible benefits that people receive from the good or service. For example, the benefits of the new park might include opportunities to exercise, enjoy nature, and socialize with friends and family.

- **Payment mechanism**: This should describe how people would be asked to pay for the good or service. For example, people might be asked to pay a one-time fee, a monthly fee, or a tax. The payment mechanism includes the following: (a) voluntary payments which are donations and gifts and (b) coercive payments which include taxes, rates, fees, charges, or prices (see Tables 1 and 3).

- **Context**: This should place the hypothetical scenario in a realistic context. For example, if the hypothetical scenario is being conducted in a country with a widespread and socially accepted

Table 3:   Elicitation formats — Some advantages and disadvantages.

Format	Advantages (A) and disadvantages (D)
Bidding game	A: Simple and assisted process. D: Anchoring or starting-point bias, an effect such that the final WTP amount at the end of the bidding game is systematically related to the initial bid value. Repeated questioning may annoy or tire respondents, causing them to say "yes" or "no" to a stated amount in hopes of terminating the interview.
Open-ended	A: Allows respondents to freely state their WTP or WTA values without any preconceived ranges or options, which may capture a wider range of values. D: Can be challenging for respondents to come up with a monetary value without any guidance, leading to a higher chance of non-response or protest responses or unreliable estimates.
Payment card	A: Presents a payment card containing a series of pre-determined payment amounts. Provides a visual aid that simplifies the response process and reduces cognitive burden. D: Fixed payment amounts on the card may influence respondents' choices and introduce anchoring bias. May not capture the full range of values, particularly if the payment amounts are not carefully designed.
Single-bounded dichotomous choice	A: Provides respondents with a fixed set of options or ranges to choose from, making it easier for them to express their preferences. Mimics behavior in regular markets (incentive compatible). D: Limits respondents' choices to predefined values, potentially leading to a loss of information and a failure to capture their true preferences. May overlook values outside the given ranges, resulting in biased estimates.
Double-bounded dichotomous choice	A: Addresses some of the limitations of single-bounded formats by providing respondents with a range of values and asking for their WTP or WTA at both ends. Helps elicit a narrower range of values and provides more information for analysis. D: Can be cognitively demanding for respondents to consider both upper and lower bounds, leading to potential response fatigue or inconsistent answers. Requires additional questions and more complex analysis. Typically fails to make clear the *decision rule* (Will governments go ahead with a project if enough respondents vote "yes" to the first amount or to the second amount asked?).

tax system, the context should mention that people would be asked to pay for the good or service through taxes.

9.1.4. *Approaches for estimating WTP*

There are different methods for estimating willingness to pay which include the following:

- For an open-ended elicitation format, the estimation approach is: Use the mean or the median WTP to estimate WTP.
  To explore the determinants of the estimated WTP, a bid function of the form

  WTP = f (Income, Age, Health, Status, Kids, Education...)

  can be estimated using regression techniques.
- Single- and double-bounded dichotomous choice.
  With yes/no responses, the WTP is estimated using logit, probit, or linear probability models, which take into account the respondent's answer to the dichotomous choice, and includes as determinants the socioeconomic factors and the bid price. The estimated WTP from these models is the price at which the probability of a respondent answering "yes" to the dichotomous choice question is equal to 0.5. This means that half of the respondents who are asked this price would be willing to pay it and half would not be willing to pay it.
- Utility difference approach (see Section 9.1.5).
- Non-parametric methods (see Section 9.1.6).

9.1.5. *Utility difference approach*

The utility difference approach (Hanemann, 1984, 1999) uses a random utility model. Following Haab and McConnell (2002), the random utility model can be described as follows: Let the utility of the jth respondent be defined as

$$U_{ij} = v_i(y_j, z_j) + \varepsilon_{ij},$$

where the deterministic part is v and the random part is ε; $i = 1$ denotes the state when the environmental change is implemented; $i = 0$ is the *status quo* (i.e., no implementation); y_j is the respondent's income; z_j is an m-dimensional vector of respondent's socioeconomic characteristics.

Suppose that a woman (respondent j) answers "yes" to the question of whether she is willing to pay the amount t_j for the implementation of the environmental program. This means that the utility of the environmental program, net of the required payment, exceeds the utility of the *status quo*, or

$$v_1(y_j - t_j, z_j) + \varepsilon_{1j} > v_0(y_j, z_j) + \varepsilon_{0j}.$$

Then the probability of a "yes" answer is defined as

$$Pr(yes) = Pr[v_1(y_j - t_j, z_j) + \varepsilon_{1j} > v_0(y_j, z_j) + \varepsilon_{0j}],$$

while the compensating variation A, which is the maximum amount that the individual is willing to pay, is defined as

$$v_1(y_j - A_j, z_j) = v_0(y_j, z_j).$$

Assuming a linear utility function

$$v_{ij}(y_j) = \alpha_i z_j + \beta_i y_i,$$

the deterministic part of the utility of the proposed environmental program is

$$v_{1j}(y_j - t_j) = \alpha_1 z_j + \beta_1(y_j - t_j),$$

while the *status quo* deterministic part of the utility is

$$v_{0j}(y_j) = \alpha_0 z_j + \beta_0 y_i,$$

with the restriction that $\beta_1 = \beta_0 = \beta$ is constant, which means that the marginal utility of income is assumed to be constant.

It follows then that the change in deterministic utility is

$$v_{1j} - v_{0j} = \alpha z_j - \beta t_j, \quad \alpha = \alpha_1 - \alpha_0.$$

Then the probability of responding "yes" is

$$Pr(yes) = Pr[\alpha z_j - \beta t_j + \varepsilon_j > 0], \quad \varepsilon_j = \varepsilon_{1j} - \varepsilon_{0j}$$

The next steps depend on the assumption made about the distribution of the error term ε.

Under the assumption that the error term ε is identically and independently distributed (iid) with zero mean, two distributions are usually used: the normal and the logistic. The normal leads to the probit model, while the logistic leads to the logit model (see Haab and McConnell (2002) for details).

To estimate a probit or a logit model, create a dependent variable, coded as $1 = $ yes and $0 = $ no, which is the "response", then regress this on the socioeconomic variables z and the payment amount t for each person, using software such as STATA or LIMDEP.

For the simplest case of the linear utility function, the mean WTP is given by

$$E(\text{WTP}_j) = \left(\frac{\alpha z_j}{\beta}\right),$$

where $\alpha z_j = \sum_{k=1}^{m} \alpha_k z_{jk}$ and m is the number of estimated parameters.

Median WTP can be calculated as the value of t for which there is a 50–50 chance that a randomly selected person would agree to pay.

9.1.6. *Non-parametric or distribution-free methods*

9.1.6.1. *The Turnbull estimator*

Let F_j be the unknown probability that the jth respondent will say "no" to price t_j. A good estimate of F_j is the proportion of all respondents asked whether they would pay amount t_j who answered "no".

A "lower bound" on WTP can be calculated using the formula

$$E(\text{WTP}) = \sum_{j=0}^{M} t_j(F_{j+1} - F_j). \tag{1}$$

An example, using formula (1) and the data in Tables 4 and 5, is shown as follows:

$$E(\text{WTP}) = (50 * 0.08) + (100 * 0.07) + (150 * 0.06) + (200 * 0.03)$$
$$+ (250 * 0.34) = 111.$$

For more details, see Haab and McConnell (2002).

Table 4: An example of data from a discrete choice contingent valuation study.

Amount offered	Number of "no" responses	Total number of people who were made this offer	F_j
€50	78	185	0.42
€100	101	200	0.50
€150	120	210	0.57
€200	135	215	0.63
€250	126	190	0.66

Note: F_j = Number of "no" responses (column 2) divided by total number of people who were made this offer (column 3).

Table 5: Transformed discrete choice data for use of the Turnbull method.

Amount offered, t	Number of "no" responses	Total number of people who were made this offer	F_j	$F_{j+1} - F_j$
€50	78	185	0.42	0.42
€100	101	200	0.50	0.08
€150	120	210	0.57	0.07
€200	135	215	0.63	0.06
€250	126	190	0.66	0.03
€250+			1	0.34

Note: F_j = Number of "no" responses (column 2) divided by total number of people who were made this offer (column 3).

9.1.7. *Aggregation*

The aggregation process in the CVM involves combining individual respondents' valuations to estimate the overall economic value of a non-market good or service. There are several important issues with regard to the aggregation process.

The choice of the relevant population is a critical aspect of the aggregation process in the CVM. The relevant population refers to the group of individuals or households for whom the estimated economic value of the non-market good or service is intended to apply.

The choice of the relevant population fits into the aggregation process in the CVM in the following way:

1. **Define the study scope**: Before conducting the CVM study, researchers need to define the scope of the analysis, which includes specifying the target population. The choice of the relevant population depends on the policy or research question being addressed. For example, if the study aims to assess the value of a public park to the local residents, the relevant population would consist of those residents who have access to or use the park.

2. **Sample selection**: Once the relevant population is defined, researchers need to select a sample of individuals or households to participate in the CVM survey. The sample should be representative of the relevant population to ensure that the aggregated results can be generalized to the broader group.

3. **Data collection**: The CVM survey is then administered to the selected sample to collect individual respondents' bid values. The survey should be carefully designed to capture the preferences and valuations of the targeted population accurately.

4. **Estimation and aggregation**: After collecting the data and estimating the econometric model, the aggregation process involves combining individual bid values and model estimates from the sample to calculate the overall economic value of the non-market good or service for the relevant population. The aggregated value represents the collective WTP or WTA of the targeted group for the specific change being studied. Moving from the sample mean to a mean for the total population could be obtained, for example, by multiplying the sample mean by the number of households in the population.

5. **Generalizability and policy implications**: Researchers need to carefully interpret the results and consider their generalizability beyond the sample used in the study. If the sample is representative of the relevant population, the aggregated results can be used to inform policy decisions or evaluate the economic significance of the non-market good or service for the entire group. If not, the

estimates may not accurately reflect the economic value for the intended group.

9.1.8. *Problems with the CVM*

The contingent valuation method can be a valuable tool for assessing non-market values, but it has certain limitations and challenges. Some of the main problems with the CVM include the following:

- **Hypothetical market bias** is one of the most significant issues with the CVM. Since respondents are asked to make hypothetical choices, their responses might not reflect real-world behavior accurately. People may overstate or understate their WTP, leading to inaccurate estimates. "Cheap talk" can be used to moderate hypothetical market bias.
- **Choice of the response mode**: Differences in the survey design (e.g., open-ended questions versus single- or double-bounded dichotomous choice), as well as the wording of the questions, can significantly influence respondents' valuation, leading to inconsistent results.
- **Anchor bias** can occur if respondents' valuation responses are influenced by an initial piece of information provided to them, known as the "anchor." For example, an initial bid, which serves as the starting point for their valuation, can act as an anchor and thus shape their perceptions and lead to biased valuation responses.
- **Strategic bias**: Respondents may strategically overstate or understate their WTP based on their perceptions of how the information will be used or how the outcome might affect them personally.
- **Voluntary vs non-voluntary payments**: In some CVM studies, respondents are asked about their WTP for a non-market good or service voluntarily. In such cases, some respondents may strategically understate their WTP to avoid paying a higher price while still benefiting from the good or service if it is provided as a public good (free riding). On the other hand, some respondents may strategically overstate their WTP, in order to signal strong support for the public good being provided.

- **Information provision**: The quality and accuracy of the information provided to respondents can influence their valuation. If participants lack knowledge about the good or service being valued, their responses may not be reliable.
- **Embedding effects**: The CVM often asks participants to value a specific change in the quantity or quality of a good or service. However, people's WTP may depend on the magnitude of the change, and the valuation might not be linear, leading to embedding effects.
- **Scope and scale issues**: The CVM often asks participants to value changes with large spatial or temporal scales. However, individuals may have difficulty comprehending the full implications of these changes, leading to unreliable estimates.
- **Cultural and social context**: Valuing non-market goods and services can be influenced by cultural and social factors that are not adequately captured in the survey, potentially leading to biased estimates.

9.2. Stated Preference Approaches II: Choice Modeling

9.2.1. *Basic concepts*

Although the CVM is a very commonly used stated preference technique, choice modeling is also widely used:

- The main purpose of the CVM is to elicit the monetary value that individuals place on non-market goods or services. In contrast, the primary purpose of choice modeling (CM) is to understand and predict consumer preferences and choices among different alternatives.
- The CVM directly asks individuals to state their WTP or WTA for a specific non-market good or service, typically using surveys or hypothetical scenarios. CM, on the other hand, presents respondents with choice sets where they are asked to select their preferred option.

- The CVM is commonly used in environmental economics to assess the value of natural resources, environmental conservation projects, and public goods like clean air, water quality, and biodiversity. CM is used to understand people's preferences and values related to environmental resources, ecosystem services, environmental policies, climate change mitigation and adaptation, and conservation projects.
- The CVM would typically be used to uncover the value of the total change in a multi-dimensional good. If policy makers require measures of the change in each of the dimensions or attributes of the good, then some variant of CM might be considered.

In summary, contingent valuation is used to estimate the monetary value of non-market goods or services, whereas choice modeling focuses on understanding choices and preferences among different alternatives which involve non-market goods or services.

9.2.2. *Alternative approaches to choice modeling*

The valuation of environmental costs and benefits in situations in which revealed preference methods cannot be used can therefore be carried out using CM methods. The most common choice modeling alternatives are described in Table 6.

9.2.3. *Choice experiments*

- In a choice experiment (CE), respondents are presented with a series of alternatives, differing in terms of attributes and levels, and asked to choose their most preferred alternative. A baseline alternative, corresponding to the *status quo* or "do nothing" situation, is usually included in each choice set.
- Table 7 provides an example of a choice set for a choice experiment valuing the conservation of tropical forests. Option 1 is the baseline or *status quo* scenario, while Options 2 and 3 propose conserving different amounts of forest area.
- Table 8 shows a sample choice set for a choice experiment to value pollution reduction in a lake. In this choice set, Option D is

Table 6: Alternative approaches to choice modeling.

Approach	Description	Elicitation method	Welfare measure
Choice experiments	Relies on the application of statistical design theory to construct a sequence of hypothetical scenarios (choice sets) which describe particular options. Respondents choose their preferred option from two or more mutually exclusive alternatives which differ with regard to their attributes and levels. One of the options is usually the *status quo.*	Choose preferred alternative	Absolute
Contingent ranking	Presents respondents with sets of items and asks them to rank them according to their preferences or importance. It helps assess relative preferences without assigning specific numerical values.	Rank several alternatives	Relative
Contingent rating	Presents respondents with sets of items and asks them to rate them based on a predefined ratings scale. Respondents are not asked to compare the different alternatives but rather to rate each separately. It helps assess the relative importance or desirability of different items.	Provide rating	Relative
Paired comparisons	Involves presenting respondents with pairs of items and asking them to select their preferred option and to indicate the strength of their preference in a numeric or semantic scale. It helps determine relative preferences between different items.	Rate difference between two alternatives	Relative
Best–worst scaling	Asks respondents to select the best and worst options from a set of alternatives. Rather than ranking or rating options, it focuses on identifying the most and least preferred choices. The focus of the BWS is on preferences for individual attributes rather than scenarios. It helps researchers understand the relative importance of different attributes or features.	Choose the most and least preferred options from a set of alternatives	Relative

Table 7: An example of a choice set from a choice experiment valuing conservation of tropical forests.

"What option would you prefer that the government went ahead with — 1, 2 or 3?"			
	Option 1 (*status quo*)	Option 2	Option 3
Tropical forest area conserved	20,000 ha	50,000 ha	100,000 ha
Biodiversity protection	Low	Medium	High
Flood risk reduction	Low	Low	High
Area to be reforested	None	2,000 ha	5,000 ha
Annual tax per household	€0	€50	€100
I prefer (please tick one box)			

Table 8: An example of a choice set from a choice experiment valuing pollution reduction in a lake.

"Assuming that the four management options below are the only choices, which one would you prefer?"			
	Management option A	Management option B	Management option C	Management option D (*status quo*)
Manage the lake to ⋯	reduce pollution by 50%	reduce pollution by 20%	maintain current pollution level	no management (condition of lake could get worse)
Improved health of ecosystem	High	Moderate	None	None
Increase in tourism	50%	20%	5%	None
Improved recreational opportunities (e.g., swimming, fishing, and boating)	High	Moderate	Low	None
Benefit to future generations	Large	Moderate	Small	None
Cost to household over 3 year period	€90	€60	€45	€0
Please check the option you prefer				

the *status quo* scenario (no management of the pollution), while Option C would take measures to maintain the pollution in the lake at its current level but not allow it to worsen. Options A and B would reduce the current level of pollution by 50% and 20%, respectively.

• The conceptual framework for a CE assumes that consumers' or respondents' utilities for a good can be decomposed into utilities or well-being, derived from the composing characteristics of the good.

9.2.3.1. *Key steps in a discrete choice experiment*

In discrete choice experiments (DCEs), which are quantitative tools used to understand decision-making and elicit preferences, participants are asked to choose between hypothetical scenarios. Participants are given multiple pairs of scenarios (choice sets) and are asked to select which scenario they would prefer. Selection of various scenarios reveals the relative impact of each attribute on participant's decision-making and the extent to which individuals are willing to trade one attribute for another. There are certain key steps typically followed in conducting a discrete choice experiment, which are as follows:

1. **Define the problem**: Select the good, service, or policy to be valued.
2. **Select the relevant attributes**: The attributes — the characteristics of a good, service, or policy that are important for decision-making — can be quantitative (e.g., cost) and/or qualitative (e.g., design of a product). Ideally, this step begins with a literature review to identify the relevant attributes; focus groups and consultations with experts are also commonly used.
3. **Define the levels**: For each attribute chosen, the specific values or options must be defined using quantitative or qualitative scales. Quantitative attributes such as cost or distance are easier to measure than qualitative attributes. When selecting attribute levels, researchers aim to include a range of options that are meaningful and representative of the choices individuals may face

in real life. It is important to choose levels that vary systematically and cover the relevant range of values for each attribute.

4. **Develop an experimental design**: Once the attributes and their levels have been selected, the next step is to decide on the specific structure and characteristics of the choice sets — the options or alternatives that participants will encounter. Researchers use statistical techniques, such as fractional factorial designs or orthogonal designs, to generate a set of choice sets with specific attribute level combinations. A *status quo* alternative should be included in each choice set so that estimated utility functions represent changes from baseline conditions.

5. **Construct choice sets**: The options identified by the experimental design are then grouped into choice sets to be presented to respondents and the questionnaire format is chosen. This stage typically includes pilot testing on a small sample of participants to evaluate clarity, understandability, and length and make any necessary revisions.

6. **Collect data**: The questionnaire is administered to a larger sample of participants. Each participant responds to a series of choice scenarios by selecting their preferred option.

7. **Analyze the data**: This step typically involves using econometric models, such as multinomial logit or mixed logit models, to estimate preference weights and calculate utilities for the different attribute levels.

8. **Interpretation of results**: The estimates obtained from the econometric models provide information about the monetary valuation of attributes included in the choice set. These valuations will support efficient decision-making regarding the environmental issue under investigation.

9.2.4. *CM and random utility models*

The random utility models presented in the previous section for the CVM can also be used for estimation in CM. This implies defining a utility function of the form

$$U_{ij} = v_i(y_j, z_j) + \varepsilon_{ij}.$$

- Following OECD (2018), let the indirect utility function for each respondent i be decomposed into two parts. The first is a deterministic part v which is typically specified as a linear function of the attributes X of the j different options (profiles) in the choice set C from which the respondent should make a choice. An example of the options and the choice set is given in Tables 7 and 8. The second is a stochastic element ε which represents unobservable effects on individual choice. Therefore, the utility of profile j for respondent i is defined as

$$U_{ij} = v\left(X_{ij}\right) + \varepsilon_{ij} = \sum_{k=1}^{K} \beta_k X_{jk} + \beta_p p_j + \varepsilon_{ij},$$

where β_k is the preference coefficient associated with attribute k, X_{jk} is attribute k in profile j, p_j is the cost of the profile, and β_p is the coefficient of the profile's cost.

- The probability that any respondent prefers option (profile) g in the choice set C to any alternative option (profile) h can be expressed as the probability that the utility associated with option g exceeds the utility associated with all other options. That is,

$$Pr[(U_{ig} > U_{ih})\forall h \neq g] = Pr[(v_{ig} - v_{ih}) > (\varepsilon_{ig} - \varepsilon_{ih})].$$

Assuming that the error terms are iid and that they follow an extreme value (Weibull) distribution, the probability of choosing profile j from set C can be written as follows:

$$Pr(g/C) = \frac{\exp\left[\mu \sum_{k=1}^{K} \beta_k X_{jk} + \beta_p p_j\right]}{\sum_{h \in C} \exp\left[\mu \sum_{k=1}^{K} \beta_k X_{hk} + \beta_p p_h\right]} = \frac{\exp\left[\mu v_{ig}\right]}{\sum_{h \in C} \exp\left[\mu v_{ih}\right]},$$

where μ is a scale parameter.

With additive separable specification of utility and assuming $\mu = 1$ (Holmes and Adamowicz, 2003), the probability of choosing g from set C is given by

$$Pr(g/C) = \frac{\exp[v_{ig}]}{\sum\limits_{h \in C} \exp[v_{ih}]}.$$

If N is the sample size and we define

$$y_{jn} = \begin{cases} 1 \text{ if respondent } n \text{ chooses option } j \\ 0 \text{ otherwise}, \end{cases}$$

then the likelihood function is

$$L = \prod_{n=1}^{N} \prod_{j \in C} (\underset{n}{Pr}(j) y_{jn}).$$

The coefficients β can be estimated by maximizing the log-likelihood function.

9.2.4.1. *Willingness to pay*

The values of the preference coefficients β show the effect on the utility of changes in the attributes. For cost–benefit analysis, we need money-metric measures of WTP. For a marginal change in an attribute, this WTP value or *implicit price* is typically given, for attribute X_k, by:

$$\text{WTP}_k = \frac{\beta_k}{\beta_p}.$$

Assume that the regression equation resulting from the choice experiment described in Table 7 has the following coefficients:

β_1 : for the attribute of forest area conserved,
β_2 : for the attribute of biodiversity protection,
β_3 : for the attribute of flood risk reduction,
β_4 : for the attribute of reforested area,
β_5 : annual cost.

Then the implicit prices for each attribute would be calculated as follows:

$$\text{WTP}_{\text{AREA CONSERVED}} = \frac{\beta_1}{\beta_5},$$

$$\text{WTP}_{\text{BIODIVERSITY PROTECTION}} = \frac{\beta_2}{\beta_5},$$

$$\text{WTP}_{\text{FLOOD RISK REDUCTION}} = \frac{\beta_3}{\beta_5},$$

$$\text{WTP}_{\text{REFORESTED AREA}} = \frac{\beta_4}{\beta_5}.$$

An applied example of how these implicit prices can be obtained and used can be seen using the implicit prices associated with a study regarding a cleaner Thames River (EFTEC, 2003). Pollution of the Thames River has been a serious problem since the 1800s, with frequent sewage overflows that degrade water quality and cause disamenity. The objective of the study was to measure people's WTP for choices between potential river cleaning solutions. The attributes of the choice set were as follows: reduce sewage litter, reduce number of days when water sports are inadvisable for health reasons, and reduce potential fish kills. The cost of cleaning would be covered by an increase in annual water bills.

More specifically, the *status quo* (present situation at the time of the study) involved 10% of total sewage litter visible, the presence of other litter, 120 days/year involving health risks for individuals engaged in water sports, and 8 potential fish deaths per year. No cost was associated with the *status quo*. The study included two options, Option A and Option B, in which:

- For visible sewage litter: 10% would be visible under A and 0% under B.
- Other litter: would be present under both A and B.
- Health risk days: would be reduced to 4 under A and zero under B.
- Potential fish deaths: would be 0 under A and < 1 under B.
- Option A would cost 15 GBP/year and Option B would cost 36 GBP/year in terms of water bill for the affected households.

Implicit prices for sewage, health, and fish were calculated (Pearce *et al.*, 2006) as follows:

$$\text{WTP}_{\text{SEWAGE}} = b1/b4 = -0.0346/-0.0190 = \text{GBP } 1.82,$$

$$\text{WTP}_{\text{HEALTH}} = b2/b4 = -0.0073/-0.0190 = \text{GBP } 0.38,$$

$$\text{WTP}_{\text{FISH}} = b3/b4 = -0.0287/-0.0190 = \text{GBP } 1.51.$$

By aggregating these unit values, the total benefits of each of the options can be evaluated. For an option that would completely eliminate the discharge of sewage into the Thames, the total benefits per household are calculated as follows:

Sewage	Health	Fish	Total

$$[£1.84 \times (10-0)] + [£0.38 \times (120-0)] + [£1.51 \times (8-0)] = £76.$$

Thus each household's annual average WTP to eliminate any sewage discharges is approximately GBP 76. The annual aggregate WTP can be obtained by multiplying this value by the number of affected households in the area. The present value of these annual benefits can be compared with the present value of cleaning costs in order to decide whether the project is desirable.

9.2.5. *DCEs and random utility models: Evaluating policies*

For a more general evaluation of alternative policies, consider two policies A and B which will result in vectors of attributes $(X_{1A}, X_{2A}, \ldots, X_{KA})$ and $(X_{1B}, X_{2B}, \ldots, X_{KB})$. The average willingness to pay (AWTP) for policy changes is determined as follows:

$$\text{AWTP} = \frac{1}{\beta_p}(V_A - V_B),$$

where V_A, V_B are calculated using the estimated coefficients $\beta_k, k = 1, \ldots, K$ as

$$V_A = \sum_{k=1}^{K} \beta_k X_{Ak}, \quad V_B = \sum_{k=1}^{K} \beta_k X_{Bk}.$$

The calculated AWTP will determine which policy is preferred.

9.2.6. CEs and the status quo option

Choice experiments are consistent with utility maximization and demand theory, at least when a *status quo* option is included in the choice set. Without a *status quo* option, like Option 1 in Table 7 or Option D in Table 8, all respondents are "forced" to choose one of the other alternatives, but some of them may prefer to choose the *status quo*. Omission of the *status quo* option in this case will lead to biased estimates of implicit prices and WTP.

9.2.7. Alternative CM approaches

9.2.7.1. *Contingent ranking*

In a contingent ranking (CR) experiment, respondents are required to rank a set of alternative options, characterized by a number of attributes, which are offered at different levels across options. For example, with reference to Table 7, respondents are asked to rank the alternatives for conserving a tropical forest (Option 1 to Option 3) according to their preferences, by assigning 3 to the most preferred, 2 to the second most preferred, and 1 to the least preferred.

9.2.7.2. *Contingent rating*

In a contingent rating exercise, respondents are presented with a number of scenarios and asked to rate them individually on a semantic or numeric scale. In Table 9, respondents are asked to rank the alternatives for valuing the conservation of a tropical forest (see Table 7). Typical instructions might be as shown in Table 9.

9.2.7.3. *Paired comparisons*

In a paired comparison exercise, respondents are presented with two scenarios and asked to choose their preferred alternative. They are also asked to indicate the strength of their preference on a numeric or semantic scale. In Table 10, respondents are asked to compare two alternatives for reducing pollution in a lake (see Table 8). Typical instructions might be as shown in Table 10.

Table 9:   Example of a contingent rating exercise.

"On the scale below, please rate your preferences for conserving tropical forest for this option, from "1" (least preferred) to "10" (most preferred)."

Option 2	
Tropical forest area conserved	50,000 ha
Biodiversity protection	Medium
Flood risk reduction	Low
Area to be reforested	2,000 ha
Annual tax per household	€50

1	2	3	4	5	6	7	8	9	10
Least preferred								Most preferred	

9.2.8.   *Strengths and weaknesses of choice modeling*

9.2.8.1.   *Strengths of CM*

• CM is well suited for handling complex situations where changes occur across multiple dimensions and where the trade-offs between these dimensions are of particular interest. This is due to the inherent ability of CM to evaluate the individual value of different attributes of a product or program, which are often provided together.

• Certain variations of CM (for example, choice experiments) can be considered more informative compared to discrete choice contingent valuation studies. In choice experiments, respondents have the opportunity to express their preferences for a desired product across a range of payment amounts, allowing for a more comprehensive understanding of their preferences.

• In CM, the explicit determination of respondents' willingness to pay (WTP) is generally avoided. Instead, CM relies on methods such as ratings, rankings, or choices among different packages of characteristics. By analyzing these responses, the WTP can be indirectly inferred.

Table 10: Example of a paired comparison exercise.

"Which of the two management options below for reducing pollution in a lake do you prefer? Please choose the number that best expresses your preference."

	Management Option A	Management Option B
Manage the lake to ...	reduce pollution by 50%	reduce pollution by 20%
Improved health of ecosystem	High	Moderate
Increase in tourism	50%	20%
Improved recreational opportunities (e.g., swimming, fishing, or boating)	High	Moderate
Benefit to future generations	Large	Moderate
Cost to household over 3 year period	$90	$60

1	2	3	4	5	6	7	8	9	10
Strongly prefer Option A							Strongly prefer Option B		

9.2.8.2. *Weaknesses of CM*

- The primary drawback of CM methods is the cognitive challenge posed by making multiple complex choices or rankings among bundles that have numerous attributes and levels. Substantial evidence exists that suggests that there is a limit to how much information respondents can effectively process when making choices. Studies have found that greater choice complexity or the greater depth of a ranking task can result in increased random errors or imprecision in responses.
- Compared to a CVM alternative, CM approaches face greater difficulty in deriving values for a series of elements implemented by a policy or a project. Therefore, when it comes to valuing the

sequential provision of goods in multi-attribute programs, it is generally more advisable to employ the CVM.
• Just as with all stated preference techniques, the welfare estimates obtained through CM are highly sensitive to the design of the study employed.

References

Carson, R. T., Czajkowski, M. (2014). The discrete choice experiment approach to environmental contingent valuation. In S. Hess, A. Daly (eds.), *Handbook of Choice Modelling* (pp. 202–235). Cheltenham, UK: Edward Elgar Publishing.

EFTEC. (2003). *The Thames Tideway: Stated Preference Study*. London: Thames Water.

Haab, T., McConnell, K. (2002). *Valuing Environmental and Natural Resources: The Econometrics of Non-market Valuation*. Cheltenham, UK: Edward Elgar Publishing.

Hanemann, W. M. (1984). Welfare evaluations in contingent valuation experiments with discrete responses. *American Journal of Agricultural Economics*, 66(3), 332–341.

Hanemann, W. M. (1999). The economic theory of WTP and WTA. In I. Bateman, K. Willis (eds.), *Valuing Environmental Preferences: Theory and Practice of the Contingent Valuation Method in the US, EU and Developing Countries* (pp. 42–96). Oxford, UK: Oxford University Press.

Holmes, T. P., Adamowicz, W. L. (2003). Attribute-based methods. In Champ, P. A., K. J. Boyle, T. C. Brown (eds.), *The Economics of Nonmarket Valuation*. Dordrecht: Springer.

Johnston, R. J., Boyle, K. J., Adamowicz, W., Bennett, J. *et al.* (2017). Contemporary guidance for stated preference studies. *Journal of the Association of Environmental and Resource Economists*, 4, 319–405.

OECD (2018). *Cost-Benefit Analysis and the Environment: Further Developments and Policy Use*. Paris: OECD Publishing.

Pearce, D., Atkinson, G., Mourato, S. (2006). *Cost-Benefit Analysis and the Environment: Recent Developments*. Paris: OECD Publishing.

Part 3

Ecosystems, Biodiversity, and the Economy

Chapter 10

The Coevolution of Ecological and Economic Systems

10.1. Ecological–Economic Systems as Complex Adaptive Systems

Current ecological–economics literature regards ecological and economic systems as being interconnected complex adaptive systems (e.g., Levin *et al.*, 2013; Arrow *et al.*, 2014; Levin and Xepapadeas, 2021). The ecological and economic systems can therefore be considered as building blocks in a higher-level complex adaptive system (CAS) in which they are interconnected and interdependent. Thus, changes in one system can have a cascading effect on the other and vice versa. This inseparability presents unique challenges for managing either system:

- CASs are self-organized through local interactions and are characterized by historical dependencies, complex nonlinear dynamics, thresholds, tipping points, and multiple basins of attraction (e.g., Carpenter *et al.*, 1999; Levin, 1999).
- In the ecology–economy CAS, there are two groups of individual agents: economic agents and ecosystem agents (Levin and Xepapadeas, 2021).
  - Economic agents, such as individuals, firms, and governments, compete for resources to maximize their well-being, which can

be measured in terms of utility, profits, or social welfare. They do this by using the services provided by ecosystems, which are natural capital, along with the services of produced and human capital.

○ Ecosystems are complex systems made up of many different agents, from individual organisms to entire populations. These agents, from the genetic level through to populations and beyond, compete for resources, exploit each other, and cooperate to accumulate natural capital, which provides useful services to the economic system.

• In the CAS, the actions of ecological and economic agents at the "microscopic" level affect the aggregate or macroscopic characteristics of the economic ecosystem, and the emergent macroscopic characteristics feed back into the system to influence the actions of individual agents.

• The actions of the economic agents in their use of ecosystem services within the CAS result in excess consumption of natural capital which causes a reduction in the quality and quantity of services provided by natural capital, i.e., the ecosystems. Economic agents may consider their way of using the ecosystem services undesirable if it causes damages to the economic system, such as local pollution or climate change damages. In such cases, governments or regulatory agencies may implement policies to promote the efficient use of these services and thus reduce damages.

To summarize, the two systems involve agents who seek to optimize their objectives by competing for resources that could be shared. These agents can be economic, social, or biological. The interconnectedness of the two systems emerges because the economic system uses the services of ecosystems and consumes the natural capital that the ecosystems accumulate. Excessive consumption and depletion of natural capital can damage the economic system, which induces policy responses from economic institutions. The two systems evolve in time through accumulation processes and in space through transportation processes. Thus, evolution in time and space — spatiotemporal evolution — creates another level of interlinkages between the two systems. For more details, see Levin and Xepapadeas (2021).

10.1.1. *Temporal dynamics and optimization*

To provide a description of temporal dynamics, consider the evolution of a resource stock y (e.g., biomass) under harvesting by economic agents which is denoted by u, at time t. The function $f(y, u)$ characterizes the temporal growth of the resource,

$$\frac{dy(t)}{dt} = f(y(t), u(t)). \tag{1}$$

In ecological–economic systems, humans interact with the resource dynamics and derive some utility $U(y, u)$ either from the amount of the stock y in the system, such as fish, trees, or water in an aquifer, or from the amount of harvest of fish, trees, or water pumping.

Humans typically are assumed to choose the level of harvest or water abstractions to maximize the discounted (at rate ρ) present value of their utility over the time horizon T they consider (which could be infinite). A common management problem is to find the path $u(t)$ such that

$$\max_{\{u(t)\}} \int_0^T \mathrm{e}^{-\rho t} U(y(t), u(t)) dt, \quad \text{subject to (1)}.$$

10.1.2. *Spatiotemporal dynamics of unified ecological–economic systems*

In ecological systems, the spatiotemporal evolution of interacting biological agents is associated with the generation and maintenance of spatial and spatiotemporal patterns (Levin and Segel, 1985). Similar spatiotemporal patterns can be induced by economic agents, such as capital flows across locations or pollution flows generated by production processes in the economic system. Endogenous pattern formation can arise from a variety of mechanisms such as differential dispersal rates as suggested by Alan Turing (1952) over 70 years ago.

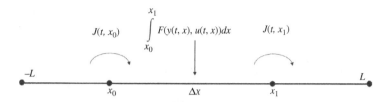

Figure 1:   Fickian diffusion.

The simplest models of spread, rest on limits of random walks or on a Fickian assumption of movement from locations of high to low concentration (see Figure 1).

The *new economic geography* has been the main driver in incorporating the spatial dimension into economic systems. The main focus of that work is the emergence of agglomerations and clusters at different spatial scales, as a result of interactions between scale economies and spatial spillovers (Krugman, 1996, 1998).

To provide a simple exposition of spatiotemporal dynamics, consider a substance (biomass, pollution stock) whose concentration at time t and spatial location x is $y(t, x)$, with harvesting $u(t, x)$ and the net growth in the spatial location determined by $f(y(t, x), u(t, x))$. Then the spatiotemporal concentration dynamics under diffusion is given by the partial differential equation:

$$\frac{\partial y(t, x)}{\partial t} = f(y(t, x), u(t, x)) + D\frac{\partial y^2(t, x)}{\partial x^2}, \quad y(0, x) = y_0(x).$$

Evolution of biomass under linear diffusion is shown in Figure 2.

10.1.3. *Spatiotemporal optimization*

In resource management, ecology and economics are linked through a harvesting process and an objective that includes the resource stock and harvesting, which is optimized. The spatiotemporal dynamics of the resource under harvesting act as constraints to the economic optimization problem (Levin and Xepapadeas, 2021). For pollution control and fishery management, these processes imply the following:

• For pollution control, the objective is to minimize the pollution cost for the entire spatial domain when the pollutant disperses across locations.

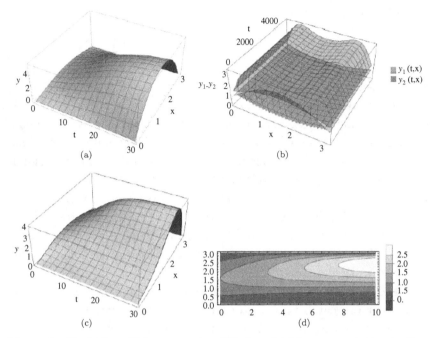

Figure 2: Evolution of biomass under diffusion. (a) Biomass evolution in time and space (t, x) of a population with logistic growth under linear diffusion. (b) Biomass evolution in time and space (t, x) of two interacting populations with logistic growth under linear diffusion (reaction–diffusion system). (c) Case (a) with advection. (d) Contours of the evolution surface of case (c).

- For fishery management, conventional models were coupled with metapopulation models to develop optimal harvesting models when fish populations move across discrete patches (e.g., Smith and Wilen, 2003; Costello and Polasky, 2008).
- In general, the objective is to optimize the present discounted value of an objective depending on state y and control u, which are defined over the entire spatial domain.
- In the context of continuous time and space, this can be regarded as the problem of a social planner or environmental regulator defined as:

$$\max_{u \in \mathcal{U}} \int_{x \in O} \int_{0}^{\infty} e^{-\rho t} U(y(t, x), u(t, x)) dt dx$$

subject to

$$\frac{\partial y(t,x)}{\partial t} = f(y(t,x),\, u(t,x)) + D\frac{\partial y^2(t,x)}{\partial x^2}.$$

- In discrete space, the problem is usually solved using metapopulation or dispersion models.
- The so-called *acid rain game*, in which acid deposits damage locations because of acid rain generated by sulfur emissions dispersing in different locations, is solved using the dispersion concept (Mäler, 1989; Mäler and de Zeeuw, 1998).
- Levin and Xepapadeas (2017) studied a two-region model with two stocks moving in space. Produced capital stock moves toward the region with the higher rate of return, and pollution stock moves from the region of higher concentration to the region of lower concentration.
- In the economics of climate change and the design of climate policy, transfer of heat from the Equator to the Poles has been used as a mechanism for explaining Polar amplification in the context of spatial models of climate science. This is important for climate policy since there is evidence that expected economic damages are associated with Polar amplification (mainly Arctic amplification). The incorporation of heat transport into integrated assessment models of climate change, either in continuous space (diffusion process) or discrete space (spatial box models), is another research area in which ecological processes are coupled with economics (see Brock *et al.*, 2014; Brock and Xepapadeas, 2017).
- In groundwater management, hydrological factors such as seepage or aquifer transmissivity induce spatial dynamics and introduce a spatial pumping externality. In this case, pumping policies with spatial structures are appropriate. Similar characteristics can be found in semi-arid systems with reaction–diffusion processes in which plant biomass and soil water interact and diffuse in space (Brock and Xepapadeas, 2010).
- The main results of this type of approach were the identification of conditions under which the coupled ecological–economic system generates spatial patterns, through an extension of Turing's mechanism for pattern generation or pattern suppression in space,

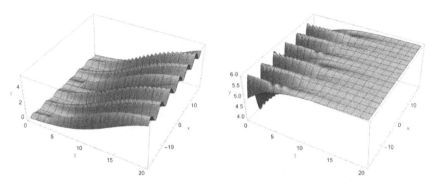

Figure 3: Emergence and dissipation of spatial patterns. Optimal patterns emergence (on the left) and optimal patterns disappearance (on the right).

and spatially structured policies of price or quantity instruments if the emergence of the spatial pattern was the socially optimal policy. Pattern generation and suppression are depicted in Figure 3.

10.1.4. *Nonlinearities and feedbacks*

The presence of nonlinearities and positive feedbacks — which amplify the impact of a forcing factor — in the temporal dynamics of ecological systems can generate multiple steady states with various stability characteristics, limit cycles, hysteresis, and flips from one basin of attraction to another, even without human interference.

Shallow lakes have been studied intensively over the last two decades and it has been shown that the essential dynamics of the eutrophication process (see Figure 4) include nonlinear dynamics and feedbacks and can be modeled by differential equation (2). See Mäler *et al.* (2003) for a detailed analysis.

10.2. The Lake Model

The temporal dynamics of the shallow lake can be described as follows:

$$\dot{P}(t) = L(t) - sP(t) + r\frac{P^2(t)}{P^2(t) + m^2}, \quad P(0) = P_0, \qquad (2)$$

where P is the amount of phosphorus in algae, L is the input of phosphorus (the "loading"), s is the rate of loss consisting of

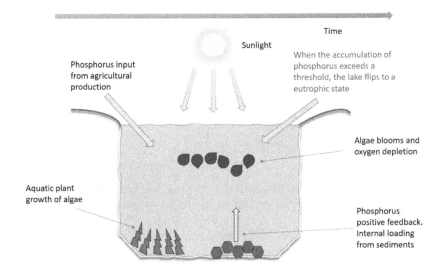

Figure 4:   Eutrophication processes.

sedimentation, outflow, and sequestration in other biomass, r is the maximum rate of internal loading, and m is the anoxic level. The dynamics of the lake model could lead to a eutrophic or oligotrophic lake, as shown in Figure 5.

By substituting $x = P/m$, $a = L/r$, $b = sm/r$ and by changing the time scale to rt/m, lake dynamics can be rewritten as

$$\dot{x}(t) = a(t) - bx(t) + \frac{x^2(t)}{x^2(t) + 1}, \quad x(0) = x_0.$$

10.2.1.   Optimal policy in the many-agent lake model

10.2.1.1.   Nonlinear lake dynamics

When $i = 1, \ldots, n$ agents load phosphorus in the lake, lake dynamics can be written as

$$\dot{x}(t) = \sum_{i=1}^{n} a_i(t) - bx(t) + f(x(t)), x(0) = x_0,$$

$$\dot{x}(t) = a(t) - bx(t) + \frac{x^2(t)}{x^2(t) + 1}, x(0) = x_0.$$

Figure 5: Aerial image of Experimental Lake Area (ELA) Lake 227 showing lakewide algal bloom. Eutrophic (on the left) vs oligotrophic lake (on the right). *Source*: https://sites.google.com/site/experimentallakearea/3/a-eutrophication-lake-227-and-226.

The flow of net benefits accruing to each agent is $U(a_i(t)) - D(x(t))$, where the phosphorus load generates agricultural benefits to agent i, but the stock of phosphorus x in the lake generates damages. Each agent chooses a strategy a_i in order to maximize the present value of net benefits over an infinite time horizon, or

$$\max_{a_i(\cdot)} \int_0^\infty e^{-\rho t}[U(a_i(t)) - D(x(t))]dt, i = 1, 2, \ldots, n.$$

Optimal policy and nonlinear dynamics could lead to multiple steady states, instabilities, and the emergence of Skiba points, as shown in Figures 6 and 7. Figure 6 shows three steady states emerging at a non-cooperative open-loop Nash equilibrium (for details, see Mäler *et al.*, 2003) with a flow of phosphorus loading a^* and phosphorus concentration x^*, (0.424, 0.099), (0.792, 0.080), and (2.180, 0.457), respectively. The first steady state corresponds to an oligotrophic steady state, while the third to a eutrophic

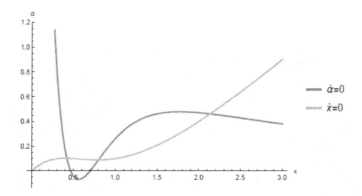

Figure 6:   Open-loop Nash equilibrium for nonlinear lake dynamics.

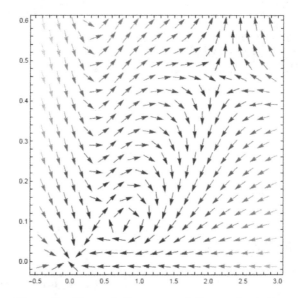

Figure 7:   Dynamic flows around the steady states.

steady state. The second is unstable. The dynamic flow around the three steady states is shown in Figure 7. For solutions at a feedback Nash equilibrium, see Kossioris *et al.* (2008).

10.3. Heterogeneity

Early models analyzing population dynamics and population interactions (e.g., Volterra, 1926) were simplified by treating all individuals within a species as identical, interacting within a homogeneous environment. These simple models have been used as a basis to answer the question about the way in which many species coexist on limited numbers of resources (Hutchinson, 1961).

As Levin and Xepapadeas (2021) point out, heterogeneity can provide the explanation: environmental heterogeneity in space or time can allow differential specialization on specific aspects of a resource and characterize the structure of populations regarding genetics, age, behavior, or spatial location.

Furthermore, evolutionary theory is founded on the genetic structuring of populations while the basis of mathematical demography is demographic models that account for age-dependent or size-dependent variation in life-history parameters, such as survival and fecundity.

10.4. Tipping Points

The mathematicians Alfred J. Lotka and Vito Volterra recognized as early as the early 1900s the existence of multiple locally stable steady states in ecological models. Multiple steady states or basins of attraction imply that a system in a given basin of attraction can, after an exogenous shock, cross a tipping point and flip to another basin of attraction.

The potential for systems to flip — either due to exogenous changes or slow evolution of endogenous variables — from one state (normally a healthy one, like an oligotrophic lake) to another (a less healthy one, like a eutrophic lake), as shown in Figure 6, is an interesting area of current research.

10.4.1. *Tipping points: The spruce budworm model*

The spruce budworm model is another example of tipping points:

- The spruce budworm is one of the most destructive native insects in the northern spruce and fir forests of the eastern United States

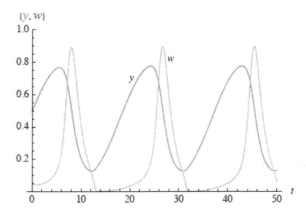

Figure 8:   Budworms vs tree foliage.

and Canada. Most of the time, the number of budworms remains at a low level. However, every forty years or so, the population of budworms explodes into huge numbers, devastating the forests and destroying many trees, before dropping back down to the previous low level. Evidence suggests these outbreaks have been recurring regularly for hundreds, if not thousands, of years.

- As forest conditions improve, budworm growth exceeds the control by predators and an outbreak occurs. On the other hand, if the forest is destroyed far enough, the predators can again regain control. For more details, see Ludwig *et al.* (1978).
- Figure 8 shows the evolution through time of the densities of budworms w and tree foliage y.

10.4.2. *Tipping points and early-warning systems*

The trade-off between the loss of ecosystem services when the system crosses a tipping point and a regime shift occurs, and the potential benefit of economic activities which induce the shift, is an important issue in the optimal management of ecosystems.

However, tipping points and regime shifts are uncertain and the optimal reaction to uncertain future tipping points is an issue which emerges naturally in climate change (e.g., van der Ploeg and de Zeeuw, 2018) or resource management (e.g., Polasky *et al.*, 2011; de Zeeuw, 2014).

Thus, the introduction of the concept of an early-warning indicator that will provide information about whether a tipping point "is being approached", and its incorporation into models of optimal management under regime shifts, is an area for further research.

10.5. Scale and Scaling

A fundamental challenge when analyzing a CAS is that phenomena evolve across multiple scales of space, time, and organizational complexity (Levin, 1992; Chave and Levin, 2003). This leads to the need to relate the processes on larger scales to those on smaller scales, essentially by developing appropriate nonlinear statistical mechanics:

- Separation of time scales (fast and slow) has important policy implications. Since population dynamics evolve rapidly, while evolution generally takes place more slowly, separate time scales are required in order to analyze coevolutionary processes. For example, management can impose strong evolutionary pressures on resources such as fish, with impacts on fast time scales (Diekert *et al.*, 2010).
- The interaction of population dynamics and mutation (or trait) dynamics operating in different time scales gives rise to the so-called Red Queen cycles which are observed in ecological systems. Modeling fast–slow systems and Red Queen dynamics has been associated with issues like biological resource management, water management, and pest control (e.g., Brock and Xepapadeas, 2003; Grimsrud and Huffaker, 2006; Crépin *et al.*, 2011).

10.6. Policy Issues and Ecosystem Management

Natural ecosystems and the species that comprise them sustain human life and support the human economy through the provision of ecosystem services (Daily, 1997). The Millennium Ecosystem Assessment (2005) connects ecosystem services — supporting, provisioning, regulating, and cultural — with the constituents of human well-being, which include security, basic material needs for a good life, health, good social relations, freedom, and choice of action.

Ecosystem services provided in a market economy have two important characteristics: (1) markets for their services may or may not exist and (2) common pool or open-access conditions emerge due to property rights that are not well defined, and this can cause overexploitation of a resource (the so-called *tragedy of the commons*).

As pointed out by Arrow (1969), when markets fail to exist, externalities emerge. An externality is the indirect (positive or negative) effect of the consumption or production of a good by an agent on the production or consumption set of another agent. As is well known in the non-cooperative competitive context, externalities lead to market failure.

10.6.1. *Policies*

Levin and Xepapadeas (2021) consider that the correction of negative externalities through decentralized schemes can, in general, be obtained either through the creation of markets in the spirit of Arrow (1969) or through the taxation of negative externalities or subsidization of positive externalities. They summarize the potential environmental policies as follows:

(1) Command-and-control policy, which corresponds to environmental policy that relies on regulation such as permissions, prohibition, standard or performance setting, and enforcement.
(2) Market-based regulatory instruments, which aim at changing the behavior of consumers or producers by providing appropriate economic incentives. These incentives change relative prices in the majority of cases.
(3) Voluntary approaches, which are not strictly speaking economic instruments but rather commitments by firms or industries to improve their environmental performance beyond legal mandates imposed by regulators (Segerson and Miceli, 1998; Dawson and Segerson, 2008; Ahmed and Segerson, 2011).

These policies should take into consideration the following points:

- The damages from pollution or excessive use of ecosystem services and depletion of stocks of natural capital. These damages are usually modeled by a damage function and provide a description of the linkages between the ecological system and the economic system.
- Deviations emerging between the socially optimal outcome, which internalizes ecosystem damages, and the privately optimal outcome, which does not internalize these effects. These deviations can be used as a basis for designing a regulatory scheme (e.g., controls, taxes, tradable permits, or agreements) which is supposed to bridge the gap between socially optimal and privately optimal outcomes. These regulatory schemes support ecosystem management which promotes the socially efficient use of ecosystem services by humans.
- The new challenges emerging from the coevolution of unified ecological–economic should be taken into account in the process of correcting the potential multiple externalities emerging from this coevolution. This goes beyond the postulation of a simple damage function.
- How should command-and-control, market-based, and voluntary policy instruments be modified when they are derived in the context of a unified co-evolving ecological–economic system?
- Are the relatively simplified "ecology only" or "economy only"-based policies sufficient to correct multiple externalities?

10.6.2. *New challenges*

Levin and Xepapadeas (2021) identify the following new challenges with regard to policy design:

(1) Spatially differentiated paths for policy instruments or additional policy instruments when the spatiotemporal dimension of the ecological–economic systems are taken into account.
(2) The actual interactions between fast and slow processes will not provide policies appropriate for the regulation of slow

variables if, as usual, the evolution of slow variables is ignored in policy design. Unregulated slow variables might cross thresholds or tipping points.

(3) The design of biodiversity policies should allow for heterogeneity.

(4) Policies which will provide early-warning indicators are important in the presence of tipping points and regime shifts.

(5) The precautionary principle should be supported by allowing for deep uncertainty and aversion to ambiguity.

(6) The existence of multiple steady states which could be "bad" or "good" in terms of the regulator's objective might be obscured by ignoring positive feedbacks and non-convexities (e.g., oligotrophic vs eutrophic steady states, permafrost thawing). This could produce a management regime which steers the unified system to an undesirable steady state.

10.7. Ecological–Economic Systems and Infectious Diseases

10.7.1. *Classic epidemiology models*

Epidemiology models seek to describe the way in which an infectious disease is spread into a large population. This is done by assuming that a small group of infected individuals are introduced into a large population. The basic problem is how to describe the spread of the infection within the population as a function of time. In the models we consider here, the total population is taken to be constant.

- Consider a disease in which recovered individuals are immune (which includes deaths, that is, dead individuals are still counted). The population can then be divided into three distinct cases: (a) the susceptible people, S, who can catch the disease, (b) the infectious people, I, who have the disease and can transmit it, and (c) the recovered class, R, namely those who have either had the disease and recovered or are immune or isolated until recovered. The progress of individuals is schematically described by $S \to I \to R$.

- Such models are often called susceptible–infectious–recovered (SIR) models.
- In contrast, diseases which do not provide immunity are described as susceptible–infectious–susceptible (SIS) models.
- SIR models can be regarded as appropriate for diseases such as measles, mumps, or SARS, while SIS models can be regarded as appropriate for diseases such as influenza, COVID-19, or tuberculosis.

The threshold for many epidemiology models is the basic reproduction number R_0, which is defined as the average number of secondary infections produced when one infected individual, I, is introduced into a host population where everyone is susceptible, S. For many deterministic epidemiology models, an infection can get started in a fully susceptible population if, and only if, $R_0 > 1$. Thus, the basic reproduction number R_0 is often considered as the threshold quantity that determines when an infection can invade and persist in a new host population. For more details, see Murray (2001).

- The epidemic SIR model is as follows:

$$\frac{dS}{dt} = -\frac{\beta IS}{N}, \quad S(0) = S_0 \geq 0,$$

$$\frac{dI}{dt} = \frac{\beta IS}{N} - \gamma I, \quad I(0) = I_0 \geq 0,$$

$$\frac{dR}{dt} = \gamma I, \quad R(0) = R_0 \geq 0,$$

where $S(t) + I(t) + R(t) = N(t)$ the population.
- Assuming constant population N, dividing the above equations by N, and denoting

$$s = \frac{S}{N}, \quad i = \frac{I}{N}, \quad r = \frac{R}{N},$$

we obtain the following:

$$\frac{ds}{dt} = \beta is, \quad s(0) \geq 0,$$

$$\frac{di}{dt} = \beta i s - \gamma i, \quad i(0) \geq 0,$$

$$r(t) = 1 - s(t) - i(t).$$

Then, $R_0 = \frac{\beta}{\gamma}$ is the basic reproduction number or contact rate, where β is the infection rate, γ is the removal rate of the infectives, $1/\gamma$ is the average infectious period, and the mortality rate μ is assumed to be zero.

The basic reproduction rate of the infection, R_0, is the average number of adequate contacts of an infective with susceptibles during the infectious period. If more than one adequate contact from one primary infection takes place, that is, $R_0 > 1$, then an epidemic spreads.

- Figure 9(a) shows phase trajectories in the susceptible–infective $(S - I)$ phase plane for the SIR model epidemic system.
- The curves are determined by the initial conditions $I(0) = I_0$ and $S(0) = S_0$. With $R(0) = 0$, all trajectories start on the line $S + I = N$ and remain within the triangle since $0 < S + I \leq N$ for all time.
- An epidemic situation formally exists if $I(t) > I_0$ for any time $t > 0$: this always occurs if $S_0 > \gamma/\beta$ and $I_0 > 0$.
- If $S_0 = 1$, then the epidemic occurs if $R_0 = \frac{\beta}{\gamma} > 1$.
- Figure 9(a) shows the paths of an SIR epidemic for which there is immunity after infection with $\mu = 0$, while Figure 9(b) shows the paths of an SIS infectious disease, such as influenza, for which there is no immunity.

10.7.2. R_0: COVID-19

R_0 estimates are complex and not as straightforward as many assume. The number is constantly changing and determining it is not an exact science. For example:

- In January 2020, the World Health Organization estimated the R_0 for COVID-19 as between 1.4 and 2.5.
- Twelve other studies published in January–February 2020 estimated an R_0 ranging from 1.5 to 6.68 (Liu *et al.*, 2020).

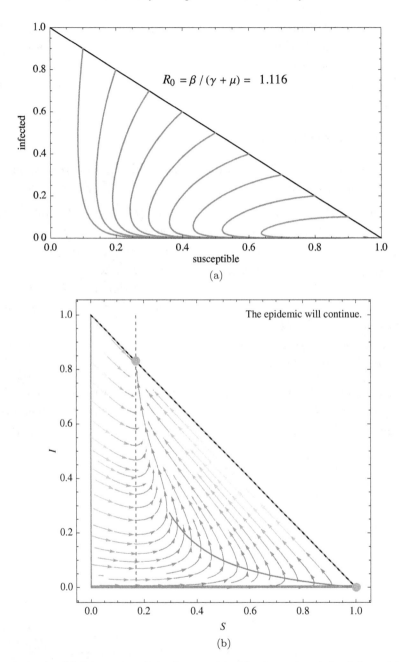

Figure 9: (a) The paths of the SIR model. (b) The paths of the SIS model.

- Preliminary studies estimated the R_0 to be between 1.5 and 3.5.
- In August 2021, the US Centers for Disease Control estimated the R_0 of the Delta variant to be about 8.5.
- In comparison, the R_0 for the common flu is 1.3 and for SARS it was 2.0.

10.7.3. *Epidemic outbreak*

An outbreak with an $R_0 > 1$ will expand, while an outbreak with an $R_0 < 1$ will gradually disappear.

Theorem (Hethcote, 2000). *Let $(s(t), i(t))$ be a solution of (2). If $R_0 s_0 \leq 1$, then $i(t)$ decreases to zero as $t \to \infty$. If $R_0 s_0 > 1$, then $i(t)$ first increases up to a maximum value $i_{max} = i_0 s_0 - \frac{1}{R_0} - [\ln(R_0 s_0)/R_0]$ and then decreases to zero as $t \to \infty$.*

The susceptible fraction $s(t)$ is a decreasing function and the limiting value s^∞ is the unique root in $(0, 1/\sigma)$ of the equation $i_0 s_0 = s^\infty + \ln(\frac{s^\infty}{s_0})/R_0 = 0$.

The solution of a classic SIR model which is described in the theorem above is shown in Figure 10.

- A typical epidemic outbreak which is described by an SIR model is an infective curve (see "infectious" in Figure 10) that first increases from an initial low near zero, reaches a peak, and then

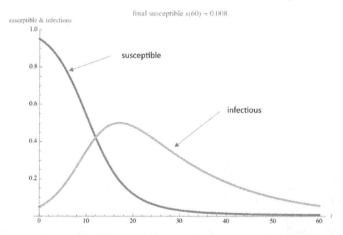

Figure 10: Solution of a susceptible–infectious–recovered (SIR) model.

decreases toward zero as a function of time. The epidemic dies out because, when the susceptible fraction $s(t)$ goes below $1/R_0$, the replacement number $R_0 s(t)$ goes below 1 and $I \to 0$.

- The results in the theorem are epidemiologically reasonable, since the infectives decrease and there is no epidemic if enough people are already immune, so that a typical infective initially replaces itself with no more than one new infective ($R_0 s_0 \leq 1$). But if a typical infective initially generates more than one new infective ($R_0 s_0 > 1$), then infectives initially increase so that an epidemic emerges.
- The speed at which an epidemic progresses depends on the characteristics of the disease (e.g., the outbreak size).

10.7.4. *Infectious diseases and human activities*

Research indicates the strong probability of a link between emerging infectious diseases and climate change and the increasing human encroachment in the natural environment resulting in pressures on disease reservoirs and continued antibiotic resistance.

- As early as 1996, Daily and Ehrlich (1996) were examining the potential impact on the epidemiological environment of biophysical aspects of global change, including population changes, land conversion, agricultural intensification, and climate change. They warned that as human populations are increasingly pushed into contact with animal reservoirs of diseases such as HIV and Ebola, the odds increase that a pathogen will invade human populations and become endemic.
- According to Cunningham (2005), the emergence of infectious diseases with high case fatality rates, such as AIDS, SARS, and H5N1 avian influenza, highlight the importance of wildlife as reservoirs or vectors for disease.
- Muehlenbein (2013) found that population, ecological, and behavioral changes that increase contact with wildlife exacerbate the emergence of zoonotic pathogens.
- Even before the COVID-19 crisis, Afelt *et al.* (2018) linked deforestation with the emergence of coronaviruses and novel

infectious diseases. The link between deforestation and infectious diseases affecting humans was stressed by Zimmer (2019).

- Jane Goodall has blamed the overexploitation of the natural world, in terms of deforestation, species extinction, and destruction of habitats, for the emergence of COVID-19 (Harvey, 2020).
- Nova *et al.* (2022) state that the emergence of novel infectious diseases and their expansion to new geographical regions have been induced by climate change, land use changes, and urbanization.
- Mora *et al.* (2022) also found evidence suggesting that a large number of infectious diseases are related to climatic hazards induced by climate change.

Human encroachment on wildlife results in stresses to the ecosystems which cause increased emergence of infectious diseases. A small cluster of individuals infected by a novel disease — such as COVID-19, as the most recent example — may emerge because of increased use of wildlife products, increasing use of concentrated animal husbandry, increasing human encroachment on nature, land use changes, and climate change. The small group of infected individuals can then infect the susceptible part of the population in the way described by the SIR or the SIS models.

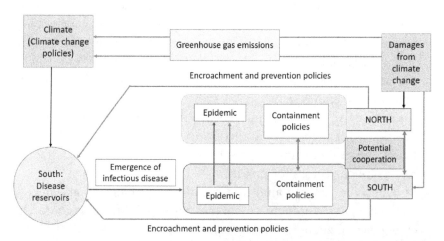

Figure 11:   An epi-econ IAM with short-run containment and long-run prevention policy options.

The links between the emergence of infectious diseases, human activities, and climate change are illustrated in Figure 11.

10.7.5. *An SIR model under climate change*

Following Brock and Xepapadeas (2020), consider the extension of an SIR model that includes the economy and climate change:

$$\frac{ds}{dt} = -\beta(C, T, u)is, \quad s(0) = 1,$$

$$\frac{di}{dt} = \beta(C, T, u)is - \gamma i, \quad i(0) = 0,$$

$$r(t) = 1 - s(t) - i(t).$$

Then, $R_0 = \frac{\beta(C,T,u)}{\gamma}$ is the basic reproduction number, where C is a composite of market-consumption goods, T is the global average temperature anomaly relative to the preindustrial period T_0, and u is disease control measures such as vaccinations, lockdowns, or social distancing. It is assumed that increasing the consumption composite and increasing global temperature increases the basic reproduction rate. On the other hand, increasing disease control measures reduces it. That is,

$$\frac{\partial \beta(C, T, u)}{\partial C} > 0, \quad \frac{\partial \beta(C, T, u)}{\partial T} > 0, \quad \frac{\partial \beta(C, T, u)}{\partial u} < 0.$$

Consider a logarithmic instantaneous utility function which is the logarithm of a Cobb–Douglas specification of a material consumption aggregate C and energy E. Damages to utility are induced by a positive temperature anomaly T relative to the preindustrial period T_0 and by the infected part of the population I. If the cost of controlling the disease through reduction of the basic reproduction number is $c(u)c' > 0, c'' > 0$, then the instantaneous utility function can be defined as follows:

$$U = a\ln E + (1 - a)(\ln C - kT - \mu I) - c(u),$$

where kT reflects climate change cost and μI the cost of the disease. Then a control problem for a social planner that chooses optimal paths for energy, consumption, and disease control can be written, normalizing $N = 1$, as

$$\max_{C,E,u} \int_0^Z e^{-\rho t}[a \ln E + (1-a)(\ln C - kT - \mu I) - c(u)]dt$$

subject to

$$C + \dot{K} + \delta K = AK, \quad K(0) = K_0,$$

$$\dot{T} = bE - mT, \quad T(0) = 0,$$

$$\frac{dS}{dt} = -\beta(C,T,u)IS, \quad S(0) = S_0 \geq 0,$$

$$\frac{dI}{dt} = -\beta(C,T,u)IS - \gamma I, \quad I(0) = I_0 \geq 0,$$

$$\frac{dR}{dt} = \gamma I, \quad R(0) = R_0 \geq 0,$$

where K is the stock of capital and the production function is assumed to be AK. If the constraint $I(Z) = 0$ is imposed, then we require that the disease is eradicated at the terminal time Z. For more details, see Brock and Xepapadeas (2020).

10.7.6. *Some policy implications*

The potential of an epidemic in terms of increased contact number or the probability of its arrival may increase with continuous growth of consumption activities, capital accumulation, and greenhouse gas emissions which result in climate change.

The framework of analysis of infectious disease policies can be considered in two stages:

o In the short run, when the infectious disease has emerged, containment policies such as vaccination or social distancing could help bring down R_0 below 1 and stop the epidemic.
o The potential of the emergence of epidemics in the medium and the long run can be reduced by economic policies directed at changing consumption patterns and addressing climate change.

References

Afelt, A., Frutos, R., Devaux, C. (2018). Bats, coronaviruses, and deforestation: Toward the emergence of novel infectious diseases? *Frontiers in Microbiology*, 9.

Ahmed, R., Segerson, K. (2011). Collective voluntary agreements to eliminate polluting products. *Resource and Energy Economics*, 33, 572–588.

Arrow, K. J. (1969). The organization of economic activity: Issues pertinent to the choice of market versus non-market allocation. In *Joint Economic Committee, The Analysis and Evaluation of Public Expenditures: The PPB System* (pp. 47–64). Washington, DC: Government Printing Office.

Arrow, K. J., Ehrlich, P. R., Levin, S. A. (2014). Some perspectives on linked ecosystems and socioeconomic systems. In S. Barrett, K.-G. Maler, E. S. Maskin (eds), *Environment and Development Economics: Essays in Honour of Sir Partha Dasgupta* (pp. 95–119). Oxford Scholarship Online.

Brock, W. A., Engström, G., Xepapadeas, A. (2014). Energy balance climate models, damage reservoirs, and the time profile of climate change policy. In L. Bernard, W. Semmler (eds.), *The Oxford Handbook of the Macroeconomics of Global Warming* (Chapter 3). Oxford: Oxford University Press.

Brock, W. A., Xepapadeas, A. (2003). Valuing biodiversity from an economic perspective: A unified economic, ecological and genetic approach. *American Economic Review*, 93, 1597–1614.

Brock, W. A., Xepapadeas A. (2010). Pattern formation, spatial externalities and regulation in coupled economic–ecological systems. *Journal of Environmental Economics and Management*, 59, 149–164.

Brock, W. A., Xepapadeas, A. (2017). Climate change policy under polar amplification. *European Economic Review*, 94, 263–282.

Brock, W. A., Xepapadeas, A. (2020). The economy, climate change and infectious diseases: Links and policy implications. *Environmental and Resource Economics*, 76(4), 811–824.

Carpenter, S. R., Ludwig, D., Brock, W. (1999). Management of lakes subject to potentially irreversible change. *Ecological Applications*, 9(3), 751–771.

Chave, J., Levin, S. A. (2003). Scale and scaling in ecological and economic systems. *Environmental and Resource Economics*, 26, 527–557.

Costello, C., Polasky, S. (2008). Optimal harvesting of stochastic spatial resources. *Journal of Environmental Economics and Management*, 56, 1–18.

Crépin, A.-S., Norberg, J., Mäler, K.-G. (2011). Coupled economic-ecological systems with slow and fast dynamics — Modelling and analysis method. *Ecological Economics*, 70, 1448–1458.

Cunningham, A. A. (2005). A walk on the wild side — Emerging wildlife diseases. *The BMJ*, 331, 1215.

Daily, G. C. (1997). *Nature's Services: Societal Dependence on Natural Ecosystems*. Washington, DC: Island Press.

Daily, G. C., Ehrlich, P. R. (1996). Global change and human susceptibility to disease. *Annual Review of Energy and the Environment*, 21, 125–144.

Dawson, N. L., Segerson, K. (2008). Voluntary agreements with industries: Participation incentives with industrywide targets. *Land Economics*, 84(1), 97–114.

de Zeeuw, A. (2014). Differential games and environmental economics. In J. Haunschmied, V. Veliov, S. Wrzaczek (eds.), *Dynamic Games in Economics. Dynamic Modeling and Econometrics in Economics and Finance* (Vol. 16, pp. 135–159). Springer.

Diekert, F. K., Hjermann, D. O., Navdal, E., Stenseth, N.-C. (2010). Noncooperative exploitation of multi-cohort fisheries — The role of gear selectivity in the North-East Arctic cod fishery. *Resource and Energy Economics*, 32, 78–92.

Grimsrud, K., Huffaker, R. (2006). Solving multidimensional bioeconomic problems with singular-perturbation reduction methods: Application to managing pest resistance to pesticidal crops. *Journal of Environmental Economics and Management*, 51, 336–353.

Harvey, F. (2020). Jane Goodall: Humanity is finished if it fails to adapt after Covid-19. *The Guardian*, 3 June.

Hethcote, H. W. (2000). The mathematics of infectious diseases. *SIAM Review*, 42, 599–653.

Hutchinson, G. E. (1961). The paradox of the plankton. *American Naturalist*, 95(882), 137–145.

Kossioris, G., Plexousakis, M., Xepapadeas, A., de Zeeuw, A., Mäler, K.-G. (2008). Feedback Nash equilibria for non-linear differential games in pollution control. *Journal of Economic Dynamics and Control*, 32(4), 1312–1331.

Krugman, P. R. (1996). *The Self-Organizing Economy*. Blackwell Publishers.

Krugman, P. R. (1998). Space: The final frontier. *Journal of Economic Perspectives*, 12, 161–174.

Levin, S. A. (1992). The problem of pattern and scale in ecology. *Ecology*, 73, 1943–1967.

Levin, S. A. (1999). *Fragile Dominion: Complexity and the Commons, Helix Books*. Reading, MA: Perseus Books.

Levin, S. A., Segel, L. (1985). Pattern generation in space and aspect. *SIAM Review*, 27, 45–67.

Levin, S. A., Xepapadeas, A. (2017). Transboundary capital and pollution flows and the emergence of regional inequalities. *Discrete and Continuous Dynamical Systems B*, 22, 913–922.

Levin, S. A., Xepapadeas, A. (2021). On the coevolution of economic and ecological systems. *Annual Review of Resource Economics*, 13, 355–377.

Levin, S. A., Xepapadeas, T., Crépin, A.-S., Norberg, J., de Zeeuw, A., et al. (2013). Social-ecological systems as complex adaptive systems: Modeling and policy implications. *Environment and Development Economics*, 18, 111–132.

Liu, Y., Gayle, A. A., Wilder-Smith, A., Rocklöv, J. (2020). The reproductive number of COVID-19 is higher compared to SARS coronavirus. *Journal of Travel Medicine*, 27, 1–4.

Ludwig, D., Jones, D. D., Holling, C. S. (1978). Qualitative analysis of insect outbreak systems: The spruce budworm and forest. *Journal of Animal Ecology*, 47, 315–332.

Mäler, K.-G. (1989). The acid rain game. In H. Folmer, E. van Ierland (eds), *Valuation Methods and Policy Making in Environmental Economics*, Vol. 36, Studies in Environmental Science (pp. 231–252). Amsterdam: Elsevier.

Mäler, K.-G., de Zeeuw, A. (1998). The acid rain differential game. *Environmental and Resource Economics*, 12, 167–184.

Mäler, K.-G., Xepapadeas, A., de Zeeuw, A. (2003). The economics of shallow lakes. *Environmental and Resource Economics*, 26(4), 603–624.

Millennium Ecosystem Assessment (2005). *Ecosystems and Human Well-being: Synthesis*. Washington, DC: Island Press.

Mora, C., McKenzie, T., Gaw, I. M., Dean, J. M., von Hammerstein, H., Knudson, T. A., Setter, R. O., Smith, C. Z., Webster, K. M., Patz, J. A., Franklin, E. C. (2022). Over half of known human pathogenic diseases can be aggravated by climate change. *Nature Climate Change*, 12(9), 869–875.

Muehlenbein, M. P. (2013). Human-wildlife contact and emerging infectious diseases. In E. S. Brondízio, E. F. Moran (eds.), *Human–Environment Interactions: Current and Future Directions* (Chapter 4). Springer Science.

Murray, J. D. (2001). *Mathematical Bioeconomics*. Springer.

Nova, N., Athni, T. S., Childs, M. L., Mandle, L., Mordecai, E. A. (2022). Global change and emerging infectious diseases. *Annual Review of Resource Economics*, 14, 333–354.

Polasky, S. A., de Zeeuw, A., Wagener, F. (2011). Optimal management with potential regime shifts. *Journal of Environmental Economics and Management*, 62, 229–240.

Segerson, K., Miceli, T. J. (1998). Voluntary environmental agreements: Good or bad news for environmental protection? *Journal of Environmental Economics and Management*, 36(2), 109–130.

Smith, M., Wilen, J. (2003). Economic impacts of marine reserves: The importance of spatial behavior. *Journal of Environmental Economics and Management*, 4, 183–206.

Turing, A. (1952). The chemical basis of morphogenesis. *Philosophical Transactions of the Royal Society of London Series B*, 237, 37–72.

van der Ploeg, F., de Zeeuw, A. (2018). Climate tipping and economic growth: Precautionary capital and the price of carbon. *Journal of the European Economic Association*, 16, 1577–1617.

Volterra, V. (1926). Variazioni e fluttuazioni del numero d'individui in specie animale conviventi. *Memoria della Reale Accademia Nazionale del Lincei 2*, 31–113.

Zimmer, K. (2019) Deforestation is leading to more infectious diseases in humans. *National Geographic*, 22 November.

Chapter 11

Biodiversity Concepts and Valuation

11.1. Biodiversity: Basic Concepts

11.1.1. *Biological diversity*

Biological diversity, more commonly referred to as *biodiversity,* is "the variability among living organisms from all sources, including terrestrial, marine and other aquatic ecosystems and the ecological complexes of which they are part; this includes diversity within species, between species and of ecosystems" (Article 2, Convention on Biological Diversity).

The term covers all variety of life that can be found on Earth (plants, animals, fungi, and microorganisms), the diversity of communities ·that they form, and the habitats in which they live. It encompasses three levels: ecosystem diversity (the variety of different ecosystems present in a particular geographical area or on a global scale), species diversity (the variety and abundance of different species present within a specific area or ecosystem), and genetic diversity (the variation in genetic information within a population of the same species).

11.1.2. *Biodiversity loss*

As was shown in Chapter 5, biodiversity is crucial to human well-being, but damage to global ecosystem services and biodiversity is acute and accelerating. According to the Millennium Ecosystem Assessment (MA) (2005), in the last century, the world has lost 35% of mangroves, 40% of forests, and 50% of wetlands. Sixty percent of ecosystem services have been degraded in just 50 years. Species loss is 100–1,000 times greater than in geological times and will get worse with climate change. Eighty percent of the world's fisheries are fully exploited or over-exploited. Critical thresholds are being passed: for example, coral reefs risk collapse if CO_2 emissions are not urgently reduced.

The Millennium Ecosystem Assessment (2005) prepared four scenarios regarding the future for ecosystems and human well-being: one in which the world becomes increasingly globalized, one in which it becomes increasingly regionalized, and two different approaches to ecosystem management — one in which problems are mostly addressed after they become obvious (reactive) and the other in which policies attempt to maintain ecosystem services for the long run (proactive).

The most important direct drivers of change in ecosystems identified by the MA are habitat change, overexploitation, invasive alien species, pollution, and climate change. Most of these direct drivers of change are currently either constant or growing in intensity. In all four MA scenarios, the pressures on ecosystems are projected to continue to grow during the first half of this century (Millennium Ecosystem Assessment, 2005).

Steffen *et al.* (2011) present data suggesting that the proportional decrease in mean species abundance increased from approximately 4% in 1750 to approximately 30% in 2000. This is a clear sign of global terrestrial biosphere degradation.

The Millennium Ecosystem Assessment (2005, pp. 2–3) reports the following:

- More land was converted to cropland between 1950 and 1980 than in the 150 years between 1700 and 1850.

- About 20% of the world's coral reefs and 35% of mangrove areas were lost in the last decades of the twentieth century.
- From 1750 to 2003, the atmospheric concentration of CO_2 increased by about 32%, mainly due to fossil fuel combustion and land use changes.

Global Biodiversity Outlook 1 (Convention on Biological Diversity, 2001) used quantitative criteria to assess species under threat of extinction: rate of decline, population size, area of geographic distribution, and degree of population and distribution fragmentation. Fragmentation, the division of a species' habitat into smaller, isolated patches due to human activities such as habitat destruction, urbanization, or infrastructure development, can lead to the isolation of populations, making it difficult for individuals to move between different patches. The report found that in 2000:

- 24% of the world's mammal species (1,130) were considered threatened,
- 12% of bird species (1,183) were considered globally threatened,
- 4% of the world's reptile species (296) and 3% of its fish species (752) were considered globally threatened, and
- 16% of conifers, cycads, etc. species (141) and 3.5% of flowering plant species (5,390), as well as many other vertebrate, invertebrate, and plant species, were also under threat.

11.1.3. *The economic perspective of biodiversity*

To provide an economic perspective of biodiversity, it is necessary to link the concept of ecosystems as assets with the concept of biodiversity as a factor that facilitates the growth of these assets:

- Ecosystems are assets (for details, see Dasgupta, 2021). This is why Nature is referred to by economists as natural capital, akin to produced capital (e.g., infrastructure, buildings, and machinery) and human capital (combinations of health, knowledge, and skills).
- The evolution of ecosystems is determined by earth-system processes and their boundaries (see Figure 1).

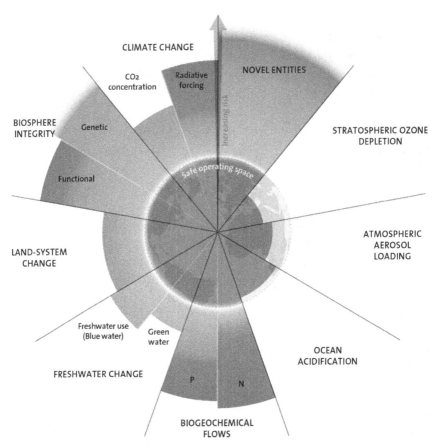

Figure 1: Planetary boundaries. Counterclockwise from top: climate change, biosphere integrity (functional and genetic), land-system change, freshwater use, biogeochemical flows (nitrogen and phosphorus), ocean acidification, atmospheric aerosol pollution, stratospheric ozone depletion, and release of novel chemicals.
Source: Azote for Stockholm Resilience Centre, based on analysis in Richardson *et al.* (2023). Licensed under CC BY-NC-ND 3.0.

- Biodiversity is not an asset. Rather, it is a descriptive feature of assets we call ecosystems. The building blocks of the economics of biodiversity are *own rates of return* on assets.
- Formally, the own rate of return on investment in an asset is the increase in the asset's size that would be expected tomorrow if one more unit of the asset were added to a portfolio today. The additional unit is the investment in question.

Some examples of the way in which the rate of return is defined in terms of natural capital are:

- The additional biomass of a fishery that would be expected tomorrow if the biomass in the fishery were increased by a unit today.
- The increase in a tree's biomass per unit of its biomass if we were to postpone harvesting. Waiting suggests that natural capital's own rate of return is its regenerative rate for a marginal unit of stock.
- The own rate of return on investment in produced capital is its marginal product.

When compared to the own rate of return on produced capital — proxied by the long-run global yield (rent or dividend) on housing and equities, which has averaged around 5% (Jordà *et al.*, 2019) — the own rate of return on planetary biomass is significantly higher. Estimates suggest that the biosphere-wide average own rate of return is around 19% a year (Dasgupta, 2021).

If the global portfolio was deemed to be efficient, we would expect capital losses on the biosphere equal to the difference between these rates of return (i.e., around 14% a year). But the global economy has been decumulating natural capital while accumulating produced capital as shown in Table 1.

This means that the accounting price of the biosphere relative to that of produced capital will have been *increasing*, which means that Nature should be enjoying "capital gains" against produced capital, not capital losses. That shows that humanity has been mismanaging

Table 1: Global composition of total capital stock (%).

Type	1990	2014
Produced capital	14.8	21.0
Human capital	50.5	56.4
Natural capital	34.6	22.6

the global portfolio of assets. Some signs of this mismanagement, and some of the reasons underlying it, include the following:

- Extinction of species due to anthropogenic influences (development and land use and climate change).
- Deterioration of ecosystems and reductions in their services (e.g., fisheries collapse).
- The fact that biodiversity has very strong public good characteristics (non-rivaled, non-excludable), which implies that unregulated private markets cannot produce the socially optimal amount of biodiversity. This market failure can be associated with species extinction and fishery collapse.
- The public good characteristics of biodiversity imply that regulation is required to correct for market failures.
- In order to have efficient regulation, we need to know the following:
  (1) How do we measure biodiversity?
  (2) How do we value changes in biodiversity?
  (3) What are the implications of measurement/valuation for policy design?

These issues are discussed in the following sections.

11.2. Measurement, Valuation, and Economic Policy

11.2.1. *Biodiversity measurement*

11.2.1.1. *Biodiversity metrics*

Biodiversity metrics, ecologically or biologically oriented, are quantitative measures used to assess and quantify various aspects of biodiversity within ecosystems or regions.

Diversity measures that have been extensively employed in biological and ecological applications are influenced by two components:

(1) *Richness*: The number of species.
(2) *Evenness*: The distribution of species.

- **Simpson Index (D)**: $D = 1 - \sum_{i=1}^{N} P_i^2$. This index takes into account both species richness and evenness, providing a single value that represents the diversity of a community. It ranges from 0 to 1, with higher values indicating higher diversity.
- **Shannon Index (H)**: $H = -\sum_{i=1}^{N} P_i \ln P_i$. This metric also considers species richness and evenness to quantify biodiversity. It provides a more sensitive measure of diversity, especially when dealing with smaller samples.

N is the number of species in a landscape (that is, species richness) and P_i is the proportion of individuals or biomass of species i in the landscape.

These metrics provide valuable information about the diversity, composition, and distribution of species, as well as the overall health and ecological integrity of an area.

11.2.1.2. *The diversity function*

In the context of biodiversity management and conservation, *the diversity function* (Weitzman, 1992) refers to the ecological role and significance of species diversity within an ecosystem:

- The diversity function is defined in terms of pair-wise DNA distances among species, with distance being a measure of dissimilarity among species.
- In biological applications, this distance is based on the DNA–DNA hybridization.
  - There is an implicit assumption that diversity measured in terms of genetic distances is desirable. This means that the most valuable species is the one most distant from the others.
- The diversity function can be used to rank conservation alternatives (most desirable alternative showing the relatively highest value for the ecological diversity function).
- In the "Noah's ark problem" (Weitzman, 1998), species are valued according to both the genetic distances and direct utility associated with the species, which is taken to reflect aesthetic or existence values. (See Section 11.3 for a more detailed analysis.)

11.2.2. *Valuation of changes in biodiversity*

The value of ecosystem services is determined through the total economic value concept which, as shown in detail in Chapter 5, includes:

- direct use values (production and consumption),
- indirect use values (ecosystem resilience and survival),
- existence value, non-use value (intrinsic value of nature),
- option values (potential future uses), in which the main ingredient is the irreversibility of a change.

The economic perspective of biodiversity is based on the fact that by generating positive externalities, it provides or enhances a number of important characteristics associated with ecosystem services and their values (Heal, 2000). We can base biodiversity valuation on these characteristics.

Biodiversity is essential for the proper functioning of an ecosystem so that it retains its ability to provide economically important services, such as watershed benefits, ecotourism, carbon sequestration services of forests, or production of non-timber forest products. Table 2 shows the main components of biodiversity and some examples of the ecosystem services they provide.

Maintaining biodiversity is important in order to promote productivity, resilience, insurance, and knowledge:

- **Productivity**: More diverse plant systems are more productive than less diverse ones. Empirical studies relating the number of species in ecosystems to plant productivity have found that functional diversity is a principal factor explaining plant productivity (Tilman *et al.*, 2005).

  o Productivity relates mainly to Provisioning Services.

- **Resilience**: Diverse systems are more resilient to exogenous disturbances. Diversity promotes stability, while monocultures tend to make ecosystems unstable.

  o Resilience relates to All Services.

Table 2: Components of biodiversity and examples of their ecosystem services.

Main components of biodiversity	Description	Examples of ecosystem services
Genetic diversity	The variation within and between species' gene pools. It allows species to adapt to changing environments and plays a crucial role in evolution.	Crop improvement, forestry, medicine
Species diversity	The variety of different species that exist in a given area. The number of species in an ecosystem can be an indication of its health, as different species often have different ecological roles.	Pollination, pest control, nutrient cycling
Ecosystem diversity	The variety of different ecosystems, such as forests, grasslands, wetlands, and oceans, that exist on Earth. Each ecosystem has unique characteristics and supports a unique set of species.	Climate regulation, water purification, carbon sequestration
Functional diversity	The variety of ecological functions performed by different species in an ecosystem. It is important because different species perform different roles in the ecosystem, such as predator, prey, decomposer, or pollinator.	Regulating nutrient cycles, controlling pests and diseases, maintaining soil fertility

- **Insurance**: It is associated with the possibility of finding genes in non-commercially used species that can be used to build resistance against lethal diseases affecting other species. Thus, genetic diversity can be used as insurance against catastrophic events or infections.

  ○ Insurance relates mainly to Provisioning and Cultural Services.

- **Knowledge**: Biodiversity can be used as a source of knowledge with which to develop new products in the biotechnology industry or pharmaceuticals.

  ○ Knowledge relates mainly to Provisioning Services.

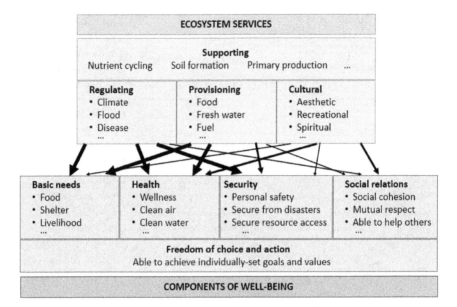

Figure 2:   Ecosystem services and human well-being.

Note: The width of the lines indicates the strength of the linkages.

Overall, these four factors are interconnected and reinforce each other in supporting biodiversity. Figure 2, based on the Millennium Ecosystem Assessment (2005), illustrates the linkages between ecosystem services and the well-being of people.

A process for valuing biodiversity through ecosystem services is shown in Figure 3. What is important in this figure is that it illustrates the need to know how changes in biodiversity affect useful services provided by ecosystems. This is the black box in the figure. Thus, in terms of Figure 3, we need to

- obtain quantifiable value concepts for biodiversity characteristics,
- estimate these values and combine them if possible,
- study policy implications and policy design.

11.2.2.1. *Biodiversity and ecosystem characteristics*

As noted above, maintaining biodiversity enhances certain desirable characteristics of ecosystems.

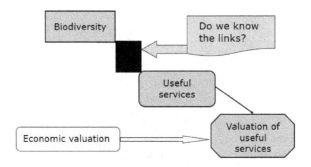

Figure 3: Are there missing links?

(a) Biodiversity and productivity

Total plant biomass is a good proxy for carbon sequestration, pollution prevention, or other desirable ecosystem services. The more diverse a system is, the more closely the traits of some species match those that lead to maximal efficiency and productivity in terms of biomass.

As shown in Tilman *et al.* (2005), when there is competition among species — perennial grassland plant species in this case — for a single resource in a spatially homogeneous and temporally constant environment, increasing species diversity, measured by the number of species, increases total community biomass. The graph of species diversity versus total community biomass in Tilman *et al.* (2005) suggests a monotonically increasing strictly concave function, which looks very similar to a strictly concave production function with one input.

(b) Biodiversity and resilience

Defining the temporal stability of an ecosystem as mean biomass divided by the standard deviation of the temporal variation in its biomass can provide a measure of resilience to external shocks.

For the same case of perennial grassland plant species, the graph of species diversity versus temporal stability in Tilman *et al.* (2005), measured by the ratio of the mean over standard deviation of biomass, suggests monotonically increasing temporal stability as the number of species increases.

(c) Biodiversity and insurance

Greater levels of biodiversity protect systems from unpredictable and irreversible effects. This offers *insurance against catastrophic events.* The existence of "redundant species" provides insurance in cases in which exogenous shocks remove some species from the system. The insurance benefits are also related to the resilience property implying that, after an exogenous shock, the system can return to its initial presumably desirable state and not move to an undesirable basin of attraction. The insurance value is almost wholly an option value.

(d) Biodiversity and knowledge

This is also related to option value. Maintaining biodiversity and protecting against irreversible changes provide the opportunity to study species and gain knowledge that might be used in the future. Thus, the utilitarian value of biodiversity can be located mainly in the potential uses of genetic material.

11.2.2.2. *Biological portfolios*

Preservation of biodiversity can be seen as a way to hold a diverse portfolio of assets with an uncertain payoff.

The concept of *biological portfolios* is related to the investment and management of biodiversity for conservation purposes. It draws an analogy between financial portfolios, where investors diversify their investments across various assets to reduce risk, and the conservation of biodiversity, where efforts are made to protect and manage a diverse range of species and ecosystems to enhance resilience and reduce the risk of biodiversity loss.

An efficient species portfolio is defined by maximizing the expected value from this portfolio over a given time horizon. In efficient portfolios,

- "value" includes use and non-use values,
- the ecosystem manager incurs conservation costs and may receive harvesting revenues,
- the biomass or the "value" of species is modeled as a stochastic process.

The success of biological portfolios depends on careful planning, adaptive management, and the involvement of local communities and relevant stakeholders. Some results indicate the following:

- Expected ecosystem values exist, leading to species portfolios that fully preserve biodiversity.
- The decision to let a species disappear by cutting conservation expenditures implies *losing the option value* to use it in the future.
- A higher option value combined with unchanged conservation costs makes conservation incentives stronger.

11.2.2.3. *Bioprospecting*

Bioprospecting is the process of exploring, collecting, and studying biological resources — such as plants, animals, microorganisms, and other organisms — to discover and develop new products, processes, or applications for various industries.

- Bioprospecting is one market-based mechanism for biodiversity protection with regard, for example, to the search for valuable products such as pharmaceuticals in biological organisms.
- Bioprospecting activities are typically carried out in the so-called "biodiversity hot spots". As shown in Figure 3 in Mutke and Barthlott (2005), hot spots — that is, diversity zones in which species richness measured by the number of vascular plants exceeds 3,000 per 10,000 square km — can be found primarily in Central and South America, South Africa, and South East Asia.
- Can private sector bioprospecting incentives be relied upon for the protection of biological diversity?

(1) The marginal value of the most promising hotspots ranges from \$14/ha (mean estimate) to \$65/ha (upper 5% quantile estimate) (Costello and Ward, 2007).
(2) These values are below what would likely be required for large-scale private-sector conservation via bioprospecting.
(3) *The bioprospecting conservation incentive is insufficient to offset development.*

(4) Therefore, to the extent that biodiversity is a public good, other incentive mechanisms will be required for its protection.

11.2.2.4.   *Valuation through the diversity function*

The diversity function can be used to value and rank conservation plans. It includes the following stages:

- Construct a diversity function from DNA differences among species (e.g., the diversity function for 15 species from the family of cranes in Weitzman (1993)).
- Determine conservation potential which is the increase in expected diversity from making a species completely safe.
- *Design conservation programs to include the combination of species that minimizes the expected diversity loss.*

11.2.2.5.   *Endogenous diversity valuation*

Endogenous biodiversity valuation is a concept used to assign economic value to the biodiversity that exists within a particular ecosystem or region and it is based on the maximization of the total value of the system. Thus, it is not based on DNA distances but rather on the value of services that an ecosystem provides when managed optimally. This is a value function approach in a dynamic programming concept (Brock and Xepapadeas, 2003) and suggests that the DNA distance between two assemblies with different diversity can tend to zero, but the value function difference of the two assemblies can be very large.

An example can be provided by the joint management of Bt-corn and non-Bt-corn:

- Bt-corn and non-Bt-corn are very close genetically.
- With a Bt-corn monoculture, increased resistance of corn borers might decrease future productivity.
- With a Bt-corn and non-Bt-corn polyculture, the value increases because resistance to corn borers is stabilized.

- Biodiversity increases productivity by protecting the group from lethal pests, although the genetic distances are very small. Productivity and the insurance value are captured together.

To summarize, methods to value biodiversity include:

- productivity relations,
- biological portfolio and real options models,
- bioprospecting,
- genetic distance functions,
- endogenous valuation through the value function.

These approaches should be regarded as complementary.

11.2.3. *Approximate valuation using accounting prices*

The methods described in the previous sections can be regarded as "exact" methods based on a rigorous theoretical framework. Given the difficulty in using these methods due to their complexity, an approximate approach can be based on the following observations:

- Biodiversity is essential for the proper functioning of an ecosystem so that the ecosystem retains its ability to provide a flow of supporting, provisioning, regulating, and cultural services.
- The particular contribution to each category of services and to items within each category is an open research area.
- These contributions will determine an economic value for biodiversity.
- Estimation of the contribution could be better accomplished on an ecosystem-specific basis which is focused on changes in an approximate aggregate value of ecosystem services (see Figure 4).

11.2.3.1. *The marginal value of a species*

A formal way to value changes in biodiversity and changes in the value of the ecosystem can be based on the marginal value of a species

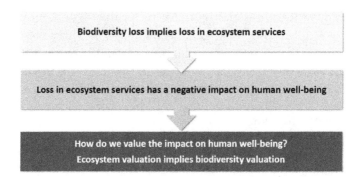

Figure 4: The economic dimension of biodiversity.

considering that the species generates a flow of benefits, or

$$\text{VS}_0 = \int_0^\infty e^{-\rho t} B_t dt, \quad B_t = \sum_{i=1}^n B_{it},$$

where B_{it} is the value associated with ecosystem service i.

The value of the service depends on the set of species $(x_1, \ldots, x_J)$, or

$$B_{it} = F_i(x_{1t}, \ldots, x_{Jt}).$$

Then, the marginal value of species j with respect to service i is $\partial B_{it}/\partial x_{jt}$.

However, unless we know the functional forms, this definition has little operational use. A framework for determining accounting prices and valuing changes in biodiversity associated with productivity, resilience, insurance, and knowledge is presented in Figures 5–10. These figures are based on the idea of comparing the value of a major service provided by an ecosystem before and after the change in biodiversity. In our example, the service is the value of timber which is a provisioning service (Figure 5).

In Figures 6–9, the link between biodiversity characteristics, changes in ecosystem services, and valuations is presented. Figure 10 illustrates a more general way of approximating accounting prices for biodiversity.

In this framework, a cost–benefit rule for a project that preserves biodiversity by increasing species richness can be described as follows: Suppose that a certain project provides gains in terms of species richness of ΔB and the project costs C. Then a cost–benefit rule for accepting the project could be $p_B \Delta B - C > 0$.

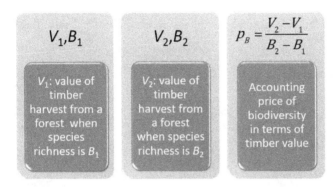

Figure 5: Accounting price for forest biodiversity.

Figure 6: A framework for valuing changes in biodiversity.

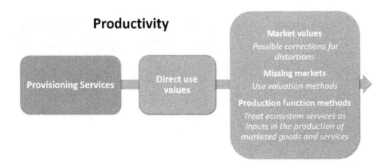

Figure 7: A framework for valuing changes in biodiversity: Productivity.

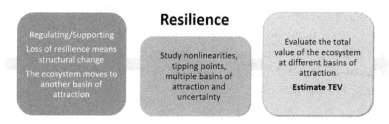

Figure 8: A framework for valuing changes in biodiversity: Resilience.

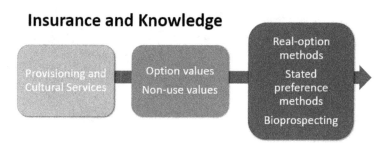

Figure 9: A framework for valuing changes in biodiversity: Insurance and knowledge.

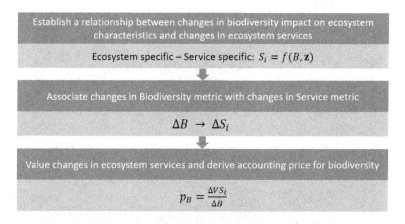

Figure 10: Summary of valuation stages.

11.2.4. *Economic policy for biodiversity management*

The discussion in the previous sections suggests that:

- Biodiversity loss implies loss in value.
- Unregulated private markets cannot prevent these losses.
- Bioprospecting incentives are weak.
  Therefore, there is a need for policy design and choice of policy instruments.

11.2.4.1. *Command-and-control instruments*

Command-and-control policy instruments are regulatory approaches used by governments and authorities to manage and conserve biodiversity and natural resources. These policies involve setting specific rules, standards, or regulations and imposing mandatory requirements on individuals, industries, or organizations to comply with conservation objectives. Examples of command-and-control policy instruments in biodiversity management include:

- Protected sites, protected species, marine or terrestrial reserves, and nature protection areas. For example,
  o NATURA 2000, Birds Directive,
  o US Endangered Species Act (ESA).
  Listing a species under the ESA can be detrimental to species recovery if not combined with substantial government funds. In contrast, listed species *with* such funding tend to improve (Ferraro *et al.*, 2007).
- Refuge strategy: Use non-Bt-corn in a fixed part of total land for resistance management, which is expected to delay the development of pest resistance to Bt-corn.
- Land-set-aside schemes/cross-compliance (Green Common Agricultural Policy, voluntary schemes).

11.2.4.2. *Market-based instruments*

Market-based instruments are economic tools and mechanisms designed to align economic incentives with conservation objectives, thus promoting the sustainable use and conservation of biodiversity. Rather than relying on regulations and enforcement, market-based instruments use market forces and economic incentives to encourage behavior that benefits biodiversity and natural ecosystems. Examples of market-based instruments in biodiversity management are:

- Allocation of property rights which involves assigning ownership or usage rights over natural resources, such as land, water, and wildlife. This approach aims to incentivize individuals and communities to manage these resources sustainably by giving them a sense of ownership and control.
- Tradable development quotas which can be used to allocate development in a way that minimizes environmental impact. They allow countries or entities with well-defined property rights to trade their quotas for development in one area for quotas for development in another area. This can help ensure that development is allocated to areas where it will have the least impact on ecosystems.
- Tradable quota systems in fishery management (bycatch, discards) which aim to prevent overfishing and promote sustainable fisheries.
- Pollution control measures such as the polluter pays principle, green taxes, and tradable emission permits which aim, in general terms, to protect ecosystems from degradation and promote the maintenance of biodiversity. The recycling of the revenues generated by these measures can be used to create biodiversity conservation funds.
- Entrance fees that visitors pay in order to access protected areas, which help support park management and conservation efforts.
- Payments for recreational activities which refer to financial transactions where individuals or groups pay to engage in various leisure and recreational pursuits or experiences.
- Payments for ecosystem services which involve compensating landowners or communities for maintaining or restoring ecosystems that provide valuable services, such as clean water, carbon sequestration, or wildlife habitats.
- Differentiated land use taxes which involve applying varying tax rates based on the land's intended use or its ecological value to incentivize landowners to use their property in ways that support

biodiversity conservation and discourage activities that may lead to environmental degradation.

- Liability and fines through which individuals or organizations that damage ecosystems and biodiversity can be held liable for their actions and pay penalties according to the law.

11.2.4.3. *Policy design for biodiversity: Research issues*

Efficient biodiversity policy design should be based on the following:

- Establishing a relation between biodiversity/conservation policies and some benefit/cost criterion. This in turn requires methods to value changes in biodiversity.
- Proper valuation requires knowledge of the links between biodiversity and flows of benefits. This is a formidable task which should be central to the relevant research agendas.

Moreover, efficient policies to protect biodiversity should take into account a number of important issues:

- Ecological and economic systems are linked coevolving systems, as shown in Chapter 10. In this context, command-and-control might not be the welfare-maximizing policy. Do we need to consider welfare-maximizing policies and concentrate on market-based instruments?
- Ecological and economic systems are characterized by nonlinearities, multiple basins of attraction, thresholds and tipping points, hysteresis, and irreversibilities. How do these factors affect policy design?
- What is the impact of deep structural uncertainty and aversion to risk and ambiguity on policies incorporating the precautionary principle and safety minimum standards?
- Asymmetric information: Free riding and moral hazard. How do we design policies? Is there a need for mechanism design?
- How should these factors be taken into account in biodiversity valuation?
- What do these factors imply for biodiversity policy design?

The answers to the questions posed above are not only scientifically interesting but also vital for the preservation of biodiversity.

11.3. Resource Conservation: The Noah's Ark Problem

11.3.1. *The problem*

The problem of maximizing biodiversity under a hard budget constraint can be regarded from the point of view of the "Noah's Ark problem" mentioned earlier. Weitzman (1998) modeled the problem in terms of Noah's Ark which would preserve the maximum diversity of species from the flood or, alternatively, in terms of libraries containing a maximum diversity of books.

Noah's Ark — which is a metaphor for the budget — has a limited capacity of B. In the Bible, the Ark has a capacity of 300 length $\times$ 50 width $\times$ 30 height = 450,000 cubits^3 (about 1.5 million cubic feet), which would be B. Thus in the metaphor, B is the total budget available for biodiversity preservation.

It is assumed that there are n existing species, indexed $i = 1, 2, \ldots, n$ and that the arrival of the flood is known to Noah. The set of all n species is denoted as S. An Ark is available to help save some species which will enter the Ark and remain there during the flood. The entire set S might be saved if resources were unlimited, that is, if the size of the Ark approached infinity.

Because the resources are not unlimited, Noah has to decide which species from set S should be saved, given the limited capacity of the Ark. Society faces a similar problem of choice: Which species are to be protected more — and which less — when there are not enough resources to fully protect everything?

If species i is not put on board the Ark, or is left unprotected in the real world, its probability of surviving the flood, or human expansion into the natural world, is $\check{P}_i$. If, on the other hand, species i is boarded on the Ark, or protected through a conservation program in the real world, its survival probability is enhanced to $\bar{P}_i$. Thus, boarding the Ark or investing in conservation increases the survival probability of a species.

The choice of life or death for a species can be modeled by setting $\check{P}_i = 0$ and $\bar{P}_i = 1$. The old testament version of the problem is most likely closest to the life or death setup.

The choice of survival probabilities implies the restriction:

$$0 \le \check{P}_i \le \bar{P}_i \le 1.$$

On the "cost" side of the problem, it is assumed that if a species i is boarded, it takes up some of the limited space on the Ark. Let this space coefficient be denoted as C_i for species i. Since overall space is limited, the amount of space a species occupies represents the cost of having a species in the Ark. For the biblical Ark metaphor, C_i is measured in units of cubits. In the real world, C_i would represent the cost of the project that increases the protection or the survival probability of species i.

11.3.2. *Conservation*

Following Weitzman (1998), let the expected diversity function of the species assembly be $W(P)$ and the expected utility of the species themselves be $U(P)$ The objective is to pick conservation policies which are equivalent to choosing survival probabilities that maximize the sum of the expected diversity function plus the expected utility of the species, taking into account the relevant budget constraint and the constraints on P.

The mathematical problem is

$$\max_{P_i}[W(P_i) + U(P_i)]$$

subject to the n individual probability constraints

$$\check{P}_i \le P_i \le \bar{P}_i \quad \text{for all} \quad i$$

and the overall budget constraint

$$\sum_{i=1}^{n} C_i \left(\frac{P_i - \check{P}_i}{\bar{P}_i - \check{P}_i} \right) = B.$$

11.3.3. *Distinctiveness and conservation*

Distinctiveness: The "distinctiveness" D_i of species i is roughly its distance from its closest resembling species. The distance of a species i from a set S of species is defined as

$$D(i, S) \equiv \min_{j \in S} D(i, j).$$

The change in expected diversity from a change in the survival probability P_i of this species is given by the distance:

$$\frac{\partial W}{\partial P_i} = D_i.$$

11.3.4. *Ranking alternatives*

Weitzman (1998) shows that the ranking of conservation alternatives can be based on the criterion:

$$R_i = [D_i + U_i] \left(\frac{\Delta P_i}{C_i} \right),$$

where ΔP_i is the change in the survival probability of species i that costs C_i.

There exists a cut-off rate R^* such that

$R_i > R^* \rightarrow P_i = \bar{P}_i$: species i is boarded, or protected by the conservation program,

$R_i < R^* \rightarrow P_i = \check{P}_i$: species i is not boarded, or not covered by the conservation program.

11.3.5. *Conservation of biological diversity: An example*

Solow *et al.* (1993) discuss the measurement of biological diversity and provide a simple application of one approach to the conservation of biological diversity in the crane family. Their approach is based on the assumption that reductions in biodiversity occur only when species become extinct. They use 14 crane species and their assumed probability of extinction at the time of the study, p, which ranges from 0.1 to 0.9. For the purposes of their application, Solow *et al.*

Table 3: Extinction probabilities for selected crane species.

No.	Common name	Latin name	p
1	South African	*Balearica regulorum*	0.1
...			
5	Siberian	*Grus leucogeranus*	0.9
...			
9	White-naped	*Grus vipio*	0.7
...			
13	Black-necked	*Grus nigricollis*	0.5
14	Japanese	*Grus japonensis*	0.7

Data source: Solow *et al.* (1993).

assume that species classified as endangered have a probability of extinction (p) of 0.9, vulnerable species have a $p = 0.7$, indeterminate species have a $p = 0.5$, and "safe" species have a $p = 0.1$. Of the 14 crane species, a total of six have a p of 0.5, 0.7, or 0.9; the remaining eight have a $p = 0.1$. Table 3 shows data for a selected five of the 14 species, taken from Table 1 of Solow *et al.* (1993).

Using genetic distances between cranes based on DNA–DNA hybridization, which range from 0.15 to 4.05, Solow *et al.* (1993) calculate and compare the loss in expected diversity from conserving various combinations of crane species threatened with extinction. Assuming that, due to cost constraints, a conservation program must be limited to just three species, they compare the value of conserving different combinations of the six threatened crane species (i.e., $p \geq 0.5$), in order to determine which combination of three threatened species would minimize the expected loss of biodiversity. Table 4 provides an example of the differences in the value of biodiversity loss of conserving species (5, 13, 14), as compared to species (5, 9, 13) and species (9, 13, 14), with the purpose of providing guidance in designing conservation policy for threatened species.

The approaches to biodiversity valuation described in this section provide some insights into an issue which is conceptually difficult but which is associated with high values generated by biodiversity

Table 4: Example of comparison of biodiversity loss from conserving different combinations of three threatened crane species.

Combinations of threatened crane species	$E_C(D_P(X))$ (Loss of expected biodiversity)
5, 13, 14	−1.755
5, 9, 13	−1.678
9, 13, 14	−2.361

Data source: Solow *et al.* (1993).

in ecosystems. These values have strong public good characteristics and their estimation using market-based approaches is very difficult, as the results about bioprospecting demonstrated.

References

Brock, W. A., Xepapadeas, A. (2003). Valuing biodiversity from an economic perspective: A unified economic, ecological and genetic approach. *American Economic Review*, 93, 1597–1614.

Convention on Biological Diversity (2001). *Global Biodiversity Outlook 1*. Montreal, Canada.

Costello, C., Ward, M. B. (2007). Search, bioprospecting and biodiversity conservation. *Journal of Environmental Economics and Management*, 53(2), 158–179.

Dasgupta, P. (2021). *The Economics of Biodiversity: The Dasgupta Review*. HM Treasury.

Ferraro, P., McIntosh, C., Ospina, M. (2007). The effectiveness of the US endangered species act: An econometric analysis using matching methods. *Journal of Environmental Economics and Management*, 54, 245–261.

Heal, G. (2000). *Nature and the Marketplace: Capturing the Value of Ecosystem Services*. Washington, DC: Island Press.

Jordà, O., Knoll, K., Kuvshinov, D., Schularick, M., Taylor, A. M. (2019). The rate of return on everything, 1870–2015. *The Quarterly Journal of Economics*, 134, 1225–1298.

Millennium Ecosystem Assessment (2005). *Ecosystems and Human-Well-Being*, Vol. 3, *Policy Responses Synthesis*. Washington, DC: Island Press.

Mutke, J., Barthlott, W. (2005). Patterns of vascular plant diversity at continental to global scales. *Biologiske Skrifter*, 55, 521–531.

Richardson, J., Steffen W., Lucht, W., Bendtsen, J., Cornell, S. E., *et.al.* (2023). Earth beyond six of nine Planetary Boundaries. *Science Advances*, 9, 37.

Solow, A., Polasky, S., Broadus, G. (1993). On the measurement of biological diversity. *Journal of Environmental Economics and Management*, 24, 60–68.

Steffen, W., Grinevald, J., Crutzen, P., McNeill, J. (2011). The anthropocene: Conceptual and historical perspectives. *Philosophical Transactions of the Royal Society A: Mathematical, Physical and Engineering Sciences*, 369(1938), 842–867.

Tilman, D., Polasky, S., Lehman, C. (2005). Diversity, productivity and temporal stability in the economies of humans and nature. *Journal of Environmental Economics and Management*, 49, 405–426.

Weitzman, M. L. (1992). On diversity. *Quarterly Journal of Economics*, 107, 363–405.

Weitzman, M. L. (1993). What to preserve? An application of diversity theory to crane conservation. *Quarterly Journal of Economics*, 108, 157–183.

Weitzman, M. L. (1998). The Noah's ark problem. *Econometrica*, 66, 1279–1298.

Part 4

Sustainability

Chapter 12

Defining and Measuring Sustainability

12.1. Sustainable Development

- The Brundtland Report (Brundtland, 1987) defines sustainable development as *development that meets the needs of the present without compromising the ability of future generations to meet their own needs.*
- The study of sustainable development as a target to be attained by modern societies is an issue of vital importance. It gives rise to a number of fundamental questions which need to be addressed.

12.1.1. *Fundamental questions*

- How can we know whether or not the actions of present generations will undermine the well-being of future generations and how can we measure the wealth of nations?
- How can we tell whether the development of a country is sustainable or not?
- What policies promote sustainability and what can firms and individuals do to help achieve sustainability?
  - For example, how can universal access to modern energy services promote development and sustainability targets?
- Furthermore, how can we assess whether the natural and environmental resources of a country are being used in a way that will provide fair benefits across the same or future generations?

- Are sustainability objectives and associated policies compatible with stabilization, development, and growth objectives?
- Is green growth a desirable and attainable target?
- Would a green economy help stabilize economies during recessions?

12.1.2. *Defining sustainability*

To answer the questions above and to make the Brundtland Report's sustainability definition operational, in the sense of being suitable for empirical applications, several "second level" definitions of sustainability have been developed over time. These include:

(1) Achieving constant utility (Solow, 1974; Hartwick, 1977).
(2) The agent's utility is forever non-declining from t onwards (Pearce *et al.*, 1990; Pezzey, 1992, 1997).
(3) Non-declining social welfare or, equivalently, non-declining intergenerational well-being, that is, avoiding any decline in intergenerational social welfare either from time t forever onwards or, much less demandingly, just at time t (Riley, 1980; Dasgupta and Mäler, 2001; Pemberton and Ulph, 2001; Arrow *et al.*, 2003).

An encompassing definition based on definition 3 is:

Definition 1: In the context of the non-declining welfare or well-being criterion, sustainable development can be defined equivalently as the maintenance of the value of the economy's productive base. Each generation should bequeath to each succeeding generation at least as large of a productive base, in value terms, as it inherited from its predecessors.

This definition can be used as a basis for developing a sustainability-promoting cost–benefit rule.

12.1.3. *Productive base and accounting prices*

The productive base which determines social well-being or comprehensive wealth consists of the economy's assets, which may include the following:

○ manufactured or produced capital,

- human capital and knowledge,
- natural capital,
- social capital, and
- health capital.

We need to value the assets that constitute the productive base in a way that is consistent with economic theory and, at the same time, provides the necessary structure and information to conduct sustainability cost–benefit analysis.

Definition 2: In the context of sustainability, an accounting price for an asset measures the change in the present value of future well-being from a change in the stock of this asset.

Definition 3: Positive genuine or comprehensive investment increases well-being, productive base, and comprehensive wealth. Thus, if genuine investment is non-decreasing over time, then well-being and social welfare are also non-decreasing, and development is sustainable.

12.1.4. *Weak and strong sustainability*

12.1.4.1. *Weak sustainability*

Linking sustainable development with the increase in the value of the productive base defines the *weak sustainability* concept, since it allows for any of the assets to increase and decrease as long as the net change valued at accounting prices is positive (Arrow *et al.*, 2003, 2012). Thus, development is weakly sustainable if the value of the productive base of the economy valued at accounting prices is non-declining at a given point in time.

12.1.4.2. *Strong sustainability*

The strong sustainability concept stresses that, in order to attain sustainability, it is necessary not to reduce natural capital in physical terms. This condition can be interpreted in different ways. One approach is to define strong sustainability as the state at which natural capital is used at rates that do not exceed natural regeneration rates. Another approach is that natural assets should not be reduced below some critical levels:

- Pearce *et al.* (1996) give an example of how the approach based on the concept of critical natural assets might operate in the case of a tropical rainforest. In their example, the preservation of some amount of the forest is considered to be essential for the well-being of humanity in the long run. Thus, a strong sustainability criterion would require that the size of the forest not fall below the critical level.
- If analysts were able to monetize critical natural assets, and thus natural forest, then the strong sustainability perspective could be considered a special case of weak sustainability. Capturing the notion of the value of a critical amount of a resource or natural asset in terms of accounting prices implies that

$$p_i \to \infty \text{ as } X_i \to X_i^*,$$

where X_i^* is the critical amount of the natural asset. In this case, as a policy change reduces the forest toward the critical level, the natural capital component of the productive base will tend to minus infinity. Thus, the productive base will be declining and development is not sustainable. The critical factor in this case is the correct calculation of accounting prices. Therefore, the use of accounting prices unifies the weak and strong sustainability criteria.
- Another approach for selecting projects subject to a strong sustainability constraint suggests that the net effect on the environment of projects in a portfolio of projects should be greater than or equal to zero.
- For cost–benefit tests, a strong sustainability constraint could be that when choosing projects that maximize net benefits, the aggregate environmental costs of all n projects that are selected for inclusion in the portfolio should be non-positive in each time period, t. That is,

$$\sum_{i=1}^{n} E_{it} \leq 0 \quad \text{for all } t.$$

- A more flexible strong sustainability constraint which might be imposed is that the net environmental effect of all projects in a portfolio should be non-positive over some longer time horizon T, where $T > t$ (Pearce *et al.*, 2006). That is,

$$\sum_{t=1}^{T} \sum_{i=1}^{n} E_{it} \leq 0.$$

The simultaneous requirements of positive net benefits and strong sustainability for a project might lead decision-making into difficulties. Assume that EB_i represents the economic — that is, the non-environmental — benefits of two projects, $i = 1, 2$, and E_i represents the environmental benefits. Then decision-making can be inconclusive under strong sustainability criteria in certain cases, as illustrated in Table 1.

Integration of strong sustainability into cost–benefit analysis can be obtained by using the "shadow or compensating projects approach" (Pearce *et al.*, 2006). According to this approach, projects that result in environmental improvements overcompensate for projects that create environmental damage.

It should be noted that if the environmental costs were to be valued in the correct accounting prices, then they could be incorporated into the project's cash flow. Then, net benefits would contain both strictly economic benefits and correctly valued environmental costs and the conflict shown in Table 1 would not emerge. The project would be accepted or rejected using standard cost–benefit criteria.

Table 1: Strong sustainability and decision-making.

Economic benefit	Environmental benefit	Decision
$EB_1 + E_1 > 0$	$E_1 > 0$	Accept
$EB_2 + E_2 > 0$	$E_2 < 0$	?
$EB_1 + E_1 < 0$	$E_1 > 0$	?
$EB_2 + E_2 < 0$	$E_2 < 0$	Reject

12.1.4.3. *Green net national product*

When environmental goods and services are taken into account, the concept of national product along an (optimal) development path of a single economy includes *goods* and *bads* (including environmental liabilities, i.e., degradation of environmental stocks, such as clean water) that negatively affect utility or well-being. A general expression for a (net) national product aggregate or *green net national product* (gNNP) is

$$\text{gNNP} = C + \sum_{i=1}^{n} p_i \dot{X}_i = C + S_g.$$

Thus, gNNP is equivalent to consumption C plus the sum of net changes in assets $\left(\sum_{i=1}^{n} p_i \dot{X}_i \right)$, each valued at its shadow price, p_i. Alternatively, this can be written as consumption plus adjusted net or genuine (or comprehensive) savings, S_g.

The changes in assets, $\dot{X}_i = \frac{dX_i(t)}{dt}$, might refer to net investments in produced, human, natural, social, and health capital, that is, investments in the stocks that constitute the productive base of the economy.

12.1.5. *Sustainability and comprehensive or inclusive wealth*

Following Arrow *et al.* (2012), let *intergenerational well-being* at time t be $V(t)$, defined as

$$V(t) = \int_t^{\infty} e^{-\delta(s-t)} U(C(s)) ds, \tag{1}$$

where $U(C(s))$ is the economy-wide utility flow and $C(s)$ is a vector of consumption flows at time s. Thus, intergenerational well-being is the discounted flow of the utilities (or felicities) of current and future generations. Let $K(s)$ be the vector of capital assets.

An economic forecast at t is the pair of vector functions $\{C(s), K(s)\}$ for $s \geq t$, $K(s) = (K_1(s), \ldots, K_n(s))$. Assume that the integral in expression (1) converges for the forecast, then the following definition (Arrow *et al.*, 2012) holds:

Economic development is sustained at t if dV/dt ≥ 0.

This can be shown as follows:

- Given $K(t)$, then $K(s)$ and $C(s)$, and therefore $U(C(s))$, are determined for all future times $s \geq t$. Hence from equation (1), $V(t)$ is determined as well. Therefore, we can write

$$V(t) = V(K(t), t). \tag{2}$$

- Differentiating $V(t)$ with respect to t in (2), and using the definition for sustained development, yields a criterion for sustainable development at t:

$$\frac{dV(t)}{dt} = \frac{\partial V}{\partial t} + \sum_i \frac{\partial V(t)}{\partial K_i(t)} \frac{\partial K_i(t)}{\partial t} \geq 0, \tag{3}$$

where $p_i = \frac{\partial V(t)}{\partial K_i(t)}$ is the accounting or the shadow price of the asset (stock of capital) i at time t.

12.1.5.1. *Defining inclusive/comprehensive wealth*

Let $r(t) = \frac{\partial V}{\partial t}$, which can be regarded as the accounting price of time, which in this context reflects the evolution of exogenous changes, such as changes in total factor productivity (TFP).

Definition 4: An economy's comprehensive or inclusive wealth is the value of all its capital assets or its productive base valued in accounting prices. That is,

$$W(t) = r(t)t + \sum_i p_i(t) K_i(t). \tag{4}$$

A small perturbation to an economy increases (decreases) intergenerational well-being if and only if — holding shadow prices constant — it increases (decreases) comprehensive wealth.

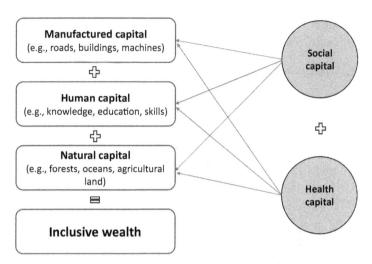

Figure 1:   Inclusive wealth and the productive base. The UNEP approach with social and health capital.

The change in comprehensive wealth is defined as

$$\Delta V(t) = \left[\frac{\partial V}{\partial t}\right] \Delta t + \sum_i \left[\frac{\partial V(t)}{\partial K_i}\right] \Delta K_i(t)$$

$$= r(t)\Delta t + \sum_i p_i(t)\Delta K_i(t) = \Delta W. \qquad (5)$$

Figure 1 shows the components of inclusive wealth and their interactions with social and health capital.

Figure 2 presents the evolution of inclusive wealth per capita in selected high and upper-middle-income countries, while Figure 3 shows a similar evolution in selected low and lower-middle-income countries. In the countries shown in Figure 2, with the possible exception of Brazil, inclusive wealth per capita is non-declining. On the other hand, in Figure 3, with the exception of the Philippines, inclusive wealth per capita seems to be declining or flat.

Figure 4 depicts the breakdown of global average wealth in terms of natural, human, health, and produced capital. It is interesting to

Defining and Measuring Sustainability

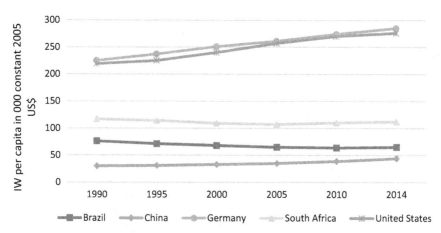

Figure 2: Inclusive wealth per capita of selected high- and upper-middle-income countries (in thousands of constant 2005 US$), 1990–2014.

Data source: Managi and Kumar (2018).

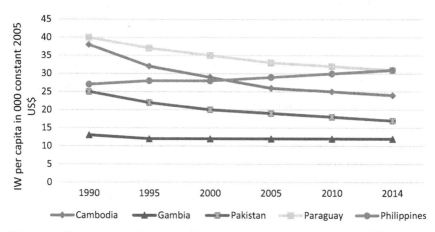

Figure 3: Inclusive wealth per capita of selected low- and lower-middle-income countries (in thousands of constant 2005 US$), 1990–2014.

Data source: Managi and Kumar (2018).

note that more than half of global wealth (59%) is induced by human capital.

In order to provide some insights into the size and the composition of inclusive wealth per capita, Tables 2 and 3 present data for

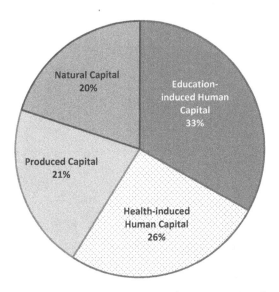

Figure 4: Global average wealth composition (mean 1990–2014).
Data source: Managi and Kumar (2018).

selected countries in different income categories. There is a striking difference in the level of human capital per capita between high-income countries and low-income countries.

12.1.6. *Comprehensive/inclusive investment or genuine savings*

In Equation (5), $p_i(t)\Delta K_i(t)$ is the accounting (shadow) value of net investment in asset i and $r(t)$ is the accounting price of time at t. Letting $I_i(t) = \Delta K_i(t)/\Delta t$, we can re-write (5) as

$$\Delta V(t) = r(t)\Delta t + \sum p_i(t)I_i(t)\Delta t. \qquad (6)$$

Let $r(t)\Delta t + \sum p_i(t)I_i(t)\Delta t = S_g$, or — when it can be assumed that $r(t) \approx 0$ — $\sum p_i(t)I_i(t)\Delta t = S_g$. This aggregate is referred to as **comprehensive investment** or **genuine savings** or **adjusted net savings**.

If $S_g > 0$, then $\Delta V(t) > 0$, and the sustainability criterion is satisfied, as shown in Arrow *et al.* (2012).

Table 2: Inclusive wealth per capita of selected high- and upper-middle-income countries, by type of capital (all values in thousands of constant 2005 US$).

Country		1990	1995	2000	2005	2010	2014
Brazil	PC	12.6	12.7	13.2	13.3	14.6	16.7
	NC	50.2	45.3	40.9	37.3	34.4	32.9
	HC	12.8	13.4	13.8	14.4	15.0	15.5
	Total IW	**75.6**	**71.4**	**67.9**	**65.0**	**64.0**	**65.1**
China	PC	1.4	2.0	3.0	4.9	8.6	13.2
	NC	8.4	7.8	7.2	6.6	6.2	5.8
	HC	20.3	21.6	22.5	23.5	24.5	25.2
	Total IW	**30.1**	**31.4**	**32.7**	**35.0**	**39.3**	**44.2**
Germany	PC	90.8	101.9	114.1	123.6	135.1	145.1
	NC	20.6	19.3	18.6	18.0	17.6	17.4
	HC	114.0	115.9	117.9	118.9	120.9	122.6
	Total IW	**225.4**	**237.1**	**250.6**	**260.5**	**273.6**	**285.1**
South Africa	PC	13.6	12.7	12.3	13.0	15.1	16.6
	NC	13.7	11.8	9.9	8.7	7.6	6.7
	HC	89.9	89.2	86.5	85.7	87.8	88.8
	Total IW	**117.2**	**113.7**	**108.7**	**107.4**	**110.5**	**112.1**
United States	PC	82.8	91.8	108.2	127.0	140.3	148.7
	NC	44.0	40.1	36.8	34.5	32.4	29.8
	HC	91.7	93.3	94.9	95.7	97.4	98.0
	Total IW	**218.5**	**225.2**	**239.9**	**257.2**	**270.1**	**276.5**

Notes: PC: Produced capital per capita. NC: Natural capital per capita. HC: Human capital per capita.
Data source: Managi and Kumar (2018).

12.1.7. *Comprehensive wealth: An estimable measure — The World Bank approach*

Hamilton and Hartwick (2005) developed an approach for estimating national wealth for a competitive economy in which output is produced by produced capital, human capital, and a natural resource (natural capital) with constant returns to scale production function, or

$$F = F(K, H, R),$$

where K is the produced capital, H is the human capital, and the natural resource flow is R. In a competitive economy, the interest

Table 3: Inclusive wealth per capita of selected low- and lower-middle-income countries, by type of capital (in thousands of constant 2005 US$).

Country		1990	1995	2000	2005	2010	2014
Cambodia	PC	0.4	0.4	0.5	0.7	1.0	1.4
	NC	27.5	21.8	17.8	15.1	13.2	11.8
	HC	9.9	10.1	10.3	10.3	10.7	10.9
	Total IW	**37.8**	**32.3**	**28.6**	**26.1**	**24.9**	**24.1**
Gambia	PC	0.7	0.8	0.9	1.3	1.4	1.4
	NC	6.0	4.3	3.7	3.0	2.5	2.1
	HC	6.5	6.8	7.2	7.6	8.0	8.4
	Total IW	**13.2**	**11.9**	**11.8**	**11.9**	**11.9**	**11.9**
Pakistan	PC	1.5	1.6	1.7	1.7	1.9	1.8
	NC	13.5	10.6	8.4	6.6	5.1	4.0
	HC	9.6	9.8	10.1	10.4	10.9	11.3
	Total IW	**24.6**	**22.0**	**20.2**	**18.7**	**17.9**	**17.1**
Paraguay	PC	4.3	4.8	4.8	4.7	4.9	5.5
	NC	27.2	23.1	21.1	18.6	17.1	15.2
	HC	8.8	9.1	9.5	9.9	10.4	10.6
	Total IW	**40.3**	**37.0**	**35.4**	**33.2**	**32.4**	**31.3**
Philippines	PC	2.9	3.0	3.3	3.5	3.8	4.2
	NC	2.3	2.0	1.8	1.7	1.5	1.4
	HC	8.8	9.1	9.5	9.9	10.4	10.6
	Total IW	**14.0**	**14.1**	**14.6**	**15.1**	**15.7**	**16.2**

Notes: PC: Produced capital per capita. NC: Natural capital per capita. HC: Human capital per capita.
Data source: Managi and Kumar (2018).

rate r is equal to the marginal product of capital and comprehensive wealth is given by

$$W(t) = K(t) + H(t) + S(t) = \int_0^\infty C(s)e^{\int_t^s r(z)dz}ds.$$

This definition of comprehensive wealth can be measured either by adding up asset values K, H (produced and human capital) and S (natural resource stock) or by measuring the present value of consumption C along the competitive development path. The intuition behind this approach is that, in the long run, a country must consume within its possibilities, which are given by the sum of all its assets or its productive base.

12.1.8. *Comprehensive vs inclusive wealth*

Arrow *et al.* (2012) are critical of the World Bank's approach to deriving an empirical estimate of total wealth because they regard the implicit assumption in the calculation of comprehensive wealth — that consumption grows at a constant positive rate — as unrealistic.

An alternative approach to wealth accounting adopted in the *Inclusive Wealth Report 2014* (UNU-IHDP and UNEP, 2014) is to estimate the aggregate value of major wealth components using shadow prices. This average is called the Inclusive Wealth Index.

A comparison of per capita comprehensive wealth and inclusive wealth in selected countries is presented in Figures 5 and 6. A comparison of the two graphs seems to indicate that natural capital

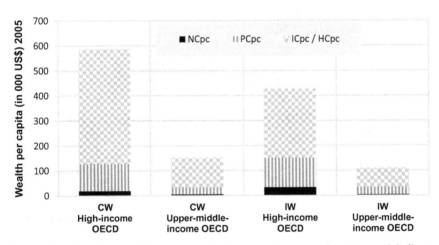

Figure 5:   Comparison of measurement of per capita comprehensive wealth (bars on the left) and inclusive wealth (bars on the right) in OECD high- and upper-middle-income countries, in 2005 values.

Notes: CW: Comprehensive wealth measurement used by the World Bank. IW: Inclusive wealth measurement used in *Inclusive Wealth 2014 Report*. *NCpc*: Natural capital per capita. *PCpc*: Produced capital per capita. *ICpc*: Intangible capital per capita (used in the Comprehensive Wealth scenario). *HCpc*: Human capital per capita (used in the Inclusive Wealth scenario).

Data source: Engelbrecht (2016).

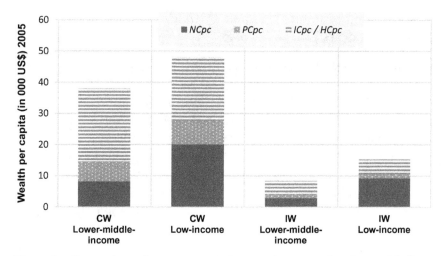

Figure 6: Comparison of measurement of per capita comprehensive wealth (bars on the left) and inclusive wealth (bars on the right) in low- and lower-middle-income countries, in 2005 values.

Notes: See notes for Figure 5.

Data source: Engelbrecht (2016).

contributes more to total wealth per capita in the lower-income countries than in the higher-income countries.

12.1.9. *Sustainability over an interval of time and TFP impact*

Arrow *et al.* (2012) define a local measure of sustainability between $s = 0$ and $s = T$ as

$$V(T) - V(0) = \int_0^T r(s)ds + \sum_i [p_i(t)K_i(t) - p_i(0)K_i(0)]$$

$$- \int_0^T \left[\sum_i \frac{dp_i(s)}{ds} K_i(s) \right] ds. \qquad (7)$$

Equation (7) indicates that, to correctly assess whether intergenerational well-being has increased between two dates, the capital gains on the assets that have accrued over the interval should be deducted from the difference in wealth between the dates. For a short time interval, under the assumption of no capital gains and approximately constant accounting prices, Equation (7) can be approximated as

$$V(T) - V(0) \approx \sum_i [p_i(K_i(T) - K_i(0))].$$

If $V(T) - V(0) \geq 0$, it can be stated that development in the time interval $[0, T]$ was sustainable.

To study the adjustments necessary in comprehensive savings if TFP is present, let $Y(t)$ denote aggregate output at t. Suppose $Y(t) = A(t)F(K(t))$, where F is a constant returns to scale production function and $A(t)$ is TFP at t.

Let γ be the rate of growth of TFP, that is, $((dA/dt)/A)$. It can be shown (Arrow *et al.*, 2012) that if the economy is in a steady state,

$$\frac{\partial V}{\partial t} = \frac{\gamma q_A(t) A(t)}{\sum_i p_i(t) K_i(t)},$$

where $q_A(t)$ is the shadow price of $A(t)$. If the rate of national savings is small, the factor $\frac{q_A(t)A(t)}{\sum_i p_i(t)K_i(t)}$ can be shown to equal one approximately. In this case, comprehensive investment is defined as

$$S_g = \gamma \Delta t + \sum_i p_i(t) I_i(t) \Delta t = \Delta V(t).$$

12.1.10. *Population change*

Up to this point, the sustainability criteria were developed under the assumption of constant population. Arrow *et al.* (2012) developed the sustainability criteria under time-varying population. Let $P(s)$ denote population at time s. Then intergenerational well-being can be defined as

$$V(t) = \frac{\int_t^\infty e^{-\delta(s-t)} P(s) U(c(s)) ds}{\int_t^\infty e^{-\delta(s-t)} P(s) ds},$$

where $c(s)$ represents per capita consumption at time s.

Let $k_i(t) = K_i(t)/P(t)$ represent the per capita stock of asset i and let $k(t)$ be the vector of per capita stocks. Then, we have the following:

Development is sustained at t if, and only if, when valued at constant accounting prices, comprehensive wealth per capita is non-decreasing at t.

12.1.11. *Evidence*

Following the estimates of Arrow *et al.* (2012), Tables 4–7 present components of comprehensive investment and growth of per capita comprehensive wealth using China (Tables 4 and 5) and Brazil (Tables 6 and 7) as examples.

Tables 8 and 9 present comprehensive investment and growth of per capita comprehensive wealth, which include health capital.

Table 10 presents the sensitivity of growth rates of per capita comprehensive wealth to the social cost of carbon, the discount rate for additional years of life, the inclusion/exclusion of health capital, and the value of a statistical life for China (Table 10(a)) and Brazil (Table 10(b)).

12.2. Sustainability: Measurement Issues

12.2.1. *Measurement of comprehensive investment or genuine savings*

As has been shown, the quantity

$$\sum p_i(t)I_i(t)\Delta t = S_g$$

is referred to as *comprehensive investment* or *genuine savings* or *adjusted net savings*.

- If $S_g > 0$, then the change in the intergenerational well-being and comprehensive wealth at t are positive (that is, $\Delta V(t) > 0$, $\Delta W > 0$) and the sustainability criterion is satisfied.
- An advantage of using comprehensive savings as an indicator of sustainability is that sustainability, resource depletion, and environmental changes can be incorporated, data for most of its components can be obtained without particular difficulties, and the concept can be understood by practitioners.

Table 4: An example of components of comprehensive investment in China (in billions of 2000 US$).

| | China | | | | | |
	Natural capital	Human capital	Reproducible capital	Oil net capital gains	Carbon damages	Total
1995 capital stock	3,854.52	8,492.93	3,706.23			16,053.680
2000 capital stock	3,847.62	9,394.69	6,471.69			19,398.916
Change 1995–2000	**−6.90**	**901.76**	**2,765.46**	**−305.80**	**−9.284**	**3,345.236**
% change	−0.18%	10.62%	74.62%			20.84%
Growth rate	−0.048%	2.04%	11.79%			**3.86%**

Data source: Arrow *et al.* (2012).

Table 5: Percentage growth rates of per capita comprehensive wealth in China, adjusted for technological change.

China

(1) Comprehensive wealth growth rate	(2) Population growth rate	(3) Per capita comprehensive wealth growth rate, accounting for population growth [(1)−(2)]	(4) TFP growth rate	(5) Per capita comprehensive wealth growth rate, accounting for TFP growth [(3) + (4)]	(6) Per capita GDP growth rate
3.86	0.94	2.92	2.71	5.63	7.60

Data source: Arrow *et al.* (2012).

Table 6: An example of components of comprehensive investment in Brazil (in billions of 2000 US$).

	Brazil					
	Natural capital	Human capital	Reproducible capital	Oil net capital gains	Carbon damages	Total
1995 capital stock	2,688.40	7,157.81	1,728.80			11,575.010
2000 capital stock	2,619.42	8,248.34	1,756.91			12,463.094
Change 1995–2000	−68.98	1,090.53	28.11	**−119.05**	**−42.526**	**888.084**
% change	−2.57%	15.24%	1.63%			7.67%
Growth rate	−0.52%	2.88%	0.32%			**1.49%**

Data source: Arrow *et al.* (2012).

Table 7:   Percentage growth rates of per capita comprehensive wealth in Brazil, adjusted for technological change.

Brazil

(1) Comprehensive wealth growth rate	(2) Population growth rate	(3) Per capita comprehensive wealth growth rate, accounting for population growth $[(1) - (2)]$	(4) TFP growth rate	(5) Per capita comprehensive wealth growth rate, accounting for TFP growth $[(3) + (4)]$	(6) Per capita GDP growth rate
1.49	1.50	−0.01	0.15	0.14	0.50

Data source: Arrow *et al.* (2012).

Table 8: An example of per capita components of comprehensive investment including health, in China (in 2000 US$).

	Natural capital	Human capital	Reproducible capital	Health capital	Oil net capital gains	Carbon damages	Total
1995 capital stock	3,199	7,049	3,076	1,710,857			1,724,181
2000 capital stock	3,047	7,440	5,126	1,719,892			1,735,256
Change 1995–2000	**−152**	**392**	**2,049**	**9,035**	**−242**	**−7**	**11,075**
% change	−4.75%	5.55%	66.62%	0.53%			0.64%
Growth rate	−0.97%	1.09%	10.75%	0.11%			**0.13%**

Data source: Arrow et al. (2012).

Table 9: An example of per capita components of comprehensive investment including health, in Brazil (in 2000 US$).

	Natural capital	Human capital	Reproducible capital	Health capital	Oil net capital gains	Carbon damages	Total
1995 capital stock	16,659	44,355	10,713	2,447,023			2,518,750
2000 capital stock	15,066	47,443	10,105	2,480,400			2,552,086
Change 1995–2000	**−1,593**	**3,088**	**−607**	**33,377**	**−685**	**−245**	**33,336**
% change	−9.56%	6.96%	−5.67%	1.36%			1.32%
Growth rate	−1.99%	1.36%	−1.16%	0.27%			**0.26%**

Data source: Arrow *et al.* (2012).

Table 10: Sensitivity analysis of growth rates of per capita comprehensive wealth under alternative assumptions.

(a) An example of growth rate of per capita comprehensive wealth for China.

Sensitivity with respect to the social cost of carbon. The per capita comprehensive wealth growth rate includes technological change but excludes health.

$50/ton cost of carbon	5.63%
$100/ton cost of carbon	5.62%
$500/ton cost of carbon	5.54%

Sensitivity with respect to the discount rate applied to additional years of life. The per capita comprehensive wealth growth rate includes technological change and health.

Low discounting (0.03)	2.88%
Base case (0.05)	2.84%
High discounting (0.07)	2.81%

Sensitivity with respect to the inclusion/exclusion of health capital.

Health capital excluded
  No TFP adjustment 2.92%
  TFP adjustment 5.63%

Health capital included
  No TFP adjustment 0.13%
  TFP adjustment 2.84%

Sensitivity with respect to the value of a statistical life (VSL). The per capita comprehensive wealth growth rate includes technological change and health.

VSL proportional to the 0.6 power of GDP	2.84%
VSL proportional to GDP	2.87%
VSL the same for all countries ($6.3 million)	2.82%
VSL the same for all countries ($1 million)	2.85%

(b) An example of growth rate of per capita comprehensive wealth for Brazil.

Sensitivity with respect to the social cost of carbon. The per capita comprehensive wealth growth rate includes technological change but excludes health.

$50/ton cost of carbon	0.14%
$100/ton cost of carbon	0.07%
$500/ton cost of carbon	−0.49%

Sensitivity with respect to the discount rate applied to additional years of life. The per capita comprehensive wealth growth rate includes technological change and health.

Low discounting (0.03)	0.53%
Base case (0.05)	0.41%
High discounting (0.07)	0.34%

(Continued)

Table 10:   (*Continued*)

Sensitivity with respect to the inclusion/exclusion of health capital.		Sensitivity with respect to the value of a statistical life (VSL). The per capita comprehensive wealth growth rate includes technological change and health.	
Health capital excluded			
No TFP adjustment	−0.01%		
TFP adjustment	0.14%		
Health capital included		VSL proportional to the 0.6 power of GDP	0.41%
No TFP adjustment	0.26%	VSL proportional to GDP	0.40%
TFP adjustment	0.41%	VSL the same for all countries ($6.3 million)	0.42%
		VSL the same for all countries ($1 million)	0.40%

Data source: Arrow *et al.* (2012).

- When comparing comprehensive savings across countries, the trade-off between myopic growth policies and far-sighted growth policies, which take into account the contribution of natural capital to growth, becomes clear. Myopic countries that pursue economic growth at the expense of natural resources will show low or even negative comprehensive savings. This suggests that growth without efficient management of natural capital might not be sustainable.
- Negative genuine savings rates imply that comprehensive wealth is declining. Policies leading to persistently negative genuine savings are unsustainable. Following the approach used by the World Bank (2006), genuine savings can be calculated from gross national savings using the method shown in Figure 7.
- Figures 8 and 9 provide an example of how genuine savings is calculated using the approach described in Figure 7. The approach shows that genuine savings as a proportion of gross national income (GNI) can be negative (Figure 8) or positive (Figure 9).
- Figures 10 and 11 show the evolution of genuine savings as a proportion of GNI for selected geographical regions. In Figure 10, it is interesting to note the convergence of genuine savings rates as a proportion of GNI for the Middle East and North Africa region

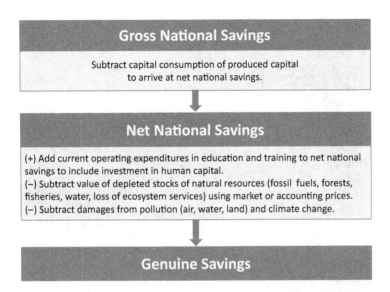

Figure 7: Calculating genuine savings using the World Bank methodology.

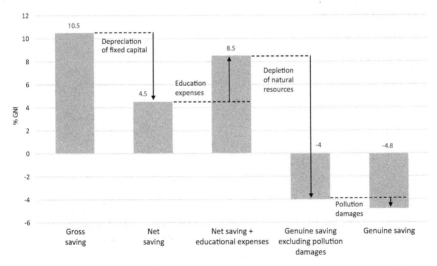

Figure 8: Adjustments in the genuine savings calculation. An example with negative genuine savings.

Notes: Depletion of natural resources includes energy depletion, mineral depletion, and net forest depletion. Pollution damages include PM_{10} damage and CO_2 damage.

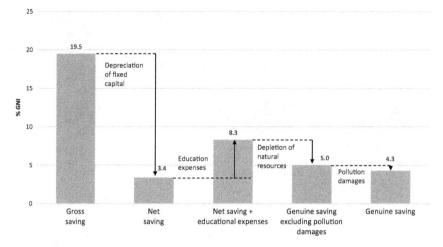

Figure 9: Adjustments in the genuine savings calculation. An example with positive genuine savings.

Notes: See notes for Figure 8.

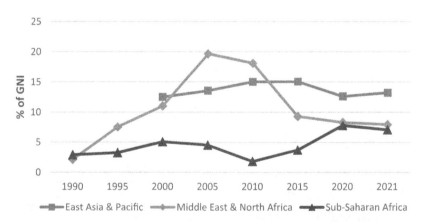

Figure 10: Genuine savings rates (% of GNI) in three geographical regions: East Asia and Pacific, Middle East and North Africa, and Sub-Saharan Africa, 1990–2021.

Notes: (1) Genuine savings is equal to net national savings plus education expenditure, minus energy depletion, mineral depletion, and net forest depletion, and minus carbon dioxide and particulate emissions damage. (2) Data not available for East Asia and Pacific for 1990 and 1995.

Data source: World Bank World Development Indicators database.

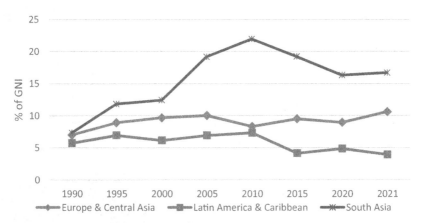

Figure 11: Genuine savings rates (% of GNI) in three geographical regions: Europe and Central Asia, Latin America and Caribbean, and South Asia, 1990–2021.

Note: Genuine savings is calculated as net national savings plus education expenditure, minus energy depletion, mineral depletion, and net forest depletion, and minus carbon dioxide and particulate emissions damage.

Data source: World Bank World Development Indicators database.

and the Sub-Saharan Africa region. The two regions start from the same level in 1990 and move in opposite directions for a long period of time before converging in 2020.

In Figure 11, although the three regions start from almost the same level in 1990, there is no sign of convergence.

- Figure 12 shows genuine savings as a proportion of GNI for different income groups of countries, while Figure 13 shows genuine savings as a proportion of GNI for the World, the OECD, and the European Union.

In Figure 12, it can be seen that the least developed countries, after being in a state of unsustainability (negative savings rates as a proportion of GNI) for almost a decade, show increasing and strong sustainability conditions starting around 2000.

It is interesting to note in Figure 13 that the sustainability status of the United States shows a sharp decrease around the period of the 2008 financial crisis. Similar but less severe signs are shown by OECD countries and the European Union.

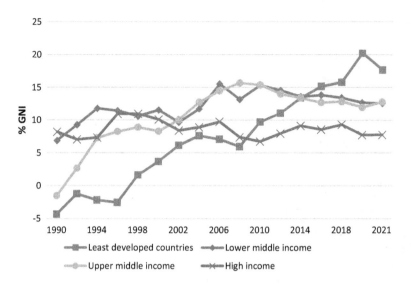

Figure 12:   Genuine savings rates (% of GNI) by income categories, 1990–2021.

Notes: (1) Least developed countries as defined by the UN. Lower-middle-, upper-middle-, and high-income countries as defined by the World Bank. (2) Genuine savings is calculated as net national savings plus education expenditure, minus energy depletion, mineral depletion, and net forest depletion, and minus carbon dioxide and particulate emissions damage.

Data source: World Bank World Development Indicators database.

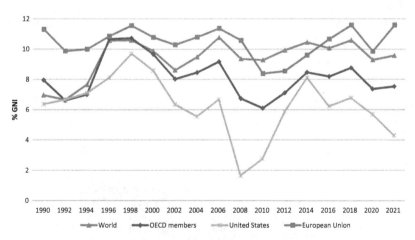

Figure 13:   Genuine savings rates (% of GNI) in World, OECD, United States and European Union, 1990–2021.

Note: Genuine savings is calculated as explained in Note (2) for Figure 12.

Data source: World Bank World Development Indicators database.

12.2.2. *GDP, GNP, NDP, NNP*

In economics, gross domestic product (GDP) is the total monetary or market value of all the final goods and services produced within a country's borders, while gross national product (GNP) is the total value of the final goods and services produced by the citizens and companies of a country, regardless of their location.

Essentially, GDP includes the value of economic activity that takes place within a nation's economy, while GNP includes the value of the economic activity generated by the nation's people. This means that GNP will count the economic activities of a country's citizens living outside its borders but GDP will not and that GDP will count the economic activities of non-citizens within those borders, but GNP will not.

Green net domestic product is calculated as shown in the following box.

Greening the national accounts from gross domestic product (GDP) to green net domestic product

GDP

MINUS capital consumption (produced capital)

= Net Domestic Product (NDP)

MINUS consumption of natural capital which includes:

Reduction in the value of stocks of exhaustible

resources (energy resources and minerals)

MINUS losses of ecosystem services

= Adjusted NDP

PLUS non-market benefit flows for ecosystem services

= Environmentally-adjusted NDP

MINUS health damages due to environmental pollution

= Green NDP

12.2.3. *Models for green national accounting*

In order to present a formal modeling of an economy in the context of green national accounting, the following notation and definitions are used:

Notation:

C = consumption
K = capital stock (produced assets)
$$\dot{K} = \frac{dK}{dt}$$
F = production
S = resource stock
R = resource extraction/harvest
p_R = resource price
f = extraction/harvest cost
f_R = marginal extraction/harvest cost
g = net natural growth of resource
D = resource discoveries
ν_D = marginal discovery cost (ν is total discovery cost)

Definitions:

$NNP = C + \dot{K} - (p_R - f_R)R$: exhaustible natural resources

$NNP = C + \dot{K} - (p_R - f_R)R + (p_R - f_R)g$: exhaustible and biological natural resources

$NNP = C + \dot{K} - \sum_{i=1}^{n}(p_{R_i} - f_{R_i})R_i$: heterogeneous deposits of exhaustible resources

$NNP = C + \dot{K} - (p_R - f_R)R + \nu_D D$: exhaustible resource with discoveries

A social welfare maximization problem for an economy with produced capital accumulation and an exhaustible resource can be written as follows (see Hartwick (1990) for details):

$$\max_{C,R} \int_0^\infty e^{-\rho t} U(C)\,dt,$$

$$\text{s.t. } \dot{K} = F(K, L, R) - C - f(R, S) - \delta K,$$

$$\dot{S} = -R, \ S(0) = S_0,$$

where S is the stock of the exhaustible resource. The first constraint indicates that net investment in produced capital equals output $F(K, L, R)$; minus consumption; minus the cost of extracting the resource $f(R, S)$, $f_R > 0$, $f_S < 0$; minus capital depreciation δK. Marginal extraction costs f_R are positive, while stock dependent extraction costs f_S are negative.

The Hamiltonian representation for this problem is

$$H(C, R, K, S, \phi, \psi)$$

$$= U(C) + \phi(t)[F(K, L, R) - C - f(R, S) - \delta K] + \psi(t)(-R).$$

The Hamiltonian representation can be used to define NNP in monetary units after a linear approximation $U(C) = U_C C$ of the utility function defined as

$$\frac{H(C, R, K, S, \phi, \psi)}{U_C} = C + \dot{K} - \frac{\psi(t)}{U_C} R$$

$$= C + \dot{K} - (F_R - f_R)R = NNP, \ F_R = p_R,$$

where $(p_R - f_R)R$ is Hotelling rent defined as the difference between the price of the resource p_R and the marginal extraction costs of natural resource f_R. The NNP definition follows directly from the optimality conditions:

$$\frac{\partial H}{\partial C} = U_C - \phi = 0, \quad \frac{\partial H}{\partial R} = \phi(F_R - f_R) - \psi = 0, \quad \frac{\psi}{U_C} = (F_R - f_R).$$

Therefore, NNP is defined as consumption, plus investment in produced assets, less Hotelling rent.

Assume that the extraction cost does not depend on the stock S. Then, from the maximum principle,

$$\frac{\partial H}{\partial S} = 0 \quad \text{and} \quad \frac{\dot{\psi}(t)}{\psi(t)} = \rho$$

This condition is the famous Hotelling's rule, which states that the scarcity price of an exhaustible resource $\psi(t)$ should grow at the rate of interest along an optimal extraction path.

12.2.4. *Adjustments to conventional NNP*

Some adjustments to conventional NNP, using the linear approximation of the utility function when exhaustible and renewable resources are taken into account, are presented below:

- **Exhaustible resources**: Start with NNP

  o Deduct current resource rents (valued as price minus the full marginal cost of extraction).
  o For heterogeneous deposits, deduct the sum of current resource rents.
  o Treat discovery expenditures as investments.

- **Renewable resources**: Start with NNP

  o Add the net natural growth of resources, valued at the rental rate (where harvest exceeds natural growth, this will be negative, while in the steady state, it will be 0).

- **Environmental services**: Start with NNP

  o Add the value of the flow of environmental services, corresponding to WTP.
  o Deduct pollution emissions, valued at the marginal cost of abatement.
  o Add environmental regeneration, also valued at marginal abatement cost (in the steady state, the value of pollution and the value of regeneration would be equal and so would cancel out).

12.2.5. Hartwick's rule, genuine savings, and the economy

12.2.5.1. Genuine savings and Hartwick's rule

The well-known Hartwick's rule seeks to answer the following question:

> "If society invests all rents from exhaustible resources in reproducible capital goods, and invests only this amount, i.e., consumes the remainder of the product, given population constant, will consumption and output rise, remain constant, or fall over time?" (Hartwick, 1977, p. 972).

- Hartwick (1977), assuming a constant returns to scale production function with inputs produced capital and an exhaustible resource which is costly to extract, shows that Hartwick's rule:

Invest all rents from the exhaustible resource in reproducible capital,

implies intergenerational equity in the Solow sense, that is, per capita consumption remains constant over time. For more details, see Asheim (2010).

- Thus, Hartwick's rule can be interpreted as suggesting that investing gross savings which are equal to the sum of depreciation of produced assets, that is, depletion of natural resources, and pollution damages, i.e., genuine savings, could satisfy the sustainability criterion. This implies that countries with a persistent negative genuine savings rate could be on an unsustainable path and welfare must fall in the future. Of course, care should be taken in interpreting the data, since important assets such as fish stock, soil erosion, and precious metals might not be included in the genuine savings calculations (see World Bank, 2006).

12.2.5.2. Genuine savings and resource rents

The relationship between genuine savings as a proportion of GNI, and fossil fuel energy and mineral rents as a proportion of GDP, is shown

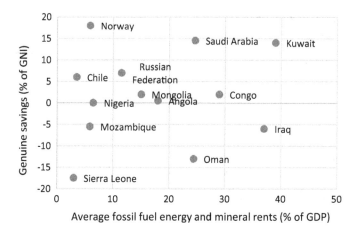

Figure 14: Genuine savings in selected resource-rich countries, 2015–2019. *Data source*: World Bank (2021).

in Figure 14. Stocks of exhaustible resources, such as oil, represent a potential source of development. The question for countries with resource endowments is whether to consume these resource rents, providing current welfare but at a cost to future generations, or to invest the rents in other assets.

12.2.5.3. *Genuine savings and growth*

It can be seen in Figure 15 that some countries, such as Nigeria, Malaysia, and Vietnam, have growing economies but negative genuine savings rates. This may be eroding the well-being of future generations.

12.2.6. *Some evidence related to total wealth*

Recent data from the World Bank (2021) provides some evidence regarding the evolution of total wealth across regions of the world and country income groups:

- Figure 16 shows the evolution of total wealth and human capital per capita in the regions of North America, and Europe and Central Asia, between 1995 and 2018. It is clear that both magnitudes exhibit an increasing trend in both regions over this period.

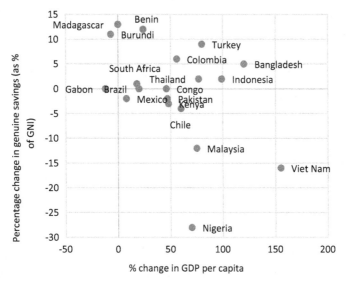

Figure 15: The relationship between change in genuine savings and change in GDP in selected countries, 2000–2018.

Data source: World Bank (2021).

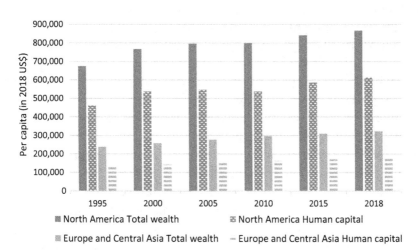

Figure 16: Total wealth and human capital per capita (in 2018 US$) in two regions: North America, and Europe and Central Asia, 1995–2018.

Note: Total wealth includes human capital.

Data source: World Bank (2021).

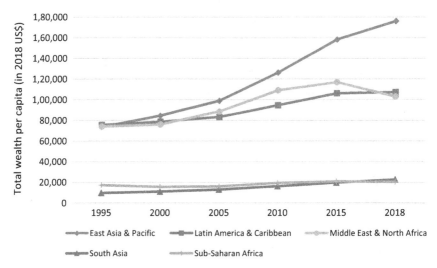

Figure 17:   Total wealth per capita (in 2018 US$) in five geographical regions, 1995–2018.

Data source: World Bank (2021).

- Figure 17 shows the evolution of total wealth per capita in five different geographical regions over the same 23-year period as in Figure 16. The different regions exhibit very different trends.

    Three of the regions start from the same level (approximately $75,000 per capita) in 1995. Of these, East Asia and the Pacific show an unbroken and rapidly increasing trend over the whole period, while the Middle East and North Africa shows solid growth until 2015, after which it declines. Latin America and Caribbean shows a slower but steady increase over the whole period.

    The other two regions start at a much lower level. Sub-Saharan Africa starts at below $18,000 per capita and has slight increases and decreases over the period, ending just slightly higher (about $20,500 per capita) in 2018. South Asia, by contrast, starts at below $10,000 per capita in 1995 but grows to almost $23,000 per capita in 2018.

- Figure 18 presents the percentage composition of total wealth broken down into human capital, produced capital, and natural capital, by income group. It can be noted that the low and

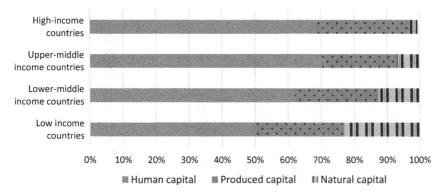

Figure 18: Breakdown of total wealth by type of capital for country income groups, 2018.
Data source: World Bank (2021).

lower-middle-income countries have a significantly higher share of natural capital than the upper-middle- and high-income countries do and that the share of natural capital is declining as country group income increases.

High- and upper-middle-income countries have a higher share of human capital than the low- and lower-middle-income countries. The percentage share of produced capital shows less variation for the four groups, ranging from 23% (upper-middle-income countries) to 29% (high-income countries).

- The change in global total wealth for the eight years between 2000 and 2018, broken down by country income groups, is presented in Figure 19. The total wealth of the World, as well as all four income groups, increased during this period. The total wealth of the world increased by more than 64%, while the total wealth of high income countries increased by just 32%. The other three income groups all showed increases above 100%, ranging from 107% for low income countries to 175% for upper-middle income countries. Although the growth of the high income countries was substantially lower than that of the rest of the income groups, the per capita inequalities are strongly in favor of the high income countries, as Figure 5 illustrates.

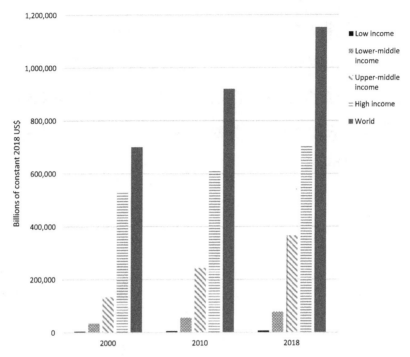

Figure 19:   Change in global total wealth, by country income groups (in billions of constant 2018 US$).

Data source: World Bank (2021).

- The percentage change in total wealth from 1995 to 2018, broken down by country income groups, is presented in Figure 20. Although the total wealth for the World, as well as all four income groups, increased in value terms during every period, the percentage growth increase ranged from 8% to 40%.

  The rate of growth was increasing from 1995 to 2010 for three of the four income groups, with only the high-income country group showing decreasing growth (which is reflected in the World rate of growth which also decreased). From 2010, the rate of growth was positive but decreasing for all of the income groups except the high income country group, which showed a slight increase in growth rate from 2010 to 2015 but which decreased from 2015 to 2018.

  The upper-middle-income countries had the highest growth rates over the entire time period, while the high-income countries

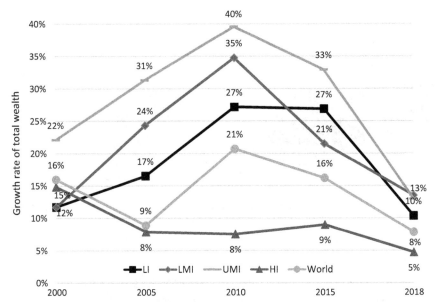

Figure 20: Percentage change in total wealth, by country income groups, 1995–2018.

Notes: (1) LI: Lower-income countries. LMI: Lower-middle-income countries. UMI: Upper-middle-income countries. HI: High-income countries. This category is the sum of high-income OECD countries and high-income non-OECD countries. (2) Value of total wealth measured in constant 2018 US$. (3) The percentage value for the year 2000 is the growth in total wealth from 1995 to 2000. The percentage value for the year 2018 is the growth in total wealth from 2015 to 2018.

Data source: World Bank (2021).

had the lowest growth rate from 2005 to 2018. It is interesting to note that the growth rate of all four income groups was lower in 2018 than in 2000.

- Figure 21 compares the distribution of global total wealth held by country income groups in 1995 and 2018. The most striking change is that the share of total wealth of the high-income countries dropped by nearly 15% (from 75.7% to 60.9%) while the share of upper-middle-income countries rose by almost 13%. The share of lower-middle-income countries rose slightly (about 2%), while the share of low-income countries stayed almost the same.

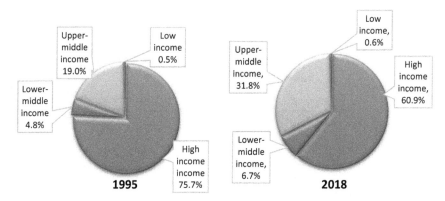

Figure 21:   Growth of global total wealth by country income categories, 1995–2018.

Data source: World Bank (2021).

The evidence presented in this section suggests that, according to the World Bank, global total wealth demonstrates a continuous upward trend for all countries, irrespective of income category. The percentage change in total wealth seems to converge for all country income groups. On the other hand, the per capita evolution of total wealth shows the strongest upward trend for East Asia and Pacific (Figure 17). For the rest of the regions, the results are varied.

References

Arrow, K. J., Dasgupta, P., Mäler, K.-G. (2003). Evaluating projects and assessing sustainable development in imperfect economies. *Environmental and Resource Economics*, 26, 647–685.

Arrow, K. J., Dasgupta, P., Goulder, L., Mumford, K., Oleson, K. (2012). Sustainability and the measurement of wealth. *Environment and Development Economics*, 17, 317–353.

Asheim, G. B. (2010). *Justifying, Characterizing and Indicating Sustainability* (Vol. 3). Springer Science & Business Media.

Brundtland, G. (1987). *Report of the World Commission on Environment and Development: Our Common Future.* United Nations General Assembly document A/42/427.

Dasgupta, P., Mäler, K.-G. (2001). Wealth as a criterion for sustainable development. The Beijer International Institute of Ecological Economics, Discussion Paper 139.

Engelbrecht, H.-J. (2016). Comprehensive versus inclusive wealth accounting and the assessment of sustainable development: An empirical comparison. *Ecological Economics*, 129, 12–20.

Hamilton, K., Hartwick, J. M. (2005). Investing exhaustible resource rents and the path of consumption. *The Canadian Journal of Economics/Revue Canadienne D'Economique*, 38, 615–621.

Hartwick, J. M. (1977). Intergenerational equity and the investing of rents from exhaustible resources. *American Economic Review*, 66, 972–974.

Hartwick, J. M. (1990). Natural resources, national accounting and economic depreciation. Working Paper No. 771, Economics Department, Queen's University.

Managi, S., Kumar, P. (2018). *Inclusive Wealth Report 2018*. Taylor & Francis.

Pearce, D., Atkinson, G., Mourato, S. (2006). *Cost–Benefit Analysis and the Environment: Recent Developments*. Paris: OECD Publishing.

Pearce, D., Hamilton, K., Atkinson, G. (1996). Measuring sustainable development: Progress on indicators. *Environment and Development Economics*, 1, 85–101.

Pearce, D., Markandya, A., Barbier, E. (1990). *Sustainable Development: Economics and Environment in the Third World*. Cheltenham, UK: Edward Elgar Publishing.

Pemberton, M., Ulph, D. (2001). Measuring income and measuring sustainability. *Scandinavian Journal of Economics*, 103, 25–40.

Pezzey, J. (1992). Sustainable development concepts: An economic analyses. World Bank Environmental Paper, 2.

Pezzey, J. (1997). Sustainability constraints versus "optimality" versus intertemporal concern, and axioms versus data. *Land Economics*, 73, 448–466.

Riley, G. (1980). The just rate of depletion of natural resource. *Journal of Environmental Economics and Management*, 7, 291–307.

Solow, R. (1974). Intergenerational equity and exhaustible resources. *The Review of Economic Studies*, 41, 29–45.

UNU-IHDP and UNEP (2014). *Inclusive Wealth Report 2014. Measuring Progress toward Sustainability*. Cambridge University Press.

World Bank (2006). *Where Is the Wealth of Nations? Measuring Capital for the 21st Century*. Washington, DC: The World Bank.

World Bank (2021). *The Changing Wealth of Nations 2021: Managing Assets for the Future*. Washington, DC: World Bank.

Chapter 13

Sustainability at the Corporate Level

13.1. The Concept of Sustainability at the Corporate Level

In a way parallel to the global or economy-level concept of sustainability defined in the Brundtland Report (1987), sustainability can also be defined at the corporate level. Dyllick and Hockerts (2002, p. 131) state that:

> Corporate sustainability can accordingly be defined as meeting the needs of a firm's direct and indirect stakeholders (such as shareholders, employees, clients, pressure groups, communities etc.), without compromising its ability to meet the needs of future stakeholders as well.

Corporate sustainability can be attained at the firm level at the intersection of economic development, environmental protection, and social responsibility. In this way, sustainability can be thought of as the response of a value-maximizing or profit-maximizing firm to environmental and social issues emerging from its operations (e.g., Engert *et al.*, 2016). This leads to the triple bottom line concept (Dyllick and Hockerts, 2002):

- The concept of the *triple bottom line* is a framework that takes into account the three dimensions of corporate sustainability:

Figure 1:   The triple bottom line.

social, environmental, and economic (see Figure 1). It suggests that businesses should not only focus on financial profits but also consider their impact on people (social), the planet (environmental), and long-term economic viability:

○ The social dimension focuses on the company's impact on society and stakeholders. It involves considering aspects such as employee well-being, labor practices, human rights, community engagement, customer satisfaction, and diversity and inclusion. Companies that emphasize the social aspect of the triple bottom line aim to create positive social change and address social issues within their operations.

○ The environmental dimension emphasizes the company's impact on the environment. It involves reducing ecological footprints, minimizing pollution and waste, conserving resources, and promoting sustainability practices. Businesses that prioritize the environmental aspect of the triple bottom line strive to operate in an environmentally responsible and sustainable manner, considering the long-term health of the planet.

○ The economic dimension focuses on financial performance and profitability. While the social and environmental aspects are essential, a company must also be financially viable in order to sustain its operations and continue its impact. However, in the context of the triple bottom line, economic success is not the **sole** focus but rather a component that must be balanced with social and environmental considerations.

13.1.1. *Corporate sustainability and the triple bottom line*

Sustainability at the global-economy level is associated with a non-declining productive base for the economy, with the productive base being defined in terms of aggregate value of produced, human, natural, social, and health capital, valued at appropriate accounting prices (see Chapter 12, Figure 1). In a parallel way, Dyllick and Hockerts (2002) suggest that at the corporate level and in the context of the triple bottom line, economic, natural, and social capital are the relevant concepts for measuring economic, environmental, and social sustainability, respectively. More specifically,

(1) An *economically sustainable* firm is one that uses its fixed and operating capital to generate sufficient cash flow to ensure liquidity and produces returns which are above the industry average for its shareholders (Dyllick and Hockerts, 2002). Economic sustainability is closely related to long-term viability: balancing short-term financial goals with the ability to sustain operations and generate profits in the long run. It involves the following:

Innovation and efficiency: Embracing sustainable technologies and practices that lead to cost savings, improve resource efficiency, and enhance competitiveness.
Supply chain management: Collaborating with suppliers and partners to promote sustainable practices throughout the supply chain, including ethical sourcing, fair trade, and responsible production.

(2) An *environmentally sustainable* firm uses renewable resources below their natural reproduction rate and depletable resources below the rate at which substitutes, or substitute technologies,

are produced. It emits pollutants at a rate below the environment's natural assimilation capacity so that pollutants do not accumulate, and finally, it does not degrade ecosystems and reduce their services through its actions. Environmental sustainability therefore requires conservation of resources, that is, implementing practices to reduce energy and water consumption, minimize waste generation, and promote recycling and reuse. To achieve this, an environmentally sustainable firm engages in

Pollution prevention: Taking measures to minimize or eliminate the release of harmful substances into the environment and adopting cleaner production techniques.

Sustainable sourcing: Ensuring that raw materials and supplies are obtained from sustainable and responsibly-managed sources, such as using renewable materials and supporting fair trade practices.

Climate action: Implementing strategies to mitigate greenhouse gas emissions, setting emission reduction targets, and adopting renewable energy sources.

(3) A *socially sustainable* firm increases human capital and social capital in the communities within which it operates and manages social capital in a way that is transparent and acceptable to its shareholders. Social sustainability implies the following:

Employee well-being: Prioritizing the health, safety, and overall well-being of employees, including fair wages, good working conditions, training opportunities, and work–life balance.

Stakeholder engagement: Actively involving and communicating with stakeholders, such as local communities, customers, and NGOs, to understand their concerns and incorporate their perspectives into decision-making processes.

Diversity and inclusion: Promoting diversity, equity, and inclusion within the company to ensure equal opportunities and foster a supportive and inclusive work environment.

Community involvement: Contributing to the local community through initiatives like volunteering, philanthropy, and supporting social causes that align with the company's values.

Moreover, to enhance social capital, a socially sustainable firm should undertake and promote:

o *Ethical governance*: Establishing transparent and accountable governance structures that prioritize ethical behavior and integrity.
o *Sustainability reporting*: Regularly disclosing information on environmental, social, and economic performance to stakeholders, thus providing transparency and accountability.
o *Sustainability policies and standards*: Developing and implementing policies and standards that guide sustainable practices throughout the organization, ensuring compliance and continuous improvement.

One difference between economy-wide sustainability and corporate sustainability is that, in the economy-wide case, the criterion for an economy being on a sustainable development path is a non-declining productive base valued at accounting prices. This overcomes the issue of weak vs strong sustainability since, if a resource is reduced below a critical level, its accounting price should become very large (in theory, it will tend to infinity; see Chapter 12, Section 12.1.4.2). In this case, the policy that will reduce a component of natural capital below its critical level will have a very large negative effect (minus infinity in theory) on the productive base, and in this case, the policy should be abandoned as unsustainable.

At the corporate level, the environmental sustainability requirement is stricter and is closer to the concept of strong sustainability because firms should improve their environmental footprint in physical terms. The substitutability issue and the trade-off between preservation of ecosystems and development at the firm level can be handled using accounting prices and valuation approaches for non-market environmental goods and services through the regulatory process.

13.2. Measuring Sustainability at the Corporate Level

As shown in Chapter 12, Section 12.1.3, the economy is on a sustainable development path at a given point in time if the productive base or, equivalently, the comprehensive savings is non-declining. To determine whether a firm is sustainable in terms of the triple bottom line, the general approach is to calculate specific metrics. These include the following:

- **financial metrics** such as cost–benefit analysis of investment programs, net present value (NPV), internal rate of return (IRR), and return on investment (ROI) which are essential to most organizations.
- **environmental metrics** which typically include reduction of electricity usage, change in fuel consumption for company vehicles, carbon emissions reductions, gallons of water saved, and increased waste diversion.
- **social metrics** which focus on all the ways companies interact with their employees and the communities in which they operate, such as employees' health and well-being, workplace diversity and inclusion, and community engagement.
- **governance metrics** which are often determined by the existence of policies on a wide range of issues, such as company values and business resilience plans.

The calculation of these metrics involves indicators which relate to each of the components and are calculated using data from the different aspects of the firm's operation. To be meaningful as tools for examining the firm's sustainability status, the indicators should be reliable, and their calculation should be transparent. The indicators can take the forms described in the following sections.

13.2.1. *Productivity/efficiency ratios*

Productivity/efficiency ratios relate value to impact. Normally, financial performance is tracked with efficiency ratios. Examples of environmental/social productivity/efficiency ratios could include the following:

- labor productivity, for example, turnover per employee,
- resource productivity, for example, sales per unit of energy consumption or output per unit of material input,
- process eco-efficiency, for example, production per unit of waste or net sales per unit of greenhouse gas emissions in tons of CO_2 equivalent,
- functional eco-efficiency of products or services, for example, fuel efficiency of a car or plane.

13.2.2. *Intensity ratios*

Intensity ratios express an impact per unit of activity or unit of value. A declining intensity ratio reflects performance improvement. Often environmental performance is tracked with intensity ratios such as:

- emission intensity (e.g., tons of CO_2 emissions per unit of electricity generated),
- waste intensity (e.g., amount of waste per production volume),
- resource intensity (e.g., energy consumption per activity or material input per service).

13.2.3. *Percentages*

Percentages indicate ratios between two like issues with the same physical unit in the numerator and denominator. Examples of percentages that are meaningful for sustainability performance include the following:

- input/output ratios (e.g., process yields),
- losses (e.g., non-product output per materials input),
- recycling percentages (e.g., percentage of waste recycled per total waste),
- fractions (e.g., percentage of renewable energy, fraction of recycled materials, or fraction of hazardous waste),
- quotas (e.g., percentage of women in upper management),

- financial performance ratios (e.g., return on equity or return on operating assets).

13.3. Environmental, Social, and Governance Reporting

The metrics and the associated indicators discussed above in either quantitative or qualitative forms are presented in firms' published environmental or sustainability reports. Similar data and indicators are generated by third-party providers and regulatory bodies. This body of information is used to produce environmental, social, and governance (ESG) scores and ratings. Thus, ESG is a framework that provides information on business practices and the performance of a firm on various environmental, sustainability, and ethical issues.

The three pillars of ESG are:

- **environmental**, which includes factors such as climate change, pollution, and resource management,
- **social**, which includes factors such as employee relations, human rights, and community engagement,
- **governance**, which includes factors such as corporate structure, executive compensation, and shareholder rights.

Some third-party providers of data and indicators related to ESG include:

Global Reporting Initiative (GRI): This is an independent international organization that sets standards for sustainability reporting. Many companies adhere to GRI guidelines to ensure that their reports are both comprehensive and comparable.

Carbon Disclosure Project (CDP): This project collects and discloses environmental data from companies worldwide, including carbon emissions, water usage, and climate change strategies.

Sustainability Accounting Standards Board (SASB): This is a non-profit organization that develops industry-specific sustainability reporting standards.

Institutional Shareholder Services (ISS): This is a financial service company that provides ESG ratings and analysis to investors.

Information by firms and third-party providers is used by ESG rating agencies that provide ESG scores for a company. There are a number of different ESG rating agencies and methodologies, each of which uses its own approach to evaluating a company's performance. For example, some agencies focus on a company's carbon footprint and energy efficiency, while others emphasize labor practices and human rights. Additionally, some agencies use a quantitative approach, analyzing data such as financial performance, while others use a qualitative approach, conducting interviews and site visits. Some of the major ESG rating agencies are ESG analytics, MSCI, Refinitiv, Sustainanalytics, RepRisk, S&P Global, Bloomberg, FTSE Russel, and ISS Global.

An example showing the way in which the ESG score is determined by Refinitiv (2022) is illustrated in Figure 2. A total of 630 ESG measures are collected at the firm level, from which the

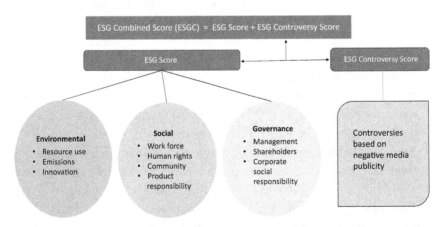

Figure 2: Calculation of ESG score.

most relevant 186 are kept. They are grouped into ten categories: three categories for environmental, four for social, and three for governance. The category scores are used to derive the three pillar scores. Then, the overall ESG score is obtained as a weighted average of the three pillar scores. Pillar weights vary across industries for the environmental and social pillars and are constant across industries for the governance pillar. The ESG score is combined with the ESG controversy score which is based on 23 ESG controversy topics. The purpose is to discount the ESG performance of a specific firm by considering negative media stories about this firm. The combination of ESG score with the ESG controversy score provides the ESG combined score (ESGC).

The ESG framework is considered important because of its potential impact in many areas. ESG can help companies to address the following:

- **Environmental risks**, by identifying and mitigating environmental risks such as transition risks associated with climate change policies, reducing pollution costs, and promoting resource savings. Reduction of environmental risks by companies could reduce global risks and promote global sustainability.
- **Social risks**, by identifying and mitigating social risks in areas such as employee relations, human rights, and community engagement. These risks can have a significant impact on a company's human capital, and if they are not properly addressed, they can damage a company's reputation.
- **Governance risks**, by identifying and mitigating governance risks in areas such as corporate structure, executive compensation, and shareholder rights. These risks can make it difficult for a company to attract and retain investors.
- **Sustainability**, by becoming more sustainable, which can reduce their environmental impact (e.g., reduce emissions and resource use) and improve their long-term financial performance.
- **Reputation issues**, by building a positive reputation, which can attract customers, investors, and employees. A strong ESG reputation can help businesses attract and retain top talent, build customer loyalty, and gain access to new markets.

- **Regulation requirements**, for which ESG is becoming increasingly important as regulators are increasingly requiring companies to disclose ESG information.
- **Innovation**, by identifying new opportunities, such as developing new products and services that are more sustainable or socially responsible.

Attainment of good performance in the above areas will promote sustainability at the corporate level. Achieving corporate sustainability across industries will promote sustainability at the economy level. The connection between corporate sustainability and sustainability at the economy level is presented in Figure 3.

13.3.1. *ESG investing*

ESG investing is a type of investment that considers environmental, social, and governance factors when making investment decisions.

There are a number of different ways to support ESG through investment. Some investors choose to invest in ESG mutual funds or exchange-traded funds. Others choose to invest in individual stocks that they believe have strong ESG profiles.

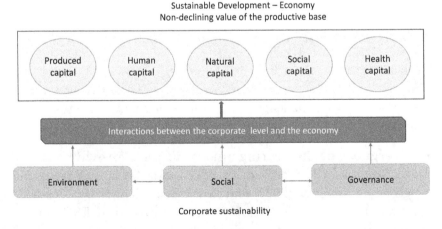

Figure 3: Corporate sustainability and sustainability for the economy.

Some of the expected benefits of ESG investing include:

- **Potential for higher returns**: There is an expectation that ESG-focused funds can outperform traditional funds over the long term.
- **Reduced risk**: ESG-focused funds could help reduce risk by investing in companies that are well managed and have strong governance practices.
- **Sustainability impact**: ESG investing can help promote sustainability and social responsibility.

ESG investing has experienced considerable market momentum, which resulted in large inflows into ESG-focused products, resulting in an average compounded annual growth rate of 27% in global assets under management between 2015 and 2021 (KPMG, 2022).

According to Bloomberg Intelligence (2022), the global total of assets under management in ESG-related funds was likely to exceed around $41 trillion in 2022, up from $22.8 trillion in 2016. Bloomberg Intelligence also estimates that ESG-related investments will surpass $50 trillion by 2025.

Europe is far ahead of other regions in terms of ESG investing. According to Bankrate (2023), Europe has 83% of all the ESG assets under management, with a value over $2 trillion. To put it into perspective, Europe holds almost five times more ESG assets than all the other regions combined.

13.3.2. *Challenges to ESG reporting and investing*

Despite the potential of ESG to characterize the sustainability of a company, and the interest it has engendered in the global community, there are numerous challenges which can be summarized in two broad categories:

- **Divergence of ESG rating among different providers**: There is an established divergence of ESG rating between ESG rating agencies. Berg *et al.* (2022) find that the correlations between ESG ratings range from 0.38 to 0.71. This is based on ESG ratings from six different raters: KLD, Sustainalytics, Moody's ESG (previously Vigeo-Eiris), S&P Global (previously RobecoSAM), Refinitiv (previously Asset4), and MSCI. This divergence has consequences which include: difficulty in evaluating and comparing ESG performance across firms, funds, and portfolios; disincentives for companies to improve ESG ratings; dispersion of ESG performance on asset prices which makes it difficult to link compensation for CEOs with ESG performance; and uncertainty in decision-making based on ESG ratings.

Berg *et al.* (2022) find that the main reason for this divergence is *measurement divergence* which is the measurement of the same attribute with different indicators, followed by *scope divergence* in which ratings are based on different sets of attributes, and *weight divergence* as a result of different weights for the relative importance of the attributes being used. From the regulator's point of view, correcting for this divergence requires standardization and harmonization of ESG disclosures.

- **ESG ratings and financial/social performance**: A major challenge in the identification of the impacts of ESG ratings in the corporate world is the understanding of the link between the corporate economic and social performance and the ESG ratings. Halbritter and Dorfleitner (2015) review earlier studies and compare them with their own results. They state that in contrast to earlier studies, they did not detect any significant return difference between companies with high and low ESG ratings. Giese *et al.* (2019) explore the links between ESG ratings, equity valuation, risk, and performance. They state that over 1000 research reports find mixed results regarding the correlation between ESG scores and financial performance, although the majority of this research found a positive correlation. They analyze possible transmission mechanisms from ESG ratings to financial performance. Their findings suggest that ESG ratings are linked with lower cost of capital, higher valuation, and higher profitability.

Cornell (2020) questions the view that ESG rating should play an important role in investment management, given the confusing and sometimes contradictory criteria in calculating the ESG scores. Gillan *et al.* (2021) indicate that although a growing body of evidence suggests that ESG activities can reduce risk and increase firm value, the issue is still under debate. They also find that a firm's ESG profile is strongly related to the firm's market leadership. Pérez *et al.* (2022) find, by analyzing the link between changes in ESG and shareholders returns, that a multi-year improvement in ESG ratings may lead to higher shareholder returns relative to industry peers. They also find that this effect has increased in recent years.

Pucker and King (2022) challenge the idea that ESG investing can solve critical environmental problems for the following reasons: the non-standardization of benefits; the E (environmental) and S (social) impacts are not clear; it has not been proven that ESG investing delivers better returns; the fees associated with ESG funds are higher than traditional funds; and ESG investing might be associated with greenwash. Bhagat (2022), making reference to recent research, challenges the idea that ESG funds perform relatively better than traditional funds and mentions research that found that companies in ESG portfolios had worse compliance records for both labor and environmental rules relative to non-ESG portfolios.

In summary, the potential advantages and challenges associated with the ESG framework suggest that more research should be devoted to exploring how resolution of issues, such as the lack of standardization, the complexity characterizing the system, or the asymmetric information due to the provision of data through self-reporting, might improve the efficiency of the framework.

References

Bankrate (2023). ESG investing statistics 2023. https://www.bankrate.com/investing/esg-investing-statistics/.

Berg, F., Koelbel, J. F., Rigobon, R. (2022). Aggregate confusion: The divergence of ESG ratings. *Review of Finance*, 26(6), 1315–1344.

Bhagat, S. (2022). An inconvenient truth about ESG investing. *Harvard Business Review*.

Bloomberg Intelligence (2022). ESG may surpass $41 trillion assets in 2022, but not without challenges, finds Bloomberg Intelligence. Press release, 24 January 2022.

Brundtland, G. (1987). *Report of the World Commission on Environment and Development: Our Common Future*. United Nations General Assembly document A/42/427.

Cornell, B. (2020). ESG investing: Conceptual issues. *The Journal of Wealth Management*, 23(3), 61–69.

Dyllick, T., Hockerts, K. (2002). Beyond the business case for corporate sustainability. *Business Strategy and the Environment*, 11(2), 130–141.

Engert, S., Rauter, R., Baumgartner, R. J. (2016). Exploring the integration of corporate sustainability into strategic management: A literature review. *Journal of Cleaner Production*, 112, 2833–2850.

Giese, G., Lee, L. E., Melas, D., Nagy, Z., Nishikawa, L. (2019). Foundations of ESG investing: How ESG affects equity valuation, risk, and performance. *The Journal of Portfolio Management*, 45(5), 69–83.

Gillan, S. L., Koch, A., Starks, L. T. (2021). Firms and social responsibility: A review of ESG and CSR research in corporate finance. *Journal of Corporate Finance*, 66, p.101889.

Halbritter, G., Dorfleitner, G. (2015). The wages of social responsibility — Where are they? A critical review of ESG investing. *Review of Financial Economics*, 26, 25–35.

KPMG (2022). Evolution of ESG investing. https://assets.kpmg.com/content/dam/kpmg/dp/pdf/2022/april/evolution-esg-investing.pdf.

Pérez, L., Hunt, V., Samandari, H., Nuttall, R., Biniek, K. (2022). Does ESG really matter and why? *McKinsey Quarterly*.

Pucker, K. P., King, A. (2022). ESG investing isn't designed to save the planet. *Harvard Business Review*.

Refinitiv (2022). Environmental, social and governance scores from Refinitiv. https://www.refinitiv.com/content/dam/marketing/en_us/documents/methodology/refinitiv-esg-scores-methodology.pdf.

Chapter 14

Sustainability and Development

14.1. Sustainability Criteria for a Model Economy

To better understand the link between sustainability and the different types of assets of an economy, we use a model of an economy with many assets and we define the sustainability criteria for this economy. The assets of the model economy and the different interactions between them are described as follows:

- Physical capital, human capital embodying labor input, fossil fuels, renewables, and services derived by ecosystems are combined to produce aggregate output denoted by $Y(t)$. This is the gross domestic product.
- The use of fossil fuels generates greenhouse gas (GHG) emissions which accumulate as a stock.
- The stock of GHGs creates damages which reduce the utility of individuals and degrade the ecosystems, thus deteriorating their services. These are the damages from climate change which can be reduced by costly adaptation.
- The stock of GHGs can be decreased by reducing the use of fossil fuels, which is mitigation, or by costly carbon capture and storage (CCS) activities.
- Energy can be produced by renewables to substitute for energy produced by fossil fuels.

- Renewable capacity or stock accumulates by undertaking costly investments in renewables.

14.1.1. *The model economy*

In this model economy,

- Climate change damages can be directly reduced by costly adaptation.
- Human capital accumulates by devoting a part of individuals' non-leisure time to human capital accumulation and the rest to the production of output.
- Adaptation capital and CCS capital accumulate through investment in adaptation and CCS.
- Ecosystems are regarded as an aggregate stock that generates a flow of useful services through the services they provide (e.g., provisioning services, such as harvesting). The stock is enhanced by natural regeneration processes and by costly human restoration activities and is reduced through the deterioration caused by climate change.
- The produced output in this model economy is distributed among consumption, net investment in physical capital and its depreciation, the cost of renewables and fossil fuel extraction, adaptation expenses, CCS expenses, and ecosystem restoration expenses.
- Social welfare at each point in time t is determined by the utility derived from consumption, less damages due to climate change.
- Intergenerational well-being or welfare at any point in time t is the discounted sum of the future flow of social welfare.

14.1.2. *The productive base*

The productive base includes physical or produced capital $K(t)$, stock of fossil fuels $X(t)$, stock of renewables $R(t)$ (e.g., wind power or photovoltaic capacity), human capital $h(t)$, the ecosystems, i.e., natural assets $S(t)$, the stock of GHGs $E(t)$, the stock of adaptation capital $A(t)$ (e.g., dams to protect against sea level rise), and the stock of CCS capital $CS(t)$, e.g., equipment and installations that allow CCS.

These stocks evolve dynamically through time, given historical, natural, and economic laws of motion.

14.1.3. *Instruments and welfare*

Instruments or controls represent human actions which change the stocks comprising the productive base of the model economy:

- These instruments include consumption $C(t)$, fossil fuel extraction $q(t)$, investment in renewables $r(t)$, proportion of non-leisure time devoted to human capital accumulation $(1 - u(t))$ which is an investment in human capital, use of ecosystem services $s(t)$, investment in adaptation capacity $a(t)$, investment in CCS capacity $c^S(t)$, and investment related to ecosystem restoration $i(t)$.
- Social welfare at each point of time $W(t)$ is determined in terms of utility from consumption $U(C(t))$ and damages from climate change after adaptation $D(E)$.
- Intergenerational welfare or well-being $V(t)$ is the discounted flow of future $W(t)$.

14.1.4. *Accounting prices and sustainability*

Let the accounting prices for stocks comprising the productive base be defined as

$$V_\Omega(t) = \lim_{\Delta\Omega(t) \to 0} \frac{\Delta V(t)}{\Delta\Omega(t)} = \frac{\partial V(t)}{\partial\Omega(t)}, \quad \Omega = K, X, R, h, S, E, A, CS.$$

Then, the change in intergenerational well-being or, equivalently, genuine savings S_g is defined as

$$\Delta V(t) = S_g(t) = [V_K(t)\Delta K(t) + V_X(t)\Delta X(t) + V_R(t)\Delta R(t)$$
$$+ V_h(t)\Delta h(t) + V_S(t)\Delta S(t) + V_E(t)\Delta E(t)$$
$$+ V_A(t)\Delta A(t) + V_{CS}(t)\Delta CS(t)]\Delta t + \left(\frac{\partial V(t)}{\partial t}\right)\Delta t.$$

According to the sustainability definition, the economy will be sustainable at time t if

$$\Delta V(t) \geq 0, \quad \text{or} \quad S_g \geq 0.$$

Setting $\left(\frac{\partial V(t)}{\partial t}\right) = TFP$ and $\Delta t = 1$, the criterion becomes

$$\Delta V(t) = S_g(t) = V_K(t)\Delta K(t) + V_X(t)\Delta X(t) + V_R(t)\Delta R(t)$$
$$+ V_h(t)\Delta h(t) + V_S(t)\Delta S(t) + V_E(t)\Delta E(t)$$
$$+ V_A(t)\Delta A(t) + V_{CS}(t)\Delta CS(t) + TFP(t).$$

An example: Assume that the physical capital is increased by $\Delta\widehat{K}(t)$, the stock of fossil fuels is reduced by $\Delta\widehat{X}(t)$, and the stock of ecosystems is reduced by $\Delta\widehat{S}(t)$ Everything else remains constant. The economy is sustainable at t if

$$\widehat{S}_g(t) = V_K(t)\Delta\widehat{K}(t) - V_X(t)\Delta\widehat{X}(t) - V_S(t)\Delta\widehat{S}(t) > 0.$$

14.1.5. *Inclusive wealth and sustainability*

Inclusive wealth is defined as

$$G(t) = V_K(t)K(t) + V_X(t)X(t) + V_R(t)R(t) + V_h(t)h(t) + V_S(t)S(t)$$
$$+ V_E(t)E(t) + V_A(t)A(t) + V_{CS}(t)CS(t) + TFP(t)t.$$

- If inclusive wealth for a country can be estimated for a number of years, then if the time series is not declining with respect to time, we may infer that the economy is on a sustainable path.
- On the contrary, if the time series is declining, then the economy is not on a sustainable path.

14.2. Development vs Sustainability Rules

In a non-optimal economy with distortions resulting from market and environmental externalities, acceptance of projects using traditional cost–benefit analysis rules that do not use the correct accounting prices does not necessarily imply that these projects promote sustainability.

Policy-makers should make clear whether a project is evaluated in terms of developmental objectives or sustainability objectives because the two criteria may not necessarily provide the same decision rule, especially when not all externalities are accounted for or when accounting prices are distorted.

14.2.1. *Comparing and combining policies*

The genuine savings definition can be used to compare policies with regard to their impact on sustainability. Assume that a policy with strict economic growth objectives will increase produced and human capital and reduce the stock of fossil fuels. The policy-maker does not consider any other potential impacts. The policy will be regarded as compatible with sustainability, in a myopic sense, if

$$S_g^m = V_K(t)K(t) - V_X(t)X(t) + V_h(t)h(t) > 0.$$

Suppose, however, that the same policy reduces natural assets and increases the stock of GHGs. In terms of "environmental sustainability", the policy will be non-sustainable since

$$S_g^e = -V_S(t)\Delta S(t) - V_E(t)\Delta E(t) < 0.$$

Thus, using strict growth objectives or strict environmental objectives could lead to conflict. The conflict can be resolved by combining the objectives as

$$S_g^* = \lambda S_g^m + (1 - \lambda)S_g^e, \quad 0 \le \lambda \le 1,$$

where λ reflects the policy-maker's preferences with respect to sustainability or development. The policy will be compatible with the sustainability criterion if $S_g^* > 0$.

The genuine investment sustainability criterion can be used to evaluate policies that might combine different policy objectives. For example:

- Select policies which promote sustainability with an increase in human capital:

$$S_g(t) \ge 0 \quad \text{and} \quad \Delta h(t) > 0.$$

- If the objective is sustainability and GDP growth, then the selection rule will be

$$S_g(t) \geq 0 \quad \text{and} \quad \Delta Y(t) > 0.$$

14.3. The Green Economy

A green economy can be thought of as one which is low carbon, resource efficient, and socially inclusive. In 2011, the United Nations Environment Programme (UNEP, 2011) defined a green economy as one that "results in improved human well-being and social equity, while significantly reducing environmental risks and ecological scarcities."

- The premise that a green economy results in improved human well-being establishes a link between the concept of a green economy and the concept of sustainable development.
- A green economy is not necessarily a sustainable economy and vice versa. For example, a green economy could be characterized by negative genuine savings if there is disinvestment in produced capital, while a sustainable economy might not be green if it is a high-carbon economy and uses a lot of natural resources. It can be argued, however, that the pursuit of a green economy could lead to a sustainable economy since it will promote resource savings and restoration of natural assets which are important elements of an economy's productive base.

14.3.1. *Public policies toward a green economy*

Some of the policies which governments can adopt in order to move toward a green economy include the following:

- development of renewable sources of energy and low-carbon production processes,
- investments in energy-efficient infrastructure,
- introduction of efficient environmental policies mainly in the form of market-based instruments,
- promotion of adaptation in view of damages from climate change,

- support for R&D spending on green technologies,
- restoration and conservation of ecosystems.

Empirical evidence (OECD, 2021) shows that although environmental policies have had relatively small effects on economic outcomes such as employment, investment, trade, and productivity, they have been effective at reducing emissions from industry. However, the policies can generate winners and losers across firms, industries, and regions, so environmental policies might need to be designed and combined with other policies to compensate workers and industries that may lose and to emphasize their positive impacts.

The EU's *European Green Deal* is a set of policies designed to boost the efficient use of resources by moving to a clean, circular economy and to restore biodiversity and cut pollution and aims to transition the EU economy to a sustainable economic model by 2050.

14.3.2. *Green growth*

In broad terms, green growth can be defined as growth that does not violate the environmental sustainability constraint or, to put it differently, as economic growth under which natural assets continue to provide the resources and environmental services on which human well-being relies.

- In terms of the analysis and criteria developed above, green growth can be regarded as requiring

$$\Delta Y(t) > 0 \quad \text{and} \quad S_g(t) > 0.$$

- A certain policy may not necessarily satisfy all the issues in question simultaneously. Such issues could be, for example,
  - sustainable development,
  - environmental sustainability,
  - the development of green economies,
  - the attainment of development or green growth.
- Sustainable development seems to be an encompassing concept, but it is not at all clear that the other concepts above are

subsets of sustainable development. This suggests using more than one criterion, depending on the combination of objectives being pursued.

14.4. The UN's Agenda 2030 and the Sustainable Development Goals

Agenda 2030 and the Sustainable Development Goals, which were adopted by all member states of the United Nations in 2015, describe a universal agenda that applies to and must be implemented by all countries, both developed and developing. Sound metrics and data are essential in order to turn the sustainable development goals (SDGs) into practical tools for problem-solving by

(1) mobilizing governments, academia, civil society, and businesses,
(2) providing a report card to track progress and ensure account-ability, and
(3) serving as a management tool for the transformations needed to achieve the SDGs by 2030. Countries around the world, including the G20, are aligning long-term development strategies with the SDGs. Similarly, businesses and other non-government stake-holders are increasingly working toward the SDGs as operational goals.

14.4.1. *The 17 SDGs*

Table 1 provides a brief description of each of the 17 SDGs, along with some of the selected targets for accomplishing the goals. A comprehensive description of the SDGs, along with a detailed description of the targets for each, can be found at https://sdgs. un.org/2030agenda.

14.4.2. *Construction of SDG indices*

The SDG index is an assessment of each country's overall perfor-mance on the 17 SDGs, giving equal weight to each goal. The score signifies a country's position between the worst possible outcome (score of 0) and the target (score of 100).

Table 1:   The 17 sustainable development goals (SDGs).

No.	Goal	Description of goal and selected targets
1	No poverty	End poverty in all its forms everywhere, including eradicating extreme poverty by 2030, ensuring that all people have equal rights to economic resources and access to basic services, and building resilience of the poor and vulnerable to climate-related extreme events.
2	Zero hunger	Create a world free from hunger and food insecurity by 2030. Double agricultural productivity and income of small-scale food producers by 2030. End malnutrition, promote sustainable agriculture, and maintain genetic diversity.
3	Good health and well-being	Ensure healthy lives and promote well-being for all people of all ages. Reduce maternal and infant mortality, achieve universal health coverage, and support R&D of vaccines and medicine. Strengthen the prevention and treatment of substance abuse. Reduce global deaths and injuries from traffic accidents.
4	Quality education	Ensure inclusive and equitable quality education for all, including access to early childhood education, free universal primary and secondary education by 2030, and equal access to affordable and quality technical, vocational, and tertiary education. Eliminate gender disparities, and increase the number of people who have relevant employment skills.
5	Gender equality	Achieve gender equality and empower all women and girls, including ending gender discrimination, eliminating all forms of violence against women and girls, recognizing and valuing unpaid care and domestic work, ensuring equal opportunities for leadership, and ensuring universal access to sexual and reproductive health and rights.
6	Clean water and sanitation	Ensure access to safe and affordable water, and adequate sanitation and hygiene for all by 2030. Improve water quality and increase water-use efficiency. Implement integrated water resource management and protect and restore water-related ecosystems.

(Continued)

Table 1: (*Continued*)

No.	Goal	Description of goal and selected targets
7	Affordable and clean energy	Ensure universal access to affordable, reliable, sustainable, and modern energy by 2030. Increase the percentage of renewable energy used globally. Improve energy efficiency. Enhance international cooperation with regard to clean energy research and technology.
8	Decent work and economic growth	Achieve sustainable economic growth, and universal full and productive employment and decent work by 2030. Increase economic productivity, and improve global resource efficiency in consumption and production. Protect labor rights and promote safe working environments. Eradicate forced labor, modern slavery, and human trafficking, and end child labor.
9	Industry, innovation, and infrastructure	Build resilient infrastructure, promote inclusive and sustainable industrialization, and foster innovation. Significantly raise industry's share of employment and GDP. Increase the access of small-scale industrial and other businesses to financial services, including affordable credit.
10	Reduced inequalities	Reduce inequality within and among countries by achieving and sustaining income growth of the bottom 40% of the population at a rate higher than the national average. Promote inclusion and equal opportunities, improve the regulation and monitoring of global financial markets, and facilitate safe and responsible migration and mobility.
11	Sustainable cities and communities	Make cities and human settlements inclusive, safe, resilient, and sustainable. Ensure universal access to safe and affordable housing and transport systems by 2030. Strengthen the protection of world's cultural and natural heritage. Reduce deaths and economic losses from disasters. Provide universal access to safe and accessible green and public spaces.
12	Responsible consumption and production	Ensure sustainable consumption and production patterns including sustainable management and efficient use of natural resources. Cut per capita global food waste in half and reduce waste generation through prevention, reduction, recycling, and reuse.

Table 1: (*Continued*)

No.	Goal	Description of goal and selected targets
13	Climate action	Take urgent action to combat climate change and its impacts. Strengthen resilience and adaptive capacity to climate-related hazards and natural disasters and integrate climate change measures into national policies, strategies, and planning. Improve knowledge and capacity regarding climate change mitigation, adaptation, and impact reduction.
14	Life below water	Conserve and sustainably use the oceans, seas, and marine resources by preventing and reducing marine pollution and sustainably managing and protecting marine and coastal ecosystems. Effectively regulate harvesting and end overfishing and other destructive fishing practices in order to restore fish stocks to maximum sustainable yield levels.
15	Life on land	Protect, restore, and promote sustainable use of terrestrial and inland freshwater ecosystems. Sustainably manage forests, combat desertification, halt and reverse land degradation, halt biodiversity loss, and end poaching and trafficking of protected species.
16	Peace, justice, and strong institutions	Promote just, peaceful, and inclusive societies. Reduce violence and related deaths, and end all forms of abuse against children. Promote the rule of law at all levels. Reduce illicit financial and arms flows, corruption, and bribery. Develop effective, accountable, and transparent institutions. Provide legal identity for all.
17	Partnership for the goals	Calls for action by all countries — developed and developing — to revitalize the global partnership for sustainable development. Targets aim at global cooperation with regard to issues including finance, technology, capacity building, trade, policy and institutional coherence, multi-stakeholder partnerships, and data, monitoring, and accountability.

The procedure for calculating the SDG Index is described analytically in Sachs *et al.* (2017). It contains four steps: (1) conduct statistical tests for normality and censor extreme values from the distribution of each indicator, (2) rescale the data to ensure comparability across indicators, (3) aggregate the indicators within and across SDGs, and (4) conduct sensitivity analysis and other statistical tests. The general approach is summarized in the following:

(a) Establish upper and lower bounds for the variables which are relevant for the specific index and linearly transform the data to a scale between 0 and 100 using the following rescaling formula:

$$x^* = \frac{x - x_{\min}}{x_{\max} - x_{\min}},$$

where x is the raw data value, *max/min* denote upper and lower bounds for best and worst performance, respectively, and x^* is the normalized value after rescaling.

(b) Each SDG index is constructed by aggregating its constituent components which are constructed by indicators obtained from the raw data in step (a). Aggregation is obtained using a constant elasticity of substitution aggregator function defined as

$$I_{ij}(N_{ij}, I_{ijk}, \rho) = \left[\sum_{k=1}^{N_{ij}} \frac{1}{N_{ij}} I_{ijk}^{\rho} \right]^{\frac{-1}{\rho}},$$

where I_{ijk} is the score of indicator k under SDG_j for country i, N_{ij} denotes the number of indicators for SDG_j, and ρ describes the substitutability across components of the indicator with a permissible range of $-1 \leq \rho \leq \infty$. The elasticity of substitution across components of the SDG Index is defined as

$$\sigma = \frac{1}{1 + \rho}.$$

Indicators for constituent k are obtained as

$$I_k = x_k^* \times 100.$$

The aggregator function defines the SDG index score I_{ij} for SDG$_j$, $j = 1, \ldots, 17$, and country i. Different values of ρ lead to different types of aggregation. For $\rho = -1$, the SDG index score is the arithmetic mean of the individual indices, while for $\rho = 1$, the SDG index score is the geometric mean of the individual components.

(c) Using the arithmetic mean, a country's overall SDG index score is estimated by aggregation within and across SDGs to obtain

$$I_i(N_i, N_{ij}, I_{ijk}) = \sum_{j=1}^{N_i} \frac{1}{N_i} \left[\sum_{k=1}^{N_{ij}} \frac{1}{N_{ij}} I_{ijk} \right],$$

where I_i is the index score for country i, N_i is the number of SDGs for which the country has data, N_{ij} is the number of indicators for SDG$_j$ for which country i has data, and I_{ijk} denotes the score of indicator k under SDG$_j$ for country i.

As an example, for the construction of SDG 8 (*Decent work and economic growth*), the indicators used, $N_{ij} = 5$ for country $i, j = 8$, are

(1) adjusted GDP growth (%),
(2) percentage of children 5–14 years old involved in child labor,
(3) adults (15 years and older) with an account at a bank or other financial institution or with a mobile-money-service provider (%),
(4) employment-to-population ratio (%), and
(5) youth not in employment, education, or training (%).

As a second example, for the construction of SDG 13 (*Climate action*), the indicators used, $N_{ij} = 4$ for country $i, j = 13$, are

(1) energy-related CO_2 emissions per capita (tCO_2/capita),
(2) imported CO_2 emissions, technology-adjusted (tCO_2/capita),
(3) climate change vulnerability index, and
(4) effective carbon rate from all non-road energy, excluding emissions from biomass.

14.4.3. *Progress toward achieving the SDGs*

14.4.3.1. *Short-term impacts of COVID-19 on the SDGs*

In the early stages of the COVID-19 pandemic, Sachs *et al.* (2020) examined its short-term impacts on the 17 SDGs and classified them into four categories: mainly positive impact, mixed or moderately negative impact, highly negative impact, and impact still unclear. Perhaps unsurprisingly, none of the SDGs were found to have been "mainly positively impacted" by COVID-19.

As shown in Table 2, Sachs *et al.* (2020) found that five of the SDGs were highly negatively impacted, and an additional eight were mixed or moderately negatively impacted. The impact on the remaining four SDGs (not shown) was unclear.

14.4.3.2. *Monitoring global progress on SDGs in 2022*

The Sustainable Development Goals Report 2022 (United Nations, 2022) reviewed the progress toward achievement of the SDGs in 2022 and found that the aspirations of the 2030 Agenda are being jeopardized by the COVID-19 pandemic, by global conflicts — the highest number since the creation of the UN — affecting some 2 billion people, and by the "full-fledged climate emergency". Some of their findings with regard to selected SDGs are summarized below. These findings reflect both progress made and obstacles faced in reaching the objectives of the 2030 Agenda.

SDG 6: Clean water and sanitation. Drinking water, sanitation, and hygiene services are vital human needs. As shown in Figure 1, left panel, access of the global population to basic drinking water increased from 88% to 90% from 2015 to 2020. Progress along this same path would result in 94% access by 2030 (dotted line), which is below the 100% target. Over the same period, global access to safely managed drinking water increased from 70% to 74%. Progress at this same rate would result in 81% access by 2030 (dashed line), which is well short of the 100% target.

Frequent and proper hand hygiene is essential to containing and controlling COVID-19 and other infectious diseases. Yet, more

Table 2: Some of the short-term impacts of COVID-19 on selected SDGs.

SDG	Goal	Impact
1	No poverty	**Highly negative impact** due to the economic lockdown and resulting job losses that disproportionately affected the poor and other vulnerable groups.
2	Zero hunger	**Highly negative impact** from reduction in global food supplies and trade, reduced incomes, reduced availability of food, higher food loss and waste, and interruption of school meals.
3	Good health and well-being	**Highly negative impact** including illnesses and deaths from COVID-19, increased deaths from other causes due to overburdened health systems, and mental health impacts, such as anxiety and depression.
8	Decent work and economic growth	**Highly negative impact** from the worldwide economic crisis that caused disruption of trade, widespread unemployment, business closures, greatly reduced tourism, and large increases in public debt.
10	Reduced inequalities	**Highly negative impact** because of the disproportionate health and economic effects on the poor, refugees, migrants, low-income workers, and other vulnerable groups.
4	Quality education	**Mixed or moderately negative impact** due to closings of schools and daycare centers, and the resulting loss in the development of human capital as well as interruption of school-provided meals.
5	Gender equality	**Mixed or moderately negative impact** including possible disproportionate economic and social impacts on women and higher mortality rates among men from COVID-19.
6	Clean water and sanitation	**Mixed or moderately negative impact** due to the limited access to clean water of disadvantaged groups, and their resulting limited ability to observe strict hygiene guidelines.
7	Affordable and clean energy	**Mixed or moderately negative impact** could be a possible reduction in incentives for renewable energy sources due to the slowdown in economic growth and resulting decrease in energy prices.

(Continued)

Table 2: (*Continued*)

SDG	Goal	Impact
9	Industry, innovation, and infrastructure	**Mixed or moderately negative impact.** Negative impacts include reduced industrial production and other effects such as closures or bankruptcies in some industries. Positive effects include scientific collaboration to find treatments and a vaccine for COVID-19, and advances in the use of digital technology for e-health, e-education, etc.
11	Sustainable cities and communities	**Mixed or moderately negative impact.** Negative impacts include increased urban poverty, shutting down of public transport, and lower access to public and green spaces. A positive effect was the sharp, short-term reduction in pollution.
16	Peace, justice and strong institutions	**Mixed or moderately negative impact** including increased pressure on governments to mitigate the health and economic consequences of the pandemic and to increase accessible health care; also increased public deficits and debt. Suspension of freedom-of-information laws and transparency policies.
17	Partnership for the goals	**Mixed or moderately negative impact** including closing of borders, slowdown in international trade, debt crisis, and possibly reduced responsiveness of international aid community to the needs of the poorest countries.

Data source: Sachs *et al.* (2020).

than 25% of the global population still does not have access to handwashing facilities with soap and water at home. Figure 1, right panel, shows the progress in this area, with access growing from 67% to 71% from 2015 to 2020. Still, progress at this rate would result in only 78% access by 2030 (dashed line).

Reaching the drinking water and hygiene targets of 100% by 2030 will require a fourfold increase in the pace of progress.

SDG 7: Affordable and clean energy. As shown in Figure 2, the global rate of access to electricity increased from 83.2% in 2010 to 90.5% in 2020. This means that the number of people without access

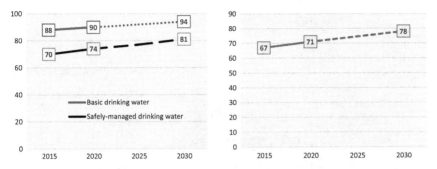

Figure 1: Global coverage of drinking water (left) and hygiene services (right), 2015–2020 (in %).

Data source: United Nations (2022).

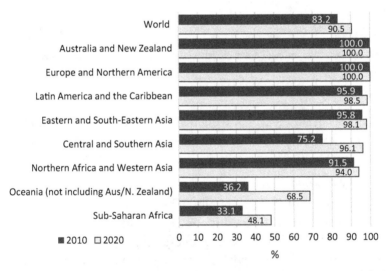

Figure 2: Proportion of population with access to electricity in 2010 and 2020, by region (in %).

Data source: United Nations (2022).

to electricity dropped from 1.2 billion to 733 million. But despite these significant gains, less than 50% of the population in Sub-Saharan Africa and less than 70% in Oceania had access to electricity in 2020.

Moreover, according to the United Nations (2022) report, the rate of progress has slowed in recent years, due to COVID-19 and

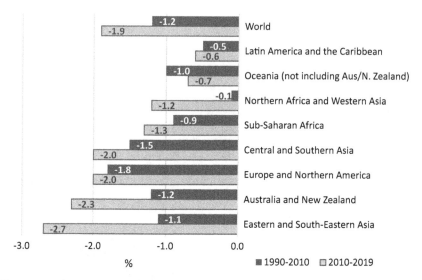

Figure 3: Average annual growth rate of primary energy intensity, 1990–2010 and 2010–2019 (in %).
Data source: United Nations (2022).

the increasing complexity of reaching those hardest to reach. In 2018–2020, the electricity access rate rose by an average of 0.5% per year as compared to 0.8% annually in the period 2010–2018.

SDG 7 (*Affordable and clean energy*) calls for an improvement in energy intensity of 2.6% annually, which is twice the rate observed between 1990 and 2010 (see Figure 3). Global primary energy intensity is defined *as the ratio of total energy supply to GDP*. It improved between 2010 and 2019, with an average annual improvement rate of 1.9%. However, to meet the target, energy intensity improvements until 2030 will need to average 3.2% a year. So far, the only region that has reached this target is Eastern and South-Eastern Asia, which had an annual average rate of 2.7% in 2010–2019, driven by strong economic growth.

SDG 8: Decent work and economic growth. According to *The Sustainable Development Goals Report 2022* (United Nations, 2022), global economic recovery has been hampered by new waves of COVID-19, rising inflation, supply chain disruptions, policy uncertainties, labor market challenges, and global conflicts. As shown

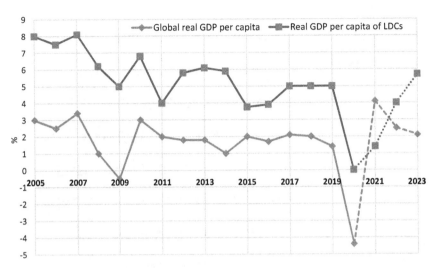

Figure 4: Annual growth rate of global real GDP per capita and annual growth rate of real GDP of LDCs, 2005–2023 (in %).

Data source: United Nations (2022).

in Figure 4, global real GDP per capita increased by 1.4% in 2019, fell sharply, by 4.4%, in 2020, and then rebounded in 2021 at an estimated growth rate of 4.4% (dashed line).

For the least developed countries (LDCs), real GDP grew by 5.0% in 2019 but had zero growth in 2020 due to pandemic-related disruptions. Real GDP of LDCs is estimated to have increased by 1.4 % in 2021 (dotted line) and is projected to rise by 4.0% in 2022 and 5.7% in 2023. However, this is still well below the 7% target envisioned in the 2030 Agenda for Sustainable Development.

SDG 10: Reduced inequalities. Labor income is an important measure of inequality. Measuring labor's contribution to GDP provides an indication of whether higher national income will lead to increased material living standards for workers. While employment is the main source of income for many workers, income derived from capital disproportionately benefits the affluent (United Nations, 2022). Therefore, the decline in the global labor share of income from 54.1% in 2014 to 52.6% in 2019, shown in Figure 5, represents upward pressure on inequality.

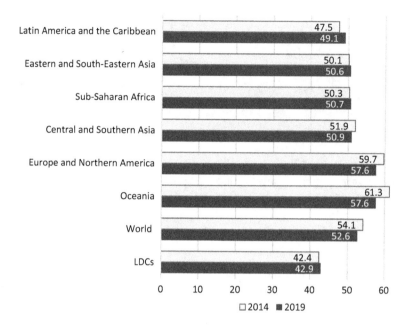

Figure 5:   Labor income as a share of GDP, in 2014 and 2019 (in %).
Data source: United Nations (2022).

The regions of Europe and Northern America, Oceania, and Central and Southern Asia experienced decline in the labor income share over the same period. In contrast, the regions of Latin America and the Caribbean, Eastern and South-Eastern Asia, and Sub-Saharan Africa showed increases in the labor income share. The LDC countries as a group also showed a slight increase in labor income as a share of GDP.

SDG 11: Sustainable cities and communities. *The Sustainable Development Goals Report 2022* (United Nations, 2022) indicates that more than 50% of the world's population live in cities and that number is estimated to reach 70% by 2050. Cities contribute more than 80% of global GDP, but they also produce more than 70% of global GHG emissions, which poses a significant threat to human health worldwide.

On the one hand, global concentrations of fine particulate matter of 2.5 microns or less in diameter ($PM_{2.5}$) have steadily decreased,

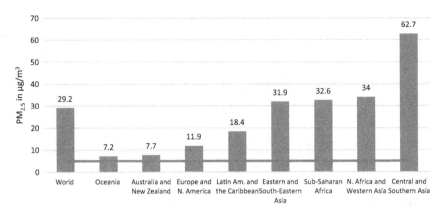

Figure 6: Annual exposure to particulate matter ($PM_{2.5}$) in urban areas (in $\mu g/m^3$), three-year average from 2017 to 2019.

Data source: United Nations (2022).

with an 11% reduction over a decade. On the other hand, despite this progress, 99% of the world's urban population lives in areas that exceed the new 2021 World Health Organization (WHO) guidelines on air quality for $PM_{2.5}$ of 5 micrograms per cubic meter ($\mu g/m^3$) or less (reduced from the previous limit of $10\,\mu g/m^3$ that was set in 2005). The vertical line in Figure 6 represents the new WHO guideline of $5\,\mu g/m^3$.

In 2019, ambient air pollution from traffic, industry, power generation, waste burning, and residential fuel combustion resulted in 4.2 million deaths which were attributed to exposure to $PM_{2.5}$ and other pollutants. People in low-income and middle-income countries are disproportionately affected by outdoor air pollution and account for 91% of the 4.2 million premature deaths.

According to data from 2017–2019, which measured three-year annual averages, cities in Central and Southern Asia have by far the worst air pollution in the world ($62.7\,\mu g/m^3$), more than two times the global average, as shown in Figure 6. The regions with the lowest concentration of $PM_{2.5}$ are Oceania, Australia and New Zealand, and Europe and North America.

The world's urban population is also struggling to cope with the mounting problem of municipal solid waste. As shown in Figure 7,

Figure 7: Municipal solid waste collection and management in controlled facilities, in 2022 (in %).

Data source: United Nations (2022).

in 2022, an average of 82% of municipal solid waste globally was being collected, but only 55% was being managed in controlled facilities.

Municipalities in Sub-Saharan Africa have an average collection rate of less than 55% and 57% in Oceania (not including Australia and New Zealand), with collection rates in the other regions ranging from 72% in Central and Southern Asia to almost 99% in Australia and New Zealand.

The percentage of waste being managed globally in controlled facilities is 55% and ranges from 18.8% to 93.9% in the individual regions. In Central and Southern Asia, the 48% gap between the collection rate and controlled management rate is larger than in other regions, suggesting that many cities there still rely on open dumpsites. The highest collection rate (98.7%) and the highest controlled management rate (93.9%) are in Australia and New Zealand.

Europe and Northern America	9.9
Latin America and the Caribbean	12.3
World	13.3
Australia and New Zealand	13.6
Central and Southern Asia	13.6
Northern Africa and Western Asia	14.8
Oceania (excl. Aus/New Zealand)	14.8
Eastern and South-Eastern Asia	15.1
Sub-Saharan Africa	21.4

Figure 8: Proportion of food loss (after harvesting and before reaching retail markets), in 2020 (in %).

Data source: United Nations (2022).

SDG 12: Responsible consumption and production. Unsustainable patterns of consumption and production are the root cause of three planetary crises: climate change, biodiversity loss, and pollution (United Nations, 2022). Domestic material consumption — the total amount of materials directly used by an economy to meet the demands for goods and services — rose by 65% globally from 2000 to 2019.

Moreover, as shown in Figure 8, over 13% of global food production is lost after harvesting and before reaching retail markets (e.g., transport, storage, and processing). Similarly, about 17% of food is wasted at the consumer level (e.g., households, stores, and restaurants), which is the equivalent of 121 kg per person per year. About 60% of this waste occurs in households.

SDG 13: Climate action. The negative impacts of climate change are being experienced all over the world. The United Nations (2022) report notes that increased occurrences of heatwaves, droughts, floods, and fires caused by climate change are already affecting

Figure 9: Carbon dioxide emissions from energy combustion and industrial processes, 1900–2021, in gigatons of CO_2.

Data source: International Energy Agency (https://www.iea.org/data-and-statistics/charts/co2-emissions-from-energy-combustion-and-industrial-processes-1900-2021).

billions of people around the world and causing potentially irreversible changes in global ecosystems.

According to the Intergovernmental Panel on Climate Change (IPCC), in order to limit global warming to 1.5°C above preindustrial levels as set out in the Paris Agreement, global GHG emissions will need to peak before 2025, then decline by 43% by 2030, and then fall to net zero by 2050. Figure 9 shows energy-related CO_2 emissions from 1900 to 2021. The 5.2% drop in 2020 — the largest decline ever — was only temporary. With the phasing out of COVID-related restrictions, the demand for coal, oil, and gas increased. As a result, CO_2 emissions increased by 6% in 2021, reaching their highest level ever.

Among the likely effects if global temperatures rise 1.5°C or higher are the following:

- sea level rise of 30–60 cm by 2100, causing more frequent and severe coastal flooding and erosion, and increased ocean acidification (IPCC, 2019),

- disappearance of between 70% and 90% of warm-water coral reefs at the 1.5°C threshold. The reefs could die off completely at the 2°C level (IPCC, 2018),
- droughts that could displace 700 million people by 2030 (United Nations, 2022),
- a 40% increase in medium- to large-scale disasters from 2015 to 2030 (United Nations, 2022).

Figure 9 shows the continuous increase over time of emissions of GHGs. As these emissions rise, so does the Earth's temperature. As can be seen in Figure 10, in 2021, the global annual mean temperature was about 1.11 ± 0.13°C above the pre-industrial level (from 1850 to 1900). Although global temperatures vary from year to year, the long-term trend shown in Figure 10 is a warming climate.

According to the World Meteorological Organization's (2022) *Global Annual to Decadal Climate Update* for the target years 2023–2027, the annual mean global near-surface temperature for each year between 2023 and 2027 is predicted to be between 1.1°C and

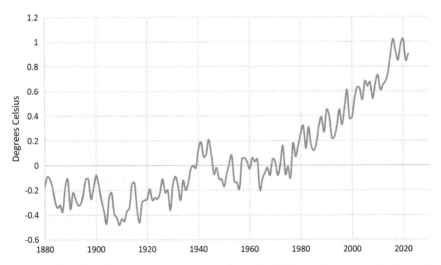

Figure 10: Global annual mean temperature (in °C) relative to pre-industrial levels (1850–1900 average), for the period 1880–2022.
Data source: National Aeronautics and Space Administration, Goddard Institute for Space Studies (https://data.giss.nasa.gov/gistemp/).

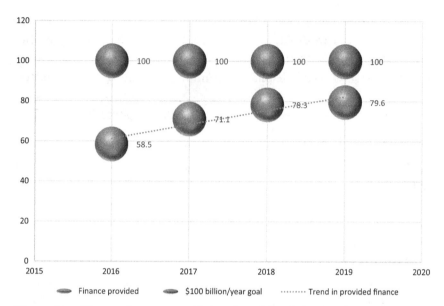

Figure 11: Climate finance provided and mobilized for developing countries, 2016–2019 (in billion US$).

Data source: OECD (2021).

1.8°C higher than the average over the years 1850–1900, and the probability of it exceeding 1.5°C above pre-industrial levels in at least one of those years is more likely than not. This will bring the world dangerously close to the lower target of the Paris Agreement.

Climate finance provided by developed countries totaled $79.6 billion in 2019 (see Figure 11) but fell short of the commitment of developed countries to mobilize $100 billion per year by 2020 for climate action in developing countries. Moreover, the $100 billion annual commitment is below estimates put forth by the IPCC, which has estimated that US$1.6 to 3.8 trillion will be needed each year through 2050 in order for the world to transition to a low-carbon future and avoid exceeding the 1.5°C benchmark.

SDG 14: Life below water. According to *The Sustainable Development Goals Report 2022* (United Nations, 2022), human activity is endangering the planet's oceans and seas and affecting the livelihoods of billions of people as a result. Some examples of the negative effects include the following:

- Increasing acidification is limiting the ocean's capacity to moderate climate change.
- Rising ocean temperatures are threatening marine species.
- Multiple sources of pollution, especially plastics and nutrient runoff, are harming marine life and finding their way into the food chain.
- Growing consumption of fish, along with inadequate public policies for managing the fishing sector, has led to depleting fish stocks.

On the other hand, marine protected areas and other measures to conserve biodiversity (including marine sanctuaries, parks, and reserves) have grown substantially and the global coverage of marine protected areas reached 8% of global coastal waters and oceans in 2021. It is expected to continue to move toward the 10% called for in the SDG target.

Moreover, although global fish stocks continue to be threatened by overfishing and other activities, the rate of decline in fish stocks has started to decrease. Measures such as regulation, monitoring, and surveillance have proven successful in reversing the trend and bringing previously overfished stocks to a biologically sustainable level in certain areas, but adoption of such measures has generally been slow.

SDG 15: Life on land. The world's ecosystems are a source of food, water, medicine, and shelter, as well as ecosystem services such as clean air and water. According to the United Nations (2022) report, despite global efforts to halt the degradation of ecosystems,

- 10 million hectares of forest are destroyed every year. However, the rate of decline has slowed slightly.
- Almost 90% of global deforestation results from agricultural expansion (49.6% from cropland expansion and 38.5% from livestock grazing).

- Biodiversity has been largely neglected in COVID-19 recovery spending, while around 40,000 species are documented to be at risk of extinction over the coming decades.

On a positive note, progress has been made on the sustainable use of genetic resources and associated traditional knowledge. In addition, nearly half of the areas identified as being key to global biodiversity are now protected areas, although the geographical coverage is uneven. Finally, although progress is slow, the number of countries that are incorporating biodiversity values into national planning processes is steadily increasing.

14.4.3.3. *Important questions regarding SDGs*

(1) Should the SDGs be linked with sustainability concepts and metrics such as comprehensive wealth and genuine investment?
(2) Is positive genuine savings compatible with the full set, or a subset, of the SDGs?
(3) What kind of trade-offs exist among the different SDGs?
(4) Once they are achieved, are the SDGs sustainable?

In summary, sustainable development — as defined in terms of comprehensive wealth and the productive base of an economy — provides an all-encompassing framework which includes the environmental and socioeconomic aspects of the issue and can be used to infer whether an economy is on a sustainable path. These lecture notes focused on the environmental aspects and, more specifically, on issues related to the natural capital part of the productive base.

The UN-SDGs provide a comprehensive framework for measuring, through indicators, the progress of an economy toward attaining socioeconomic and environmental objectives which are at the core of sustainable development objectives. Both concepts — sustainable development and the UN-SDGs — complement each other and provide a framework for designing policies that will help countries put their economies on a sustainable path of development and, at the same time, attain conditions which will enhance the well-being of their citizens.

References

IPCC (2018). *Global Warming of 1.5° C. An IPCC Special Report on the Impacts of Global Warming of 1.5° C above Pre-industrial Levels and Related Global Greenhouse Gas Emission Pathways, in the Context of Strengthening the Global Response to the Threat of Climate Change, Sustainable Development, and Efforts to Eradicate Poverty,* V. Masson-Delmotte, P. Zhai, H.-O. Pörtner, D. Roberts, J. Skea *et al.* (eds.). Cambridge University Press.

IPCC (2019). *IPCC Special Report on the Ocean and Cryosphere in a Changing Climate,* H.-O. Pörtner, D.C. Roberts, V. Masson-Delmotte, P. Zhai, M. Tignor, *et al.* (eds.). Cambridge University Press.

OECD (2021). *Assessing the Economic Impacts of Environmental Policies: Evidence from a Decade of OECD Research.* Paris: OECD Publishing.

Sachs, J., Schmidt-Traub, G., Kroll, C., Durand-Delacre, D., Teksoz, K. (2017). *SDG Index and Dashboards Report 2017.* Bertelsmann Stiftung and Sustainable Development Solutions Network.

Sachs, J., Schmidt-Traub, G., Kroll, C., Lafortune, G., Fuller, G., Woelm, F. (2020). *The Sustainable Development Goals and COVID-19. Sustainable Development Report 2020.* Cambridge University Press.

UNEP (2011). *Towards a Green Economy: Pathways to Sustainable Development and Poverty Eradication.* United Nations Environmental Programme.

United Nations (2022). *The Sustainable Development Goals Report 2022.* United Nations, Department of Economic and Social Affairs (DESA).

World Meteorological Organization (2022). *Global Annual to Decadal Climate Update for the target years 2023–2027.* World Meteorological Organization.

Printed in the USA
CPSIA information can be obtained
at www.ICGtesting.com
JSHW010754180524
63072JS00002B/13